THE PENRY PENALTY

Capital Punishment and Offenders with Mental Retardation

Emily Fabrycki Reed

UNIVERSITY
PRESS OF
AMERICA

Lanham • New York • London

Copyright © 1993 by
University Press of America®, Inc.
4720 Boston Way
Lanham, Maryland 20706

3 Henrietta Street
London WC2E 8LU England

Library of Congress Cataloging-in-Publication Data

Reed, Emily F. (Emily Fabrycki).
The Penry penalty : capital punishment and offenders with mental
retardation / by Emily Fabrycki Reed.
p.   cm.
Includes index.
1. Capital punishment—United States.   2. Mentally handicapped
offenders—United States.   I. Title.
HV8699.U5R32   1993
364.6'6'0973—dc20   92–44124 CIP

ISBN 0–8191–9019–5 (cloth : alk. paper)
ISBN 0–8191–9020–9 (pbk. : alk. paper)

 The paper used in this publication meets the minimum requirements of
American National Standard for Information Sciences—Permanence
of Paper for Printed Library Materials, ANSI Z39.48–1984.

Other Works by This Author

"Viewpoint: The Death Penalty's Inequities," *Delaware Today* (March, 1992): 6.

"States Restrict Executions of the Mentally Retarded," *State Legislatures* (November, 1991): 7.

"Halfway Houses and Electronic Monitoring Effective in Delaware," *Overcrowded Times* (September, 1991): 8.

"Legal Rights of Mentally Retarded Offenders: Hospice and Habilitation," *Criminal Law Bulletin*, 25 (Sept.-Oct. 1989): 411-443.

"Systems of Personnel Deployment in Correctional Institutions and Their Legal Foundations," *Criminal Justice Journal*, 10 (Fall 1987): 1-25.

Law, Policy and Population: Issues in A New Field. With Larry D. Barnett, Houston: Cap & Gown Press, 1985.

Book Review of C. Sneider & M. Vinoskis (eds.), *The Law and Politics of Abortion,* Lexington, MA: D.C. Heath, 1980, in *Population Research and Policy Review*, 2 (Feb. 1983): 106-107.

"Tilting at Windmills? The Massachusetts Low and Moderate Income Housing Act," *Western New England Law Review*, 4 (Summer 1981): 105-132.

Exclusionary Zoning and the Urban Ecology, Ph.D. Dissertation, University of Massachusetts, Amherst, MA (1981).

To All Those Who Work to Prevent The Execution
of Offenders with Mental Retardation

Acknowledgements

From Margaret Blair, telephone conversation with author, 26 August 1991. Reprinted by permission of Margaret Blair.

From John Blume and David Bruck, "Sentencing the Mentally Retarded to Death: An Eighth Amendment Analysis," 725-764; Donald Hermann, Howard Singer, and Mary Roberts; "Sentencing of the Mentally Retarded Criminal Defendant," 765-808. Sandra Garcia and Holly Steele, "Mentally Retarded Offenders in the Criminal Justice and Mental Retardation Services Systems in Florida: Philosophical, Placement, and Treatment Issues," *Arkansas Law Review* 41 (1988): 809-859. Reprinted by permission *Arkansas Law Review* (c) 1988.

From Philip L. Fetzer, "Execution of the Mentally Retarded: A Punishment without Justification," *South Carolina Law Review* 40 (Winter 1989): 426. Reprinted by permission of Philip L. Fetzer and the South Carolina Law Review (c) 1989.

From Ian Gray and Moira Stanley, eds., "Introduction;" Watt Espy, "American Gothic;" Reverend Joseph Ingle "Strange Fruit;" Darryl Bell, "Checkmate;" Bryon Eshelman, "Death Row Chaplain;" Clive Stafford Smith, "An Englishman Abroad;" and James W.L.Park, "Amazing Grace;" *A Punishment in Search of a Crime* (New York: Avon Books, 1989). Reprinted by permission of Edward J. Acton, Inc. (c) 1989.

From Robert Perske, telephone conversation with author, 27 March 1992. Reprinted by permission of Robert Perske.

From Robert Perske, *Unequal Justice* (Nashville, TN: Abingdon Press, 1991). Reprinted by permission of Robert Perske and Abingdon Press (c) 1991.

From Joshua N. Sondheimer, "A Continuing Source of Aggravation: The Improper Consideration of Mitigating Factors in Death Penalty Sentencing," *Hastings Law Journal* 41 (1990): 409-446. Copyright 1990 Hastings College of the Law, reprinted from 41 Hastings L.J. 409-446 by permission.

Quotes on pages 17, 47, and 48. From OF MICE AND MEN by John Steinbeck. Copyright 1937, renewed (c) 1965 by John Steinbeck. Used by permission of Viking Penguin, a division of Penguin Books USA Inc.

Contents

THE *PENRY* PENALTY

CONTENTS

CONTENTS

THE *PENRY* PENALTY

CONTENTS

Foreword

Dr. Emily F. Reed presents here a solid argument against the application of the death penalty to persons suffering from mental retardation who have been convicted of capital crimes. While there are those of us who may not share her very apparent general aversion to the death penalty as an aspect of our criminal justice system, it is hard to see how anyone, even the most convinced advocate of capital punishment, can fail to feel the impact of this information-packed, persuasive and passionate book.

Even before proceeding with Dr. Reed's argument, many readers may well wonder why it should even have to be made: it will appear to many to be self-evident that the law should deal with adult citizens whose retardation confines their mental and emotional development to that of a child of 12 or younger in the same way it deals with such a child. Unfortunately, the justice of that argument has not been self-evident to the United States Supreme court, which held in its 1989 *Penry v. Lynaugh* decision that convicted capital offenders with mental retardation may indeed be executed, provided judges and juries consider their mental retardation in arriving at the death sentence. The Court recognized that the case involved a general principle, but left it to individual judges and juries to apply that principle, as best they might, case by case. That, the justices held, was sufficient.

Dr. Reed disagrees, vigorously and vehemently, in a book that combines comprehensive, no-nonsense scholarship with an acutely human sensitivity to the effect applying the death penalty to persons with mental retardation has not only on that small but extremely vulnerable fragment of our population, but also on our very body politic and the sense of justice with which we endeavor to endow it. Dr. Reed makes, I believe, a valuable contribution to the dialogue, both because she has assembled an enormous body of fact and because she does not hesitate to express the feelings addressing those facts should arouse in the heart of any compassionate person who confronts them.

Over the past 20 or 30 years, writing on matters of public policy has become very nearly a major industry unto itself. The bookstalls and even the best-seller lists are replete with volumes of earnest, often very well-informed treatises on almost every subject that might conceivably become the object of government action, not to mention hundreds of books on other subjects we all may well hope never achieve their authors' aspirations for public-policy status: most of us today believe that government is already overburdened with objectives both beyond its jurisdiction and beyond its means.

But even when the policy objectives they espouse are well taken, these well-meant volumes too often display a defect that has, in my judgment, tended to infect the whole political dialogue in this country - an attempt to achieve, or at least project, "objectively" by subduing the natural human response to whatever problem is at issue. The result is a politics that takes on the appearance, and all too often the character, of cold-bloodedness, the very opposite of what a healthy political system should encourage and express.

Obviously, a politics and a public policy long on passion and short on facts is certain to end in impertinence, frustration, injustice and downright despotism. The long span of human history and brutal annals of the century now drawing to a close provide us with incontrovertible evidence on that score. But I would argue, and I believe Dr. Reed makes the case here, that a coldly dispassionate politics that takes no account of the human spirit and human feelings is sure to produce even more inhumane consequences. If we can not feel, and if we can not engage our feelings in our politics, we are bound to fall short of the quality of justice we have historically aspired to as a nation and a people.

A special feeling about children and how we should treat them has long held a place of respect in our American tradition, and that attitude is reflected in our law. There is no reason we should withhold that feeling nor the benefit of the law when we consider those "children" fate has lodged in adult bodies but deprived of adult faculties, and there is every reason why our feelings should be engaged in the controversy over the death penalty and mental retardation. Dr. Reed has given us the facts and expressed the feelings we all should share about them. Her argument is scholarly, disciplined and factually complete, but in the end it appeals as much to the heart as to the head -- and that is very much as it should be.

Joseph R. Biden, Jr.
United States Senator
Chairman, Senate Judiciary Committee

September, 1992

Illustrations

Figures

Preface

The Supreme Court has long held a certain fascination for me. Almost three decades ago, as an young and idealistic undergraduate student, I had the pleasure of learning Constitutional Law and Civil Liberties from the Rev. Vergil Blum, a distinguished Jesuit lawyer, in a year long course taught at Marquette University. It was here that my now deep-seated senses of equality and justice, what I consider to be the most basic of American values, began to develop. The course also gave me a profound admiration for the role the Court plays in protecting these values. When the occasional juridical decision seems to stray from the role of protection of equality and justice to one of violation, then my enduring adherence to these values also seems violated. *Penry v. Lynaugh* is such a case.

The outrage that was expressed over the *Penry* decision at a President's Commission on Mental Retardation conference on mentally retarded offenders which I attended in Washington, D.C. in September, 1989 piqued my conscience and set my pen in motion. If nothing else, I would argue the case once more for an opposite outcome to this decision, and a subsequent universal ban on executions of offenders who suffer from mental retardation.

What started out as an article ended in a book length manuscript. The effort took more than two years. During that time, a small and scattered group of persons around the nation who shared a common purpose and my sense of violation has worked at great odds to pass legislation to remedy the injustice of the *Penry* penalty. I have participated in that struggle, although unsuccessfully, in the Delaware General Assembly during the last two legislative sessions. Perhaps this book will contribute to a different outcome this year or the next. I hope so.

As I put the finishing touches on this manuscript, I must stop to express my gratitude to those who haved help to make it possible. Many thanks go to Representative Jane Maroney (R-Talleyville) for her courage and tenacity in sponsoring and pushing for legislation in Delaware to ban the death penalty for persons with mental retardation; to Bob Cunningham of Senator Joseph R. Biden, Jr.'s staff, whose always discerning observations helped to keep me in focus and on track; to Robert Perske for his insightful comments on Chapter 1; and to Tom Reed for his infinite patience, understanding and support.

1

The *Penry* Case

To sit in solemn silence in a dull, dark dock, In a pestilential prison, with a lifelong lock, Awaiting the sensation of a short, sharp shock, From a cheap and chippy chopper on a big black block! A dull, dark dock, A lifelong lock, A short, sharp shock, A big black block!
-- Gilbert & Sullivan, *The Mikado*

INTRODUCTION

On June 26, 1989, the United States Supreme Court issued a landmark decision in handicapped law, one which sent echoes of disbelief and dismay reverberating across the nation. The case is *Penry v. Lynaugh*.[1] The Court announced in *Penry* that the death penalty as applied to people with mental retardation does not violate the prohibition of cruel and unusual punishment contained in the Eighth Amendment of the Constitution of the United States. Persons having mental retardation who are convicted of capital crimes can be executed on a case-by-case basis as "long as judges and juries consider their" mental retardation before sentencing.[2]

THE FACTS

The defendant in the case, John Paul Penry, is a man with mental retardation in his mid-thirties and a convicted Texas killer, a mental child in a full-grown body.[3] His I.Q. falls somewhere between fifty and sixty-three, making him either moderately or mildly retarded.[4] He suffers from organic brain damage which likely occurred during and after his breach birth. His father was a Seventh Day Adventist who did not believe in blood transfusions.[5] His mother was only eighteen when he was born and almost died from loss of blood during his difficult birth. She suffered a nervous breakdown from the trauma and was committed to a mental hospital for the first ten months of John Paul's life.[6]

When she returned home, she began a decade long campaign of abuse and torture of the child whose difficult birth had nearly cost her life. She beat Penry severely and repeatedly. Savage blows to the head over the ten year period are undoubtedly related to his brain damage. Throughout his childhood, Penry was burned with cigarette butts all over his body. His left arm was broken several times.[7] As was common treatment for people with mental retardation at the time, he was regularly locked in a room alone for lengthy periods, where he was without toilet facilities.[8] His mother sometimes forced Penry to eat his own feces and to drink his urine.[9]

Now in his mid-thirties, Penry's mental age, intellectual development and accumulated learning are comparable to those of an average second grader (about a seven-year-old), the maximum capability of a person with his degree of retardation.[10] He dropped out of school during the first grade because he could not learn. He has the affects and social development of the average fourth grader (nine to ten-years-old). He was in and out of state schools and hospitals up to the age of twelve. At this time, he went to live with his aunt who spent a year painstakingly trying to teach him how to print his name.[11]

On October 25, 1979, at the age of twenty-two, Penry, intent on rape, entered the home of Pamela Moseley Carpenter, a white woman, also twenty-two, in the small Texas town of Livingston.[12] The victim was the sister of Mike Moseley, the professional football star.[13]

Ms. Carpenter was making Halloween decorations with a pair of scissors nearby. As Penry attempted to rape her she struggled and used the scissors against him, wounding him superficially. He became enraged at this affront and stabbed her to death with her own scissors. He later stated that he had killed her to prevent her from identifying him.[14]

The damage that was done to Penry's intelligence possibly at birth and certainly during his childhood indicate that he did not have the mental prowess to voice internally to himself that, "'Wait a minute, I'd better not do this.'"[15] Once in the course of struggling with the victim, he was incapable of braking his violence until she was dead.[16]

Despite the heavy evidence of mitigation of his crime by his organic brain damage, child abuse and mental retardation,[17] in 1980 Penry was convicted and sentenced to death.

THE DECISION

The First Issue: The Jury's Application of the Texas Death Statute

The *Penry* case presented two major legal issues. The first issue involved a challenge to the Texas statute that required that the death penalty be imposed by the jury if three conditions ("special issues") were fulfilled.[18]

First, the statute required that the killing act be "committed deliberately with a reasonable expectation that . . . death" would result.[19] Second, it required that future dangerousness be present, that is, that the defendant be likely to commit additional violent acts and be a continuing "threat to society."[20]   The third condition required that the mortal act be unreasonable in relation to the victim's provocation, if any.[21] If all three conditions were present in the case, then the death penalty would automatically be imposed on the defendant.[22]

When the jury considered these questions in the *Penry* case and made its determination of deliberateness, dangerousness, and victim provocation, it was required by precedent to consider and weigh mitigating factors.[23] Although the statute itself contained no reference to mitigation, all previous case law concerning the Texas death statute had established this obligation.[24]

Consideration of mitigating factors was required because they are relevant to the defendant's moral culpability. Courts had previously ruled that mental or emotional illness and a "disadvantaged background" may affect the degree of culpability and the extent to which a defendant can be held liable for the criminal acts he or she commits.[25] This concept was based on a societal belief that we cannot hold a person entirely responsible when some of his or her faculties are deficient.[26] Consequently, no "new rule" outside established precedent would be created by requiring mitigating factors to be considered in the jury's interpretation of the Texas death penalty statute as applied to Penry.[27]

Mitigating factors to be considered could include characteristics of the offense or of the offender.[28] In Penry's case, the mitigating factors were his offender characteristics.   These included his mental retardation, organic brain damage, lack of mental capacity, poor impulse control, and physically abused childhood background.[29]

In making its charge to the jury concerning the three statutory conditions, the trial court failed to instruct the jury that it needed to consider mitigating factors in its determination of the presence of the three special conditions. If Penry's offender characteristics could have mitigated any of the three conditions, then the death penalty should not have been imposed.[30]

The *Penry* jury did not consider Penry's mitigating conditions and found that all three special conditions (deliberateness, dangerousness, and lack of victim provocation) were present in the murder. Therefore, the death penalty was automatically assessed in the penalty phase of the trial.[31]

The Supreme Court did not accept the outcome of the penalty hearing. It reasoned that Penry's mental retardation and abused childhood may have been related to his moral culpability and to his ability to act intentionally.[32]   He may not have been able to act deliberately and, consequently, may not have been completely culpable and deserving of death.[33] Yet the jury did not have the opportunity to consider the degree of culpability nor whether it mitigated against the death penalty. Therefore, the death penalty should not have been imposed in relation to the question of deliberateness.[34]

The resolution of the first issue thus seemed like a victory for Penry and advocates for persons with mental retardation. The case was remanded for consideration of mitigation and reconsideration of the imposition of the death penalty.[35] On its face, there seemed to be a great deal of hope that, given Penry's substantively disabled state, he would not be considered completely culpable nor have the death penalty imposed a second time. Thus the specifics concerning Penry himself seemed to have won the day. He would get a second chance to be removed from Death Row.[36]

However, subsequent events and the Supreme Court's resolution of the second issue turned this first milestone into a Pyrrhic victory. In 1990, Penry was tried again. The prosecution repeatedly stated throughout the trial that Penry was faking mental retardation and was fully culpable for his acts.[37] Evidently, the jury believed this, because it sentenced him to death again despite the overwhelming evidence to the contrary.

THE SECOND ISSUE: INTERPRETATION OF THE EIGHTH AMENDMENT

When the Supreme Court considered the second issue in its review of Penry's original trial, it refused to broaden the specifics of the application of mitigation into a general rule that all persons with mental retardaton by reason of their impairments are less than totally responsible for their acts. The Court continued to allow the death penalty to be imposed on individuals with mental retardation on a case-by-case basis.[38]

The second issue shifted from Penry's specifics to a general constitutional question, that is, whether it is cruel and unusual punishment under the Eighth Amendment to the U.S. Constitution to allow any person with mental retardation, including Penry, to be executed.[39] Generally, the defendants argued that the death penalty should be prohibited when applied to all persons with mental retardation because they, by definition, lack normal mental capacity. Therefore, *per se* they also lack the moral culpability necessary to be executed.[40]

The Supreme Court would not accept this reasoning.[41] The defense's arguments progressed from the specifics of Penry's lack of culpability to the generalized prohibition of death for all defendants with mental retardation. The Court debunked each associated argument one by one.[42]

"New Rule" Argument. In an opinion written by Justice Sandra Day O'Connor, the Court first addressed a procedural matter. It held that a "new" rule would be established if the Eighth Amendment were interpreted to prohibit the execution of all convicts with mental retardation.[43] Contrary to the application of mitigating factors to the special issues of the Texas death penalty statute where no new rule was established, no precedent existed here in case law for such a broad interpretation.[44] It would be legally intolerable to declare a new rule which places "a certain class of individuals beyond the State's power to punish by death."[45] Such a rule would be analogous to "placing certain conduct beyond the State's power to punish at all."[46]

"Societal Consensus" Argument. Second, the Court reasoned that no societal consensus existed for prohibiting persons with mental retardation from being executed. The Court recognized that society's interpretation of "standards of decency" evolve over time, that changes in societal mores "mark the progress of a maturing society," and that changing societal standards should be applied to its interpretation of what constitutes cruel and unusual punishment.[47] It acknowledged that its opinions reflect the viewpoint of the society at large and that societal opinion is critical to its decision-making.[48]

However, it found no societal consensus for prohibiting execution of people with mental retardation.[49] A major source of testing societal consensus lies in the laws passed by state legislatures, but only one state (Georgia) to that time had passed legislation prohibiting imposition of death on persons with mental retardation. One state could by no means be considered a national consensus.[50]

A second source of looking at societal consensus is the common law. At a minimum, the Eighth Amendment prohibits execution of those who would not be executed under the common law. Idiots and lunatics were held by common law not to be liable for their actions and therefore punishment of any sort could not be imposed on them.[51] However, by "idiots" the common law meant what is comparable to the "severe" and "profoundly" retarded, not the mild or moderately retarded as is Penry. Penry was not considered to be an idiot in the common law sense because he was found to be competent to stand trial and to have a "rational and factual understanding of the proceedings against him."[52]

Juries and Prosecutors. In passing, the Court indicated that the defense presented no evidence as to how previous juries and prosecutors viewed the issue of applying the death penalty to people with mental retardation, and that such evidence could be used to support a position that the imposition of the death penalty on persons with mental retardation is cruel and unusual punishment.[53]

Public Opinion Polls. The defense had presented evidence that public opinion was strongly against execution of individuals with mental retardation. Polls cited included those in Texas, Georgia and Florida, all of which showed strong opposition.[54] The Court also made reference to the American Association of Mental Retardation's (AAMR) stated opposition.[55]

Nonetheless, the justices found that none of this was sufficient to show a national consensus, nor objective enough evidence such as legislation, to prohibit the death sentence "categorically" for all defendants with mental retardation under the Eighth Amendment's stricture against cruel and unusual punishment.[56]

Punishment Purposes and the Proportionality Argument. Two of the stated purposes of punishment generally, and capital punishment specifically, are retribution and deterrence.

The central concept of retribution is proportionality. Proportionality says that the degree of punishment must be proportional and directly related to the defendant's blameworthiness. In Penry's case, the defense argued that the death penalty would be disproportional to his degree of moral responsibility because he had the limited reasoning capacity of a seven-year-old. It would therefore be cruel and unusual punishment to execute him.[57]

They then carried the argument one step further. Not only is the death penalty disproportionate and cruel and unusual for Penry, but also for all convicts who have mental retardation. All persons with mental retardation have "substantial cognitive and behavioral disabilities"[58] that limit their moral culpability and make the death penalty retributively disproportional, cruel and unusual.[59]

The Court rejected this argument. It found the concept of "mental age" problematic.[60] No finding had been made at trial that Penry had the mental capabilities of a young child. There are degrees of mental retardation. Individuals with mental retardation have "diverse capacities and life experiences."[61] Some criminals with mental retardation have the degree of understanding and mental capacity required to equate their criminal culpability to the death penalty under the Eighth Amendment.[62] By precedent, courts have refused to rely on mental age as a legal concept to determine culpability. Doing so could have the counter-productive effect of denying individuals with mental retardation the right to marry or enter into contracts.[63]

Court's Conclusion. Based on these arguments, the Court chose to conclude that people with mental retardation as a class are not exempt from capital punishment.[64] At some point in the future, a societal consensus upon which to base such a generalization may exist. Until such time, imposition of death on the persons with mental retardation must be determined individually and on a case-by-case basis.[65]

Thus the Court left the decision up to juries and judges as to whether to impose capital punishment on persons with mental retardation. Whether imposition of the death penalty conforms to the concept of proportionality and fulfills the retributive and deterrence goals of punishment are issues that are "best left for juries to decide."[66] The Court could not find such imposition cruel and unusual punishment in all instances.

WHAT IT MEANS

The United States is one of the last democracies in the world to utilize execution as a criminal punishment.[67] Other culturally and technologically advanced civilizations find it ethically intolerable to execute criminals. About fifty countries, including most Latin American and all European nations have banned the death penalty.[68] West Germany (abolished in 1949), Great Britain (banned in 1973) and France (ended in 1981), all have fairly extensive histories of doing without executions with apparently no ill effects on their capital crime rates.[69] More recently such nations as Romania, Haiti, Cambodia, Namibia,[70] South Africa, Argentina, Cyprus and El Salvador, none of which are noted for their emphasis on civil liberties, have also banned capital punishment.[71]

Given that we use a questionable penalty of such brutality that it is rejected by other civilized nations, whether to take or spare a human life, particularly one of a mentally disabled person, must be weighed as a decision of profound gravity and the most crucial concern.[72] The question is not one of compassion or empathy for the murderer, but of a profound conviction that an advanced civilization should not require such an abominable punishment for such vulnerable defendants.[73]

The fundamental fallacy of the Supreme Court's reasoning to allow the persons with mental retardation to be sentenced to death is its thesis that some persons with mental retardation have sufficient comprehension of the criminality of their actions to be fully morally culpable and therefore eligible for execution. Based on this premise the Court left it to the discretion of judges and juries whether to condemn persons with mental retardation to death or not.

The legal community, both judges and attorneys (nonetheless lay jurors!) have yet to comprehend fully how the capacity of persons with mental retardation to "reason, understand moral issues, to make decisions and to protect their own legal rights"[74] are undermined and limited by their retardation. As one expert stated:

> The problem is that no one knows anything about this stuff. . . . There are very few specialists who know what being mentally retarded is, and how it affects a person's ability to reason and to make judgments.[75]

Allowing juries the discretion to determine that persons with mental retardation can be executed leaves them to decide in ignorance because the effects of mental retardation, until recently, have rarely been presented to them adequately by the defense.

Ethicists, the knowledgeable public, and experts in mental retardation viewed this decision of the Supreme Court as "morally repugnant"[76] and a "tragic injustice."[77] Some were "downright horrified,"[78] because " . . . the American public has evolved to a level of decency that rejects such cruelty."[79] The vision of a person with mental retardation sitting on Death Row *ad infinitum*[80] and then strapped into the electric chair or hanging from the yard arm with little understanding of why it should be thus began a national steamroller to change this decision.

Within this context of national consternation, several straightforward rationales can be advanced to countermand the Supreme Court's reasoning and to support a comprehensive ban on the mentally retarded death penalty. The following chapters clarify these responses to the Court's ill-conceived holding. The dignity of the human being cries out for the legal community to comprehend these principles and to use them in their legal reasoning and court decisions.

Notes

[1]Penry v. Lynaugh, 492 U.S. 302, 106 L.Ed 2d 256, 109 S.Ct. 2934 (1989).

[2]Al Kamen, "Death Penalty Upheld for Killers in Mid-Teens," *Washington Post*, 27 June 1989, sec. A.

[3]Sandra Torry, "High Court to Hear Case on Retarded Killer," *Washington Post*, 11 January 1989, sec. A.

[4]Editorial, "Execute a 7-Year-Old?" *Washington Post*, 9 June 1989, sec. A.

[5]Robert Perske, telephone conversation with author, 27 March 1992.

[6]Robert Perske, *Unequal Justice* (Nashville, TN: Abingdon Press, 1991), 63.

[7]Ibid.

[8]Penry v. Lynaugh, 109 S.Ct. 2934, 2942 (1989). *See also* Torry, "High Court," sec. A.

[9]Perske, *Unequal Justice*, 63, 71.

[10]Editorial, "Execute a 7-Year-Old?" sec. A.

[11]Penry, 109 S.Ct. 2934, 2941 (1989). *See also* Torry, "High Court," sec. A.

[12]Penry, 109 S.Ct. 2934, 2941 (1989).

[13]Torry, "High Court," sec. A.

[14]Ibid. *See also* Editorial, "Execute a 7-Year-Old?" A.

[15]John J. Gruttadaurio, "Consistency in the Application of the Death Penalty to Juveniles and the Mentally Impaired: A Suggested Legislative Approach," 58 *Cincinnati Law Review* (1989): 217 quoting Petition for Writ of Certiorari, Joint Appendix at 18, Penry v. Lynaugh, petition for cert. filed, 57 U.S.L.W. 3024 (U.S. 4 Jan 1988), cert. granted, 108 S.Ct. 2896 (1988)(No. 87-6177)(testimony of Dr. Jerome Brown, 35.)

[16]Penry, 109 S.Ct. 2934, 2941 (1989).

[17]Ibid., 2941-2942, 2958.

[18]Ibid., 2942.

[19]Ibid.

[20]Ibid.

[21]Ibid., 2942.

[22]Ibid., 2952.

[23]*See* Jurek v. Texas, 428 U.S. 362, 49 L.Ed. 929, 96 S.Ct. 2950 (1976); Woodson v. North Carolina, 428 U.S. 280, 49 L.Ed 2d. 944, 96 S.Ct. 2978 (1976); Lockett v. Ohio, 438 U.S. 586, 57 L.Ed 2d 973, 98 S.Ct. 2954 (1978); and Eddings v. Oklahoma, 455 U.S. 104, 71 L.Ed 2d, 102 S.Ct. 869 (1982).

[24]Penry, 109 S.Ct. 2934, 2945, 2947-2948 (1989).

[25]*See* ibid., 2949, quoting California v. Brown, 479 U.S. 538, 545, 933 Ed. 2d 934, 107 S.Ct. 837 (1987)(concurring opinion).

[26]Penry, 109 S.Ct. 2934, 2947 (1989).

[27]Ibid., 2946.

[28]Ibid., 2941, 2947.

[29]Ibid., 2943, 2947.

[30]Ibid., 2943.

[31]Ibid., 2942, 2947, 2949, 2958.

[32]Ibid., 2949.
[33]Ibid., 2949, 2958.
[34]Ibid., 2958.
[35]Ibid., 2957.
[36]Ibid.
[37]Perske, 67-75.
[38]Penry, 109 S.Ct. 2934, 2952 (1989).
[39]Ibid.
[40]Ibid., 2958.
[41]Ibid., 2952-2958.
[42]Ibid., 2952-2953.
[43]Ibid.
[44]Ibid., 2952.
[45]Ibid.
[46]Ibid., 2955.
[47]*See generally* Larry Barnett and Emily Reed, *Law, Society and Population, Issues in a New Field* (Houston: Cap and Gown Press, 1985) for a elaboration of the thesis that the Court adopted here.
[48]Penry, 109 S.Ct. 2934, 2955 (1989).
[49]Ibid., 2955.
[50]Ibid., 2954.
[51]Ibid.
[52]Ibid., 2955.
[53]Ibid.
[54]Ibid., 2955-2956.
[55]Ibid., 2955.
[56]Ibid., 2957.
[57]Ibid., 2956.
[58]Ibid.
[59]Ibid., 2957.
[60]Ibid.
[61]Ibid.
[62]Ibid., 2958.
[63]Ibid.
[64]Ibid.
[65]Editorial, "Evolving Standards of Decency," *Washington Post*, 28 June 1989, sec. A.
[66]Penry, 109 S.Ct. 2934, 2955 (1989).
[67]Andrew Malcolm, "Capital Punishment Is Popular, But So Are Its Alternatives," *New York Times*, 10 September 1989, sec. 4.
[68]Anthony Lewis, "A Rage to Kill," *New York Times*, 18 May 1990, sec. A.
[69]Colman McCarthy, "Death Row's Macabre Death Watch," *Washington Post*, 2 April 1990, sec. A.
[70]"The Politics of Death," *Economist Newspaper Ltd.*, 24 March 1990, 25.
[71]McCarthy, sec. A.
[72]Joshua N. Sondheimer, "A Continuing Source of Aggravation: The Improper Consideration of Mitigating Factors in Death Penalty Sentencing," *Hastings Law Journal* 41 (January 1990):431 quoting Gregg v. Georgia, 428

U.S. 153, 189 (1976).

[73]Editorial, "A Friend in the Electric Chair," *New York Times*, 22 July 1989, sec. A.

[74]Peter Applebome, "2 States Grapple With Issue of Executing Retarded Men," *New York Times*, 13 July 1989, sec. I.

[75]Ibid.

[76]Editorial, "Evolving Standards," sec. A.

[77]Kamen, "Death Penalty Upheld," sec. A.

[78]Alain Sanders, "Bad News for Death Row," *Time Magazine*, 134 (10 July 1989):48.

[79]Editorial, "Evolving Standards," sec. A.

[80]American Bar Association, ABA House of Delegates, "Recommendation," February 1989, 3.

2

Theoretical Arguments Against The Death Penalty for Offenders with Mental Retardation

> *. . . the execution of mentally retarded individuals is "nothing more than the purposeless and needless imposition of pain and suffering,". . . and is unconstitutional under the Eighth Amendment.*
> -- Justice William Brennan, *Penry v. Lynaugh*

INTRODUCTION

This chapter responds to the Supreme Court's reasoning in the *Penry* case with straightforward reasons and simplified rationales as to why individualized sentencing of offenders with mental retardation should be abandoned in capital cases. It presents a comprehensive case for the abolition of executions of persons with mental retardation.

CULPABILITY AND THE *PER SE* DEFINITION ARGUMENT

DEFINITION OF MENTAL RETARDATION

Individuals with mental retardation are special, uncomplicated people. According to the American Association on Mental Retardation, mental retardation means "significantly subaverage general intellectual functioning existing concurrently with deficits in adaptive behavior and manifested during the developmental period."[1] This definition can be divided into three parts to clarify its meaning.

The first part, "significantly subaverage general intellectual functioning," means that the retarded person has an Intelligence Quotient (I.Q.) score of seventy or less.[2] I.Q.s below seventy are at least "two standard deviations below" the average person's or "mean score" for the whole population. The average American has an I.Q. of one hundred.[3] Ninety-seven to ninety-eight percent of the population has I.Q.s of seventy or more.[4] Thus the mentally retarded fall into the bottom two to three percent of the U.S. population in intellectual functioning.

Adults with mental retardation never have a mental age greater than twelve years old. Alfred Binet, the creator of the I.Q. test, also developed the concept of "mental age." Mental age means that "an adult with certain types of mental deficiencies cannot function in terms of reasoning and understanding beyond the level of an average child" of a given age.[5] Adults with mental ages of children always have "a substantial mental disability."[6] By definition, they perpetually have "significant limitation in . . . effectiveness in meeting the standards of maturation, learning, personal independence, and/or social responsibility that are expected for [their] age level and cultural group."[7] Their handicap pervades "in every dimension" of their "functioning, including . . . language, memory, attention, ability to control impulsivity, moral development, self-concept, self-perception, suggestibility, knowledge of basic information, and general motivation."[8]

The second part of the definition, "deficits in adaptive behavior," means that people with mental retardation have behavioral problems and deficient life skills that derive from their intellectual inadequacies.[9] By definition, they have lower than average "'ability to cope with and function in the everyday world.'"[10] These deficits prevent the retarded from surviving in the world without the help of an extensive familial and/or social service support system.[11]

The third part, manifestation of the handicap "during the developmental period" means that onset of the low I.Q. and lack of adaptive skills began prior to age twenty-two.[12]

Although it may seem like a tautology to state, it is important to clarify that all three elements of the definition must be present for an individual to be classified as mentally retarded. If any one of these elements is missing, the person by definition is not mentally retarded. The importance of this definition and inclusion of all elements, especially the first two, is that the prohibition of capital punishment for all persons with mental retardation *per se* hinges on the content of these elements.

MENTAL RETARDATION ATTRIBUTES

In more detail, the inherent cognitive disability of persons with mental retardation is made up of multiple handicapping attributes.

First, persons with mental retardation are characterized by cognitive impairment which includes limited understanding, basic knowledge, memory, and communicative skills.[13] They have few concepts of basic facts and life. Their lack of elemental formal knowledge is often aggravated by improper childhood habilitation and schooling. Their sparse mental aptitude contributes to their inability to speak logically.[14] They are simple people.

I.Q.: 65

When he was twelve, Limmie Arthur was socially promoted from third grade. He couldn't print his name, despite trying patiently to learn to do so. He left school at the age of sixteen. He had never been in special education classes.

When he killed "Cripple Jack," Arthur did not grasp that leaving his bloody shirt at the crime scene was incriminating evidence that would be used against him. That he hid in an attic with his feet sticking out is almost humorous. Yet it is also a pathetic sign of his inability to cope with the enormity of his crime.

After one court hearing, Arthur was happy because he thought all had gone well. He failed to recognize that the judge had refused his pleas for a new trial and a reduction of sentence. When asked what happened, he said, "I don't understand a whole lot of what was going on. . . . I had to listen real close . . . and I get lost very quick . . . . It's bad. It's bad to be retarded."[15]

Second, although some mentally retarded people can distinguish right from wrong, all the mentally retarded have limits in moral development and reasoning.[16]

. . . moral reasoning ability develops in stages, incrementally over time, and is dependent on an individual's intellectual ability and developmental level. . . . Mental retardation limits the ability of individuals to reach full moral reasoning ability.[17]

Limmie Arthur believed that he was sentenced to death because he couldn't read. He diligently tried to learn so he could earn his GED because he thought he would get a reprieve if he was successful.[18]

Thus all individuals with mental retardation have "immature concepts of moral blameworthiness."[19]

Third, this cognitive deficit is evidenced by an inability to grasp the basic relationship between cause and effect, a lack of foresight, and an inability to foresee the consequences of actions.

I.Q.: 62-66

Morris Mason asked a legal aid what he should wear to his funeral because he couldn't understand that he would not be alive after his execution.

Typically, adults with mental retardation, like children, cannot comprehend the finality of death.[20]

Fourth, people with mental retardation lack intellectual flexibility, a deficit which prevents them from learning from their past mistakes. They have "a pattern of persisting in behaviors even after they [such behaviors] have proven counterproductive or unsuccessful."[21]

Fifth, the mentally retarded have short attention spans and lack full impulse control.[22] These problems lead to deficits in "attention focus and selectivity in the attention process."[23] Lack of ability to attend leads to impulsivity. They act on "strong emotion without the intervention of judgment."[24]

I.Q.: 50-63
While raping his victim, John Paul Penry became enraged when she superficially stabbed him with scissors. Once in the course of struggling with her, he was incapable of braking his violence until she was dead.[25]

Conversely, they lack the *mens rea* needed to formulate fully the specific intent to commit a criminal act. Under the concept of diminished capacity, their limited understanding of their own culpability circumscribes their liability and blameworthiness so that their degree of guilt is never total or complete.[26]

Thus although there are variations in the degree of mental retardation, and the severe and profoundly retarded[27] have greater disabilities than the mild and moderately retarded,[28] ALL mentally retarded people are below the threshold of normal intellectual and adaptive functioning. Even those with I.Q.s in the 60-70 range have low intellectual capacity.

It is important to say in passing that the word "mild" is an unfortunate and misleading choice of words for persons with I.Q.s in the 55-70 range. Whereas mild is meant to indicate the degree of disability relevant to the other categories of mental retardation, it inadvertently connotes a meaning of not being qualitatively different from normal intelligence. In fact, however, persons in the mild range of mental retardation have real deficits in intellectual and adaptive behavior which grievously limit their life abilities.[29] As a prominent member of the Association for Retarded Citizens said, "Why don't we talk about amputation and say that a person is mildly amputated if they lost one leg?"[30]

Even in the upper range of mild retardation (65-70 I.Q.), the mentally retarded lack the capacity to make adequate and sufficient distinctions between right and wrong. Persons with mild retardation are capable of completing at the most about the sixth grade,[31] and when they reach chronological maturity, they require "guidance and assistance when under unusual social or economic stress."[32]

A Georgia district court's opinion illustrates these points. The court gave a straightforward explanation of the limitations of accused murderer, William A. Smith, I.Q. sixty-five, that is, in the high mild category. It clarified that the defendant "had poor reading and verbal skills and that his memory, reasoning ability, and other skills . . . were severely impaired."[33]

Similarly, persons with moderate retardation can finish about the second grade. As adults they require "supervision and guidance when subjected to even mild social or economic stress."[36]

> I.Q.: 65
> William Smith senselessly killed "Old Dan," the storekeeper whom he had known all his life and who had been good to him. In the illogical thinking of the mentally retarded, Smith chose a friendly person to rob, but "went berserk" when attacked by the victim with a hammer. Smith later showed remorse. He said he hadn't meant to kill Dan but only to get money for a new car.[34]
> The 11th Circuit Court held that Smith's mental retardation prevented him from voluntarily confessing and waiving his Miranda rights.[35]

DIFFERENCE BETWEEN MENTAL RETARDATION AND MENTAL ILLNESS/INSANITY

> *"It jus' seems kinda funny a cuckoo like him and a smart guy like you travelin' together," [said Slim, the cowboy philosopher.]*
> *"He ain't no cuckoo," said George. "He's dumb as hell, but he ain't crazy."*
> *"Used to play jokes on 'im 'cause he was too dumb to take care of 'imself. But he was too dumb to even know he had a joke played on him*
> *. . . .*
> -- John Steinbeck, *Of Mice and Men*

Mental retardation is completely different from mental illness or insanity. Mental retardation is a permanent condition. It is a condition of low intelligence. There is no cure for it. Mental illness, on the other hand, is a disease of the mind. It is a psychological sickness that can be treated with therapy and medication. Although much mental illness is chronic and incurable, many mentally ill persons get better.[37]

The topic of discussion here is mental retardation, not mental illness or insanity. The following arguments refer only to mental retardation.

DEFINITION OF CULPABILITY

That individuals with mental retardation do not commit crimes in any greater numbers than the general population and that there is no direct causal link between mental retardation and criminality is now widely accepted among the criminal justice community and experts in mental disabilities.[38] When persons with mental retardation do commit crimes, their cognitive deficits, their intellectual capacity which is less than that of ninety-seven percent of the rest of us, their mental age of twelve or younger, their lack of foresight and inability to comprehend causation and consequences, their lack of full moral development, their intellectual rigidity, short attention spans and impulsivity, all bear on their legal and ethical culpability.

Two factors make it is essential to comprehend what moral culpability is. First, understanding of culpability is necessary in order to grasp how it relates to the significant impairments of persons with mental retardation in all areas of their lives, and to the imposition of the death penalty on them.

Second, it is important to grasp the meaning of culpability because a basic principle of American society holds that the degree of punishment for criminal acts must be "directly related"[39] to the degree of culpability. Culpability and punishment comprise a scale of equations of equality. The level of the punishment must equal the level of culpability. Full culpability is required in order for the most severe of crimes, murder, to receive the ultimate punishment, death. Diminished culpability requires a diminished penalty. The most severe punishment, death, cannot be imposed when there is any degree of diminished culpability. In the words of the Japanese Mikado, "My object all sublime--I shall achieve in time--to let the punishment fit the crime."[40] FIGURE 2.1 is a stylized picture of the relationship of these three elements - crime, culpability, and punishment.

Let us look then at what culpability means. A short definition states that culpability is "'personal responsibility and moral guilt.'"[41]

In more depth, culpability is comprised of a number of ingredients or characteristics. These ingredients are precisely those characteristics that persons with mental retardation lack. A murderer must have a full measure of each of these ingredients in order to be fully culpable and to be justly executed. Simply stated, because people with mental retardation lack this full measure, they cannot be executed.

First, full culpability requires the abilities to understand the relationship between cause and effect and to predict the consequences of actions. It is based on the ability to understand the options available and to select an appropriate course of action to deal with stressful situations.

Second, full culpability requires enough basic comprehension of general facts, legal terminology, and the law itself, to understand criminal processes such as the meaning of the Miranda warning and the right to an attorney, and the rights of victims to live free from terror and brutality. A person must be competent to accept and use the legal rights that the Constitution and the law afford to defendants. Such an understanding and competency is vital for a lawbreaker to be held legally responsible for actions that violate victims by depriving them of life.

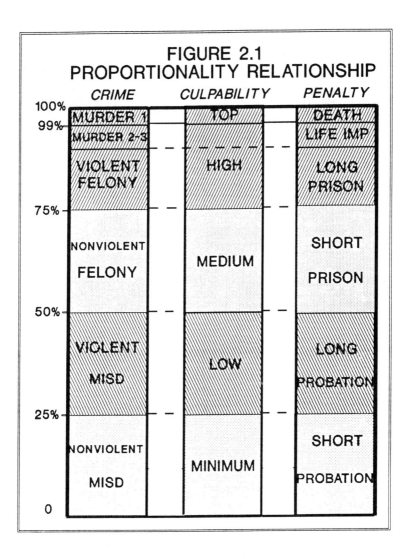

FIGURE 2.1
PROPORTIONALITY RELATIONSHIP

Third, culpability depends on the level of a person's ability to control impulses and to conform his or her conduct to the requirements of the law. This deficit of persons with mental retardation - impulsivity - makes it especially difficult for them to stay within the boundaries of legal norms.[42]

A fourth ingredient of culpability is the attainment of full moral reasoning ability and the ability to distinguish right from wrong. To be fully culpable a defendant must not only know right from wrong but also have full knowledge of why and how his or her acts are morally unacceptable. Full moral development and understanding of the concept of culpability itself must be present to attain the level of blameworthiness that justifies punishment by death.[43]

A fifth major ingredient of culpability is the defendant's deliberateness and purposefulness in committing the criminal act. He or she must first be capable of forming the specific intent to commit the crime and then to actually do so. The more intentionally, purposefully and deliberately a person is in committing the crime, the more serious it is, and, therefore, the greater ought to be the punishment.[44]   Conversely, lack of complete "purposefulness of a defendant's criminal acts or impairment in his or her understanding of them and their consequences limits the degree of culpability and warrants a less severe penalty than capital punishment."[45]

In sum, full culpability is defined as full understanding of causation, culpability and consequences, full ability to select appropriate actions under stress, full control of impulses and ability to conform to the law, full personal responsibility and moral guilt based on full moral reasoning ability, and full intention and deliberateness.

APPLICATION OF CULPABILITY COMPONENTS TO PERSONS WITH MENTAL RETARDATION

Let us look at each of the characteristics of culpability and see how they relate to the characteristics of persons with mental retardation and the imposition of punishment on them.

First, all defendants with mental retardation lack understanding of causality and consequences to some degree. All have deficits in "strategic thinking" which prevent them from generating and selecting appropriate actions in "stressful situations."[46]

Second, all defendants with mental retardation have serious impairments in general comprehension and cognition. All such defendants have the intellectual age of children. All lack basic general information and specific facts of law.[47] All defendants with mental retardation are in the bottom two to three percent of the nation's general intellectual functioning. Their substantial intellectual deficits lessen their culpability and the penalty that should be imposed on them.[48]

Third, all defendants with mental retardation lack impulse control and the ability to postpone reactions to emotional stimuli. Persons with mental retardation by definition always suffer from impulsivity. All lack sufficient understanding to conform to the intricate behavioral restraints of society. Thus their culpability is diminished, and they do not deserve the death penalty.[49]

Fourth, even though some offenders with mental retardation may know the difference between right and wrong as children do, all persons with mental retardation have deficits in ethical and moral reasoning ability to a greater or lesser degree. People with mental retardation by definition do not attain full moral development with an understanding of their own blameworthiness.[50] To the degree that the mentally retarded lack the capability to comprehend culpability, they are not culpable and cannot be held morally and legally liable for their criminal acts.

Fifth, all defendants with mental retardation lack complete purposefulness in their actions. By definition the degree of deliberateness of people with mental retardation is substantially impaired. To the degree that they are unable to intend what they do, their degree of moral culpability is lessened. Therefore, since all defendants who have mental retardation have some lack of purposefulness and diminished culpability, their criminal acts do not warrant the ultimate penalty, death.[51]

In sum, the combination of these crippling limitations in every aspect of the lives of a people with mental retardation is directly relevant to the degree of their moral blameworthiness. To the extent that defendants with mental retardation lack the characteristics of this laundry list of intellectual capacities and adaptive behaviors, they cannot be held morally responsible. The greater the degree of impairment, the lesser the culpability. Each deficit lessens the degree of culpability in its own right. The cumulative diminishing effect on culpability of each characteristic superimposed upon the others prevents ALL defendants with mental retardation from having the ability to act with the complete degree of culpability that is absolutely essential to justify the imposition of the complete and irrevocable penalty, death.[52] Mental retardation, by its very nature and definition, is "sufficiently severe" to prevent any person disabled by it who commits a capital crime from crossing the threshold into maximum culpability where the punishment equals death.[53] The definitions of mental retardation and culpability dictate that it is impossible for persons with mental retardation to possess that degree of culpability necessary for the death penalty to be imposed under the Eighth Amendment.[54] All persons with mental retardation *per se* do not have the level of moral responsibility essential for them to be executed. Because of their limited capabilities and culpability, death is always a disproportionate punishment. It is the "barbarous" elimination of "the least culpable on Death Row."[55] It is always excessively cruel and unusual and prohibited by the Eighth Amendment of the Constitution.

The federal and state court systems have failed to account for the severity of the handicap of persons with mental retardation.[56] It is time that they do so.

THE DISPROPORTIONALITY ARGUMENT

Equality consists in the same treatment of similar persons.
-- Aristotle, *Politics*

The culpability argument is based on the concepts of proportionality and disproportionality. Culpability can be elaborated into the argument of proportionality.

The proportion in question contains two elements. One is the death penalty. The other is complete culpability. The death penalty must be totally correlated with culpability for proportionality to exist. Any lack of culpability is disproportionate to the death penalty.

Let us look first at why this is true and second at why the death penalty is always disproportionate when imposed on persons with mental retardation.

PROPORTIONALITY

Capital punishment is the most severe penalty that a civilized society can constitutionally impose. In theory at least, it is reserved for the most brutal, vicious and heinous of crimes and perpetrators. A mass murderer randomly and senselessly slaughters innocent strangers. Multiple victims, police officers in the line of duty, babies, children, the elderly or handicapped are murdered. The victims are tortured or brutalized. The perpetrator is without conscience and shows no mercy. Nothing in his makeup or actions mitigates in his favor. He is totally and completely culpable for his crimes. He deserves death.

Death is unalterably final. Therefore, the evil of actions and intent and complete culpability described above must be present for a murderer to be sentenced to death.

Supreme Court *dictum* holds that the Constitution requires that the offender and offense characteristics be equal to the highest degree of culpability for death to be a proportionate punishment.[57] Federal and state death penalty statutes also have elaborate and detailed safeguards to prevent the death penalty from being applied undeservedly.

The legal strictures and safeguards of the rights of the accused result in sentencing bodies imposing death in only a very few capital cases. The Supreme Court has held that death must not be imposed arbitrarily and capriciously.[58] There must be a legitimate penological rationale for selecting which murderers will receive the death sentence from among the many who are convicted.[59] That reason is maximum culpability and a full measure of personal responsibility.[60]

Because judges and juries are limited by law and frequently have reasonable doubts that complete culpability exists, only a small segment of murderers, one to two percent, are actually sentenced to death. Only a tiny portion of these are actually executed.[61] Thus justice aims for surety in imposing the death penalty. That surety of the personal guilt of murderers with mental retardation is always lacking because of their limited intellectual and moral capabilities. Consequently, they should never be among the few who are executed.

ONE PERCENT/TWO PERCENT

The second part of the disproportionality argument looks at persons with mental retardation in relation to the crime-culpability-death proportion. Since any lack of complete culpability is disproportionate to the death penalty, and since people with mental retardation always lack complete culpability as previously stated and as evidenced by their last place in the nation in intellectual functioning, the death penalty applied to offenders with mental retardation is always disproportionate and unconstitutional.

By definition, all persons with mental retardation fall in the bottom two percent of the population in intellectual functioning. Because they have I.Q.s of seventy or below and the mental age of twelve or less, ninety-eight percent of the nation has greater mental and reasoning capabilities than they. Since culpability is related to capability, " . . . However moral blameworthiness is measured or estimated . . . " people with mental retardation "are never in the top one or two percent of defendants convicted of murder in the level of their personal culpability," "understanding, . . . foresight and responsibility."[62] A wide gap lies between the lowest two percent in terms of capabilities and culpability and the top one percent (or less) who are sentenced to death because they have the highest degree of culpability.[63]

If people with mental retardation receive the death penalty, then we must logically infer that they are in the highest one percent of the population in their culpability, based on their "appreciation and understanding" of the evil of their crime, despite the fact that they are in the lowest two percent of the population in intellectual capabilities. Such a conclusion is highly unreasonable, because, pragmatically, the gap is so wide between the two that *"no one can be in both categories."*[64] FIGURE 2.2 illustrates this disproportionality.

Based on the discrepancy and disproportionality of the relationship between the top one percent in culpability and the bottom two percent in capability, punishment of offenders with mental retardation by execution is highly discrepant, disproportionate and unreasonable.[65] It is constitutionally unacceptable because it "'is nothing more than the purposeless and needless imposition of pain and suffering.'"[66]

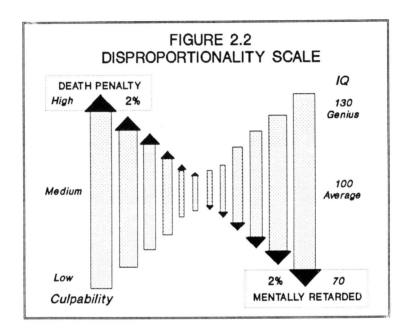

FIGURE 2.2
DISPROPORTIONALITY SCALE

DEATH PENALTY

High   2%

Medium

Low

Culpability

IQ

130
Genius

100
Average

2%   70
MENTALLY RETARDED

THE ANTI-DETERRENCE ARGUMENT

> *We are all dangerous until our fears grow thoughtful.*
> -- John Crank, *The Strongest Everything*

INTRODUCTION

As stated above, the Supreme Court has ruled that a legitimate punitive purpose must exist for determining which among the many criminals convicted of capital crimes will receive the death sentence.[67] A punishment must make a "measurable contribution" to a valid punitive purpose to be permissible under the Eighth Amendment.[68] There are two such purposes. One is deterrence. The other is retribution.[69]

Deterrence is a primary purpose of capital punishment. It means that potential criminals avoid crime because they fear punishment. Deterrence rests on the presumption that people think about and appreciate the consequences of what they do. Essentially, individuals must premeditate for deterrence to work.[70]

SPECIAL DETERRENCE

There are two kinds of deterrence. Special deterrence means that the offender himself will be dissuaded from further criminal activity by the punishment imposed on him. Special deterrence is also called incapacitation. If we execute the murderer, we know that he will never kill again. The death penalty is the ultimate incapacitation and deterrent. The offender is gone from this life and cannot commit more crimes.

Nonetheless, mentally impaired murderers can be deterred from further murders and incapacitated equally as well by life in prison. Imprisonment has the humanitarian benefit of preserving life. It allows for the murderer to be rehabilitated and for the murderer who is mentally retarded to be habilitated. Even though special deterrence works through the death penalty, life in prison works equally well and fits better with the humanitarian standards of a civilized society.

GENERAL DETERRENCE

The second kind of deterrence is general deterrence. In theory, general deterrence means that punishing an individual or all offenders deters potential criminals from similar criminal actions because they fear punishment. Capital punishment deters individuals from committing capital offenses. Murders are avoided because of the fear of the death penalty.

In the instance of the death penalty for the mentally retarded, general deterrence refers to the whole population of potential murderers at large and to mentally retarded potential murderers.

General Deterrence of Non-Mentally Retarded Persons. Looking first at the issue of general deterrence of non-mentally retarded potential killers, we can assume that they understand the deterrence relationship. Yet it does not necessarily follow that they will act on it and be deterred from murdering because persons with mental retardation are executed. No conclusive evidence exists that general deterrence works at all, that is, that execution of people with mental retardation deters further murders.

The deterrence theory assumes that people act rationally. We see that murder results in execution, so we don't murder. However, many people, especially murderers, do not reason this out. Murder is often a crime of passion. In the heat of the act, murderers do not think of being caught and suffering the most severe punishment. If they do think about this at all, they believe that they will get a few years in prison and then go free. As appeals of the death sentence take longer and longer, many beyond ten years, the certainty of punishment diminishes, and the deterrence value is lessened.

Assuming *arguendo* that deterrence does work for the majority of the population, taking out the small number of killers with mental retardation from the pool of those who can be executed is highly unlikely to make any difference in this value of deterrence for most potential killers who will continue to be subjected to the threat of the death penalty.[71] That the person being executed has mental retardation has no known effect on deterrence or the lack thereof.

General Deterrence of Persons with Mental Retardation. The probability that a person with mental retardation will be deterred from a capital offense because he knows that he and other persons with mental retardation may be executed is even less likely than for persons of normal intelligence.[72] Persons with mental retardation do not have the intellectual capacity and maturity of adults to understand the deterrence relationship. By definition they have "significantly subaverage intelligence" and "deficits in adaptive behaviors."[73] They lack the capacity that persons of ordinary intelligence have

> to 'premeditate,' . . . plan and calculate a criminal offense, . . . [and] . . . to understand its consequences. . . . [C]apital punishment serves as a deterrent only when the murder is a result of at least some premeditation and deliberation. . . .[74]

Such premeditation and deliberation is beyond the capability of people with mental retardation.

A potential murderer who has mental retardation lacks complete rationality. Persons with mental retardation do not understand that death is unalterably final.[75] They do not recognize what ceasing to exist means so that, additionally, they cannot comprehend that committing murder may cause them to cease to exist. The potential murderer with mental retardation may not know that murderers are or are not executed in his state nor understand why executions take place. The behavior of Alton Waye in wanting to tell everyone what he had done and his final words that he had no understanding of the death penalty evidence this point.[76] Consequently, since the threat of capital punishment has no meaning, it also is powerless over persons with mental retardation.[77] The death penalty has little chance of deterring a person with mental retardation from murdering.

Assuming *arguendo* that people with mental retardation do understand the correlation between murdering and the possibility of the death penalty, the probability that they will act on it is even less than that of the average person because part of their handicap is diminished impulse control.

Thus the special deterrence capacity of execution of offenders with mental retardation for other persons with mental retardation is "hardly sufficiently plausible to justify the punishment."[78]

SUMMARY

Persons with mental retardation do not have the mental capacity to understand the deterrence effect of capital punishment. Even assuming that they do, their impulsivity makes it unlikely that they would be deterred from murder by the death penalty.

Thus capital punishment for offenders with mental retardation cannot be justified on any count on the basis of deterrence. Deterrence lacks validity as a penological purpose for execution of persons with mental retardation. It simply does not work. There are better ways to hold the handicapped accountable for their actions than by executing them.

THE ANTI-RETRIBUTION ARGUMENT

Thou shalt give life for life, eye for eye, tooth for tooth, hand for hand, foot for foot, burning for burning, wound for wound, stripe for stripe.

Exodus 21:23-25

Retribution is the second constitutionally permissible punitive purpose of the death penalty. The idea of retribution is elaborated in two theories. The first theory, "just desserts," holds that the offender deserves the punishment by reason of and in proportion to the offense. In the second theory, retribution justifies society's demand for vengeance for harm done. The public takes its pound of flesh in satisfaction for being morally wronged.

THE "JUST DESSERTS" THEORY

Definition. The first sense of retribution, just desserts, is the Bible's Old Testament version of "an eye for an eye, a tooth for a tooth."[79] A life for a life.

The constitutional application of just desserts parallels the culpability and proportionality arguments. In embodying this theory in case law, the Supreme Court has held that the degree of retribution must be proportional to the measure of the individual's personal responsibility and blameworthiness. A criminal must literally get what he deserves.[80]

Just Desserts and Persons with Mental Retardation. When the proportionality of just desserts as stated above is applied to people with mental retardation, one must unavoidably draw the conclusion that they never deserve execution. By definition, their mental handicap prevents them from ever having a full measure of responsibility and blameworthiness.[81] Offenders with mental retardation can never deserve death,[82] the ultimate retribution.

Equality of Desserts Scales. Even allowing for the sake of argument that death for offenders with mental retardation is retributively valid, just desserts requires only that the scales of crimes and punishments be equal. The most serious crime receives the most serious penalty. The penalties become less severe as the crime and culpability of the offender become less severe. At the top of the scale, justice is served just as well by life imprisonment for offenders with mental retardation. There is no just retributive need to execute persons with mental handicaps.

Validity of Life Imprisonment. Today, life in prison for offenders with mental retardation no longer means warehousing, exploitation by other inmates, and general degeneration of existing skills, as it formerly did. Prison systems, some under the mandate of federal court orders,[83] have developed programs to house and habilitate offenders with mental retardation in safe and nurturing environments. These programs are in response to both a recognition of their need and a comprehension that their criminal behavior is more the result of a lack of understanding or, misunderstanding, of societal and legal norms than of deliberate intent to do wrong.[84] Thus the argument that life imprisonment is a crueler punishment than death for offenders with mental retardation has no merit today, if it ever did.

SOCIETAL VENGEANCE

Definition. In the second theory of retribution, society demands vengeful equalization for unspeakable acts committed against its members. Intentional murder done without mitigation or extenuating circumstances, more than any other crime, damages the social fabric of a nation. This harm can be set aright only by a punishment of equal degree - the death of the murderer. By deliberately and purposefully violating the right to life of others, the murderer has forfeited his own life.

Barbarism of Vengeance. However, "vengeance is mine sayeth the Lord."[85] Retribution is the old law. When applied to the handicapped, it is a barbaric theory that is unjustified in an advanced, civilized society. Retributive actions against the persons with mental retardation echo the Third Reich philosophy of elimination of the imperfect. Modern religions teach forgiveness and mercy. Retribution has been replaced by a kinder and gentler philosophy. Civilized societies do not demand revengeful just desserts of their disabled citizens. They do not execute the people with mental retardation. Exacting death from mentally handicapped persons is a barbaric concept of retribution. Our society should protect itself "from [this] barbarity of exacting mindless vengeance."[86]

Life in prison without parole punishes a person with mental retardation in proportion to his or her understanding. The needs of victims' families for consolation are better served by mercy and the sparing of the lives of those who do not have complete understanding of what they have done, than by their execution.

Sum. To summarize, the use of the death penalty as retribution in any of its theories holds no validity for persons with mental retardation. "Where neither retribution nor deterrence is furthered by executing . . .[a mentally retarded] defendant, the death sentence is inappropriate."[87]

THE SOCIETAL CONSENSUS ARGUMENT

Your representative owes you . . . his judgment; and he betrays
instead of serving you if he sacrifices it to your opinion.
-- Edmund Burke, *Speech to the Electors of Bristol*

CRITIQUE OF THE COURT'S METHODOLOGY

The *Penry* Court reasoned that the actions of the country's selected political representatives at the grass roots state level are the best indicators of American society's viewpoints. It strongly relied on state legislative enactments,[88] and found insufficient evidence of a national consensus in them because only one state, Georgia, had banned the mentally retarded death penalty to that time.

This methodology of the Court has been severely criticized by legal scholars as well as by the dissenting opinion of Justice William Brennan. Experts argue that the Supreme Court is more than a mere "political instrumentality" which simply mirrors state statutes and societal consensus. It is the highest and most august legal body of the nation - charged with interpreting the Constitution based on its learned knowledge of legal principles. By simply looking to a survey of state laws it abdicates its responsibility to interpret the Constitution and to make final legal judgments. "If all the Justices can do is survey the legislative scene and declare a winner, you don't need a court. All you need is someone who can count."[89]

In the *Penry* dissent, Justice William Brennan excoriated his colleagues for relying on political consensus. "'We have never insisted that a punishment [be] rejected unanimously by the States before we . . . judge it cruel and unusual.'" Justice Brennan accused the court of "shirking its constitutional duties by allowing 'political majorities . . . to' define the contours of the Eighth Amendment. . . ." He stated that "'[t]he very purpose of a Bill of Rights was to withdraw certain subjects from the vicissitudes of political controversy, to place them beyond the reach of majorities.'"[90] Thus the Court's reliance on the lack of political consensus of the state legislatures leaves much to be desired as a decision-making methodology where the lives of disabled citizens hang in the balance.

DIALECTICAL REVERSE

> *A universal feeling, well or ill founded, cannot be safely disregarded.*
> -- Abraham Lincoln, *Peoria (Illinois) Speech*

Nonetheless, assume *arguendo* that the Supreme Court's methodology of using the people's political representatives as litmus for societal consensus and constitutional decision-making has some legitimacy. Then the mentally retarded offender death penalty ought to be banned, since, contrary to the Court's limited interpretation, there is in fact ample evidence of a societal consensus for this policy decision.

The plight of persons with mental retardation in American society generally and the criminal justice system particularly has received growing attention during the last two decades.[91] Evidence abounds of the positive changes in contemporary American attitudes towards this issue as it has become more visible in the political arena. Solid evidence also exists of changes in attitudes toward mentally retarded executions.

The judicial standard which measures the constitutionality of legal punishments under the Eighth Amendment is whether such punishments violate the "evolving standards of decency that mark the progress of a maturing society."[92] The thesis advanced here is that the Supreme Court misjudged public consensus in the *Penry* case, and that there is a plethora of objective and convincing evidence that the mentally retarded death penalty "offends humanity"[93] and violates present canons of decency.[94]

According to multiple indicators of national attitudes, execution of mentally disabled citizens in a modern and equitable legal system is abhorrent and illegitimate.[95] Banning executions of persons with mental retardation accurately reflects a national consensus that it is unacceptable, inequitable and inhumane to put mentally "fragile and vulnerable"[96] disabled persons to death. Thus the conclusion follows that the Supreme Court erred in its assessment that insufficient evidence of a national consensus exists for banning the death penalty for individuals with mental retardation.

Attitudinal indicators which lead to this conclusion include public opinion polls, development of habilitative programs for persons with mental retardation, judges' and juries' sentencing decisions that have evolved into case law, and federal statutory enactments.[97]

PUBLIC OPINION POLLS

Within the past few years, several national and state public opinion polls have examined the question of applying the death penalty to persons with mental retardation. All have resulted in the same conclusion. A substantial majority of the American public, including a majority of people who support the death penalty, do not want the offender with mental retardation executed. Pervasive popular support exists for prohibiting such executions because[98] the vision of persons with mental retardation languishing on Death Row through years of legal procedures that they barely comprehend, and finally being strapped into the electric chair without comprehension of why, is "deeply disturbing to most Americans."[99]

The next section examines each of the polls in sequence.

NATIONAL DATA

All national survey data on the topic demonstrate that the American public opposes execution of persons with mental retardation. In a nationwide poll conducted by Louis Harris for the Washington Post during June-September, 1988, about a year prior to the *Penry* decision, seventy percent of the U.S. population opposed executions of persons with mental retardation, and only twenty-two percent favored them.[100] During the same time period, between seventy-two and seventy-nine percent of the country favored the death penalty for persons convicted of murder and other serious crimes, the highest support for the death penalty ever.[101]

In a national poll conducted shortly after the *Penry* decision, three quarters of those surveyed favored the death penalty generally, but they also strongly disapproved of executing the retarded. Only one-quarter of those surveyed were in favor of it.[102]

Thus in both time periods, about three times as many people favored the death penalty generally as favored it for people with mental retardation.

STATE DATA

Public opinion surveys have also been conducted in several states concerning this topic, particularly in those states in which an offender with mental retardation has been on the verge of being, or actually has been, executed. These include Georgia, Florida, Texas and South Carolina.[103] A similar poll was conducted in New York which does not have the death penalty.[104]

In Georgia, polling data showed that seventy-five percent favored the death penalty generally, yet two-thirds were against execution of persons with mental retardation. Seventeen percent were in favor, and another sixteen percent thought it depends on the degree of retardation.[105]

In Florida, seventy-one percent were against execution of offenders with mental retardation, and twelve percent were in favor. This is "extraordinary" both in itself and when compared to the more than seven times as many (eighty-four percent) in favor of the death penalty generally, and the thirteen percent against it.[106]

In Texas, eighty-six percent favored the death penalty, but seventy-three percent opposed it for people with mental retardation.[107]

In a poll conducted in South Carolina in 1987, seventy-two percent favored the death penalty generally, but only twenty-nine percent favored it for offenders with mental retardation.[108]

In New York in May, 1989 just prior to *Penry*, eighty-two percent were against executing people who are mentally retarded.[109]

On the average in the states surveyed in the pre-*Penry* period, seventy-nine percent favored the death penalty generally, but only twenty-two percent favored it for persons with mental retardation. The contrast is great between the two. By itself, that only about one in five persons thinks people with mental retardation should be executed is strong evidence of societal consensus for this position. In contrast to the four out of five who favor the death penalty generally, there could be no more definitive and irrefutable evidence of societal consensus. FIGURE 2.3 summarizes the national and state survey data which evidence the societal consensus that persons with mental retardation should not be executed.

FIGURE 2.3
AMERICAN ATTITUDES ON THE DEATH PENALTY

	Percent Favor Death Penalty		Percent Favor MR Death Penalty	
	1986-8	1989	1986-8	1989
Nationwide	72	79	22	27
States				
Georgia	75	-	17*	-
Texas	86	-	27**	-
Florida	84	-	12	-
South Carolina	72	-	29	-
New York	-	-	-	18
Average	78	79	21	23

*Another 16 % said it depends on how retarded the offender is.
**No figure is given for those favoring. This figure is based on 73 % opposed.
With "undecideds" and "don't knows" included, the figure is probably less than this.

Development of Habilitative Programs for Persons with Mental Retardation

In the last two decades, American society has advanced tremendously in its understanding of the needs of persons with mental retardation and its responsibilities to address those needs. The trigger for this raised consciousness is a growing recognition of the service system's long-term ill-treatment of this disabled group.[110]

Title V, Section 504 of the Rehabilitation Act of 1973[111] and two years later the Education for All Handicapped Children Act of 1975,[112] provided the first impetus for the expansion of national consciousness and responsive programming. Special education, sheltered workshops, and group homes have been developed in acknowledgement of these laws and in response to public recognition that the mental and developmental handicaps of people with mental retardation call for specialized supportive care. We now recognize as a nation that such care is essential for people with mental retardation to function in the community, that society has a responsibility to provide this supportive care, and that, with such care, individuals with mental retardation can become productive and self-supporting taxpayers.[113]

Dedicated programs in community and prison correctional settings have also been instituted.[114] Prison systems, some under the mandate of federal court orders,[115] and community corrections have implemented programs to supervise, house, habilitate, teach life skills, provide job training and job coaching, and generally to nurture the special needs of offenders with mental retardation so that they can become law-abiding and tax-paying citizens. The Lancaster County, Pennsylvania, Special Offender (Probation) Program, and the Georgia, Texas, South Carolina and California inmate rehabilitation units are prime examples.[116] At least fourteen states had such prison and community programs by the early 1980s,[117] and other states have implemented them since or are working toward their implementation.[118]

These programs respond to both a national recognition of the need of the mentally retarded offender and a comprehension that their criminal behavior is more the result of a lack of understanding or, misunderstanding, of societal and legal norms than intentional wrong-doing.[119] The programming represents a fundamental change in societal attitudes and a consensus that society has a responsibility to protect the rights of mentally retarded offenders because they cannot do so for themselves.

Society now acknowledges its responsibilities on this lower plane. It also recognizes, as all polling data indicate, a similar responsibility to respect and protect the even more fundamental right to life of the person who is mentally handicapped. This right precedes the right to habilitation and is presupposed by it. In the past, people with mental retardation have been incapable of protecting their fundamental rights because of their handicapping conditions. Society took advantage of these weaknesses and discriminated against those who were mentally retarded in every way, including considering their mental retardation and assumed associated dangerousness as a reason to execute them. Current statutes and programs that provide for the basic human rights of persons with mental retardation to housing, habilitation, training and education indicate that we are now in the process of remedying those wrongs and making up for past maltreatment and discrimination.[120] Our actions as a society for the care and treatment of people with mental retardation indicate that, because of their handicapping conditions, diminished criminal culpability, and our own previous cruelty and inhumanity to them, we support taking the last step to rebalance the scales of past injustices. Societal consensus supports barring the death penalty for persons with mental retardation.

CASE LAW: JUDGES' AND JURIES' SENTENCING PRACTICES

The body of case law surrounding the application of the death penalty to mentally retarded persons is sparse. The *Penry* Court indicated that the defense offered no case law precedents to support its contention that a contemporary American consensus exists opposing the death penalty for persons with mental retardation.[121] The implication is that there are no such precedents.[122]

Indeed, such case law is sparse. The dearth of legal precedents is evidently due to the reluctance of sentencing authorities to apply the death sentence to persons with mental retardation. This alone is a manifestation that judges and juries disavow such executions.[123] Some precedents do exist, nonetheless, and the *Penry* defense erred in failing to cite them. Those state court appellate decisions that do exist duplicate the revulsion sentencing judges and juries have toward inflicting capital punishment on persons with retardation.[124]

Over a period of more than forty years, at least four state supreme courts have ruled that the retarded are less blameworthy in capital cases than defendants with average intelligence, and that, therefore, they should not be executed.[125] Between 1944 and 1987, the supreme courts of Idaho, Nebraska, Florida and North Carolina vacated death sentences of defendants with, respectively: a) "a pronounced subnormal mind,"[126] b) "a `high-grade imbecile' with an I.Q. of sixty-four,"[127] c) an I.Q. "between 50-70"[128] and d) an I.Q. of sixty-three.[129]

Also in 1987, a Georgia district court held that William Alvin Smith, an accused murderer with an I.Q. of 65, that is, in the high mild category, "had poor reading and verbal skills and that his memory, reasoning ability, and other skills" were sufficiently impaired to prevent him from legitimately waiving his Miranda rights. His death sentence was remanded for rehearing and later reduced to life on this basis.[130]

While not case law but similar in point, the Governor of Louisiana commuted the death sentence of a killer who has mental retardation in the period immediately prior to the *Penry* decision.[131]

Thus what case law and precedents there are do indeed suggest that sentencing bodies and the American people shun execution of mentally retarded persons. At the grass roots state level, sentencing authorities who directly or indirectly reflect the people's attitudes point to this societal consensus. Their unanimity of mind is an enduring one, rooted in the second world war time period and increasingly more prevalent in sentencing authorities' decisions in the years just prior to *Penry*.

In conclusion, solid and convincing evidence in sentencing practices denotes that a mature society's standards of decency have evolved to a point where the American people do not want to see individuals with mental retardation executed.

FEDERAL STATUTES

The method of passing the Anti-Drug Abuse Act of 1988 prior to the *Penry* decision, and the proposal of the "Prohibition of the Death Penalty Clause" in the 1990 Crime Control Act after it, show a full consensus of the national political representatives of the American people for this action. The following section examines the consensus found in the provisions of these national statutes.

Anti-Drug Abuse Act of 1988.[132]   Congress specifically excluded defendants with mental retardation from the death penalty in the Anti-Drug Abuse Act of 1988, even though this law includes capital punishment for major drug smugglers.

In the floor debate in the House of Representatives prior to passage, all segments of political opinion from liberal Democrats to conservative Republicans supported the amendment to bar executions of persons with mental retardation.   The amendment was introduced by Representative Sander Levin of Michigan and was simply stated as, "A sentence of death shall not be carried out upon a person who is mentally retarded."[133]

Representatives George Gekas of Pennsylvania, Judd Gregg of New Hampshire, Arthur Ravenal of South Carolina, and Steve Bartlett of Texas all spoke in favor of the bill.[134] Representatives Levin and Bartlett both read the AAMR definition of mental retardation [significantly subaverage general intellectual functioning existing concurrently with deficits in adaptive behavior and manifested during the developmental period] into the record to create a legislative history to guide courts, prosecutors and defense attorneys in their interpretation of the single sentence clause. Representative Bartlett put the standard I.Q. of seventy or below with the mental age of a twelve-year-old or less into the record for the same purpose.

Many of the arguments against the death penalty for persons with mental retardation elaborated in this chapter were also referenced in the debate. That Georgia had reacted to Jerome Bowden's execution by passing the first mentally retarded death penalty prohibition act in the nation; that we do not execute children nor should we execute the childlike persons who have mental retardation; that the definition is scientifically measurable and precludes false claims of mental retardation; that individuals with mental retardation have impaired ability to control their actions, understand the nature of legal proceedings and of the death penalty, and to assist in their own defense; that the death penalty cannot deter persons with mental retardation who cannot premeditate and act deliberately; and that the death penalty, as the ultimate penalty, is reserved for those who are most blameworthy and personally culpable.[135] Subsequently, both the House and the Senate unanimously voted for passage of this amendment to the Anti-Drug Abuse Act.[136]

Thus the people's representatives understood the inhumanity of executing people with mental retardation and articulated this theory for the sake of legislative history and the public they represent. The Supreme Court in *Penry* did not consider this substantial evidence of a national consensus.

Senate Action in the Crime Control Act of 1990. Beginning in the spring of 1990, both prior and subsequent to the U.S. Supreme Court's ruling in the *Penry* case, the federal Congress once again considered a major omnibus crime bill, the Crime Control Act of 1990.[137] Once again, as it did in 1988, the Senate made the people's wishes known in opposition to the Supreme Court. The Senate reaffirmed the principle of banning executions of people with mental retardation.

In the debate prior to passage of the provisions which prohibited the death penalty for persons with mental retardation, Senator Joseph R. Biden, Jr. (D-DE) argued that the law was not being changed. The 1990 bill reaffirmed the national consensus found in the 1988 statute.[138]

The ban on executions for people with mental retardation in the context of the 1990 Act is significant. While the death penalty clauses authorized a major extension of capital punishment for thirty new crimes such as genocide, taking hostages, racketeering murder and murder-for-hire,[139] the death penalty for people with mental retardation was one of only two provisions in the act (the other banned execution of juvenile murderers aged seventeen and under) to negate the death penalty.[140] Clearly, the Senate supported the death penalty where it found it justified. However, it did not find it defensible when applied to juveniles or individuals who have mental retardation. It is a significant sign of the strength of legislative intent that these classes were exempted among a generally "get tough" death penalty policy.

However, these death penalty provisions did not become a part of the 1990 Act. In the words of President George Bush as he signed the bill into law, "Despite the fact that each of these [death penalty] proposals passed one or both Houses of Congress . . . [a]t the eleventh hour these reforms were stripped from the crime bill by the conference committee."[141] Nonetheless, prohibition of the execution of persons with mental retardation had once again found substantial support among the people's representatives.

CONCLUSION

In conclusion, the Court should have resolved the *Penry* penalty issue based on constitutional principles rather than societal consensus and political considerations. Nonetheless, if they were going to use this methodology, they should have weighed all the evidence of a societal consensus, because it is substantial enough to tip the scales of justice in favor of banning the mentally retarded death penalty. Public opinion polls, mentally retarded habilitative program development, judges', juries' and gubernatorial sentencing practices, and federal death penalty statutes all weigh heavily in favor of letting the mentally retarded offender live.

ARGUMENT FROM AUTHORITY

The function of wisdom is to discriminate between good and evil.

-- Cicero, *De Officiis*

Experts, professionals and knowledgeable persons with direct interest in the field of mental retardation have all reached the same conclusion. People who have mental retardation should not be executed.[142]

AMERICAN ASSOCIATION ON MENTAL RETARDATION (AAMR)

The American Association on Mental Retardation (AAMR), the oldest and largest professional organization of mental retardation experts in the country, opposes the death penalty for persons with mental retardation. In January, 1988 its Board of Directors unanimously adopted a resolution that "no person who is mentally retarded should be sentenced to death or executed."[143] It based this resolution on the fact that "mental retardation is a substantially disabling condition" affecting the "ability to conform . . . conduct to . . . the law." Consideration of mental retardation as mitigating "has failed to prevent the unjust sentencing of several mentally retarded persons to death" whose "competence . . . to stand trial or enter a guilty plea, and to face execution are always in question."[144] The AAMR also filed an extensive brief in the *Penry* case which argued against allowing persons with mental retardation to be executed.[145] Thus the AAMR is one of the strongest opponents of mentally retarded offender capital punishment. Its statements should carry substantial weight in the debate on the issue.

PENRY AMICUS BRIEF

AAMR was joined in its filing of the *Penry* brief by ten other distinguished mental disability groups. These include "the Association for Retarded Citizens of the United States (ARC), the American Psychological Association (APA), the Association for Persons with Severe Handicaps

(TASH), the American Association of University Affiliated Programs for the Developmentally Disabled (AAUAP), the American Orthopsychiatric Association, the National Association of Private Residential Resources, the New York State Association for Retarded Children, Inc. (NYSARC), the National Association of Superintendents of Public Residential Facilities for the Mentally Retarded, the Mental Health Law Project, and the National Association of Protection and Advocacy Systems."[146]

These organizations reflect a wide range of perspectives within the mental retardation professional community.[147] That all groups knowledgeable in the treatment of people with mental retardation oppose the death penalty for them is persuasive evidence for this position.

THE AMERICAN BAR ASSOCIATION STANDARDS

In 1983, the American Bar Association (ABA) adopted standards which are interpreted to exclude persons with mental retardation from execution. This interpretation arises from the inability of individuals with mental retardation to aid in their own defense and to understand the legal process. Standard 7-5.6(a)(b) says:

> Convicts who have been sentenced to death should not be executed if they are currently mentally incompetent. . . . A convict is incompetent to be executed if, as a result of . . . mental retardation, the convict cannot understand the nature of the pending proceedings, what he or she was tried for, the reason for the punishment, . . . the nature of the punishment . . . [or] lacks sufficient capacity to recognize or understand any fact which might exist which would make the punishment unjust or unlawful, or lacks the ability to convey such information to counsel or to the court.[148]

Thus the ABA enumerated precisely those characteristics of mental retardation which lessen the mentally retarded offender's culpability and which make him ineligible to be executed. It also stated that such persons should be spared not because of any "sympathy" for their plight, but because "the integrity of the criminal justice system" would be "eroded" if persons with reduced culpability and lack of understanding of what is happening to them are executed.[149]

Subsequently, in 1989, the ABA House of Delegates made the interpretation of Standard 7-5.6 precise and explicit. It adopted a recommendation that "no person with mental retardation . . . should be sentenced to death or executed; and . . . that the American Bar Association supports enactment of legislation barring the execution of defendants with mental retardation."[150]

UNITED NATIONS

In 1988, the United Nations Committee on Crime Prevention and Control made a recommendation that member nations which retained the death penalty exclude persons with mental retardation from its aegis.[151]

CONCLUSION

Virtually every group in the United States that has expertise in the areas of mental retardation and handicapped law understands the implications of the mentally retarded death penalty for the national legal fabric, the public consciousness, and the mentally retarded themselves, and consequently opposes it. The reasoned conclusions based on extensive knowledge of the subject matter of professionals and groups who are authorities should be given the greatest consideration and weight in making determinations of critical policy choices. A crucial decision of what course of action to take which has far-reaching consequences for the national soul and the integrity of the criminal justice system should be informed and fashioned by the best knowledge available on the subject. In making the *Penry* decision, the Supreme Court, a generalist policy-making body lacking in extensive and in-depth knowledge of the characteristics of mental retardation, neglected this principle. It took on the role of informed authority and overlooked the expertise of the proven authorities. In doing so, it made a critical policy error.

OVERREPRESENTATION OR STATISTICAL ARGUMENT

How sour sweet music is. When time is broke and proportion kept. So it is in the music of men's lives.
                              -- William Shakespeare, *Richard II*

Mentally retarded persons represent roughly two to three percent of the United States population.[152] The preponderance of empirical evidence substantiates that the mentally retarded don't commit crimes or murders in any greater numbers than the general population.[153] In fact, at least one professional maintains that they commit fewer crimes than persons of normal intelligence.[154] Thus it logically follows that not more than three percent, and possibly less, of the murders in the U.S. are committed by the mentally retarded. Yet the mentally retarded are larger proportions of all criminal populations, including those incarcerated, those on Death Row, and those executed.

Experts estimate that from ten to twenty-five percent of the incarcerated population in the United States has mental retardation.[155] Approximately 2,500 incarcerated offenders nationally are under death sentences,[156] and an estimated twelve (300 persons) to twenty percent of these (500 persons) are mentally retarded.[157] In a broader and less clearly defined sense of mental handicap which includes the mentally retarded, impaired or incapacitated, estimates are as high as thirty percent (750 persons) of Death Row inmates.[158]

Of the approximately 2,650 total offenders condemned since the death penalty was reinstated by the Supreme Court in 1976,[159] approximately 157 have been executed.[160] At least eleven of these (and one prior to 1976[161]), a total of seven percent of the executed) who were known to be mentally retarded have died at the hands of the State. This is more than two to three times the percentage of persons with mental retardation in the population at large. An idealized picture of the above analysis appears in FIGURE 2.4.

Others who were not identified as retarded may also have been executed. The exact number is not known because the mentally retarded are not systematically identified, screened, and evaluated in any states except Texas, Georgia, and South Carolina where the requirement to do so for all incarcerated criminals is a mandate of federal court orders.[162]

The explanation for this overrepresentation in criminal populations is fairly simple. Because mentally retarded persons are frequently not recognized as such by the police and the courts; because they do not understand Miranda warnings;[163] because they desire to please authority figures and readily confess to crimes or are easily coerced into confessing (sometimes even when they didn't commit the crime);[164] because many are poor and minorities who do not have the best of private counsel, and are most frequently represented by inexperienced Public Defenders with only marginal understanding of capital trial techniques, the nature of mental retardation and the effects of retardation on culpability;[165] because their mental deficiencies prevent them from adequately participating in their own defense; because they do not understand prison rules, have more infractions than the average prisoner, lack the capacity to prepare a viable parole plan and frequently have no family or other place to go even if they were released, they are rarely paroled;[166] in sum, because they have poorer defenses than most offenders accused of murder and fewer opportunities to have their sentences reduced, the mentally retarded are overrepresented in all facets of the criminal justice system, including prison populations, Death Row residents, and those who are executed.

In a nation based on the principles of protection of the rights of minorities from a tyrannical majority and promotion of minorities' equal participation in, and sharing of, the benefits of society, it is unjust for a virtually unprotected minority, the mentally retarded, to receive the most severe punishment that a majoritarian society can dish out in unequal proportion to the general population and to that applied to other criminals.

Like the intellectual children that they are, offenders with mental retardation should receive the special protection and safety that is given to defenseless persons, rather than being more extensively and severely punished than other criminals of the same ilk. Principles of representativeness, justice and fairness demand it.

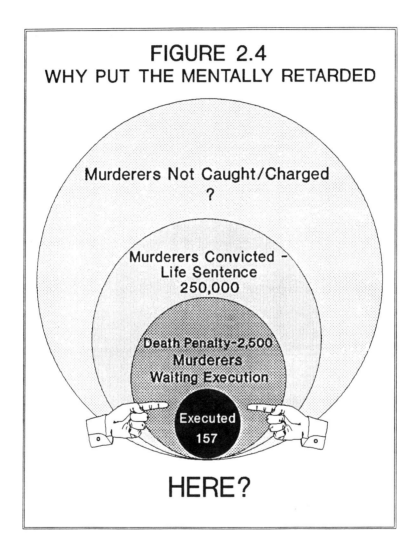

FIGURE 2.4
WHY PUT THE MENTALLY RETARDED

ANTI-MITIGATION ARGUMENT

A false balance is abomination to the Lord: but a just wedge is his delight.

-- *Proverbs, 11:1-169*

MENTAL RETARDATION MITIGATION

Early on in the law of mental retardation, legal experts recognized the need for mitigation in sentencing persons with mental retardation. "The American Bar Association's Criminal Justice Standards, adopted by the ABA House of Delegates in 1984, take this position: 'Evidence of . . . mental retardation should be considered as a possible mitigating factor in sentencing a convicted offender.'"[167]

On an elementary level, the statutes of most states that authorize capital punishment require the consideration of mitigating factors in the sentencing of capital criminal defendants.[168] Further, the Supreme Court has consistently held that the Constitution requires that "the mitigating nature of the defendant's mental state" be considered in imposing the sentence.[169]

The *Penry* case followed this interpretation. The Supreme Court reasoned in the *Penry* decision that the Constitution was violated because the trial court did not inform the jury that it needed to consider the possible mitigating effects of the defendant's mental retardation as required by the Texas death penalty statute.[170]

Under the *Penry* holding, evidence that a defendant has mental retardation must be presented to the judge and jury in order to reference at least one mitigating factor and to cross the threshold into the statutory and constitutional mitigation area.[171]

The mitigating effects of mental retardation must be delineated in each specific case because they are relevant and essential to the determination of an equitable and proportionate punishment,[172] particularly to the decision as to whether to impose the death penalty.

Model statutes and case law have substantiated several aspects of mental retardation mitigation that are pertinent, including the ability to intend the crime,[173] the defendant's degree of participation in the crime,[174] his or her character and criminal history,[175] and his or her level of mental and behavioral maturity.[176]

First, a defendant with mental retardation lacks the full ability to premeditate and form the specific intent to commit criminal acts because of his limited moral reasoning ability and behavioral impulsivity. Alternatively, if he has some limited degree of such ability, he did not use it in this instance to intend the crime prior to its commission.[177] Mental retardation mitigation exists because of a mentally retarded defendant's limited capacity to premeditate and specifically to violate the law.

Second, the defendant's role in the crime is relevant. If he is not the major perpetrator, (and since this is the case for many mentally retarded who are led into crime by more intelligent and malicious criminals),[178] the mentally retarded person's degree of culpability is diminished.

Third, the defendant's character is relevant. No prior criminal history or a limited one without previous felony convictions suggests an ordinarily non-criminal character. Mitigation is substantiated when there is evidence that the mentally retarded defendant is normally law-abiding and that this act represents an aberration that is out of character.

Fourth, the Court has determined that some factors carry greater weight than others in determining sentencing mitigation. Although the youth of a minor defendant does not necessarily prevent the death penalty from being imposed,[179] nonetheless, the younger the murderer, the more heavily must age be weighed as a factor in favor of life.[180]

Mental retardation is akin to youth because no mentally retarded person has a mental age greater than twelve. Whereas children are chronologically juveniles, persons with mental retardation are "functional juveniles."[181] Like childhood, mental retardation must be weighed heavily in the determination of the level of mitigation and the sentencing decision as to whether to impose the death penalty.

> I.Q.: 50-63
> John Paul Penry never completed the first grade because he was unable to learn. As an adult, his intellectual development and accumulated learning are comparable to an average seven year old's. He has the affects and social development of the average fourth grader.[182]

The child-like level of intellectual and behavioral maturation of the mentally retarded offender creates "a legal presumption in favor of life"[183] which includes the constitutional exclusion of the death penalty.[184]

In sum, "the greater the degree of mitigation and lessened culpability, the less appropriate is the death penalty."[185] Each factor of mitigation associated with the nature of mental retardation must be weighed independently, and the accumulated weight of all such factors creates a preponderance of evidence substantial enough to establish the presumption of life and bar the death penalty for persons with mental retardation.

AGGRAVATION

The reverse of mitigation is, of course, aggravation. While mitigating factors diminish punishment, and in the instance of the death penalty, argue for a presumption of life and the exclusion of death, aggravating factors enhance the penalty and argue for the imposition of the death penalty in capital cases.

Factors which aggravate the seriousness of a crime include "future dangerousness, sadism, and brutality."[186] In the case of people with mental retardation, aggravating circumstances include an extremely brutal, violent and sadistic crime which showed no mercy to the victim(s) and which may have included mental and physical torture. The extreme brutality of the crime evidences that the individual with mental retardation did not comprehend that such conduct is legally and morally reprehensible and anathema. His lack of understanding shows that the possibilities of habilitation or moral rehabilitation are slim, and that he is likely to do it again.[187] His likelihood of committing future criminal acts argues in favor of the death penalty.

BALANCING ACT

In the individualized[188] case-by-case formula or "totality of circumstances approach"[189] demanded by the *Penry* decision, mitigation, evidenced by a lack of specific intent, understanding and culpability, will be weighed against aggravation, illustrated by brutality, lack of understanding and tendency to commit more crimes.[190] If mental retardation is offered in evidence as a mitigating factor, then the door is opened for the prosecution to tick off the aggravating circumstances of the crime and the defendant's potential dangerousness.[191] If at least one statutory aggravating factor is proven, then the defendant becomes "'death eligible.'"[192] Once the threshold is crossed, the severe aspects of the offense or the continuing threat to public safety of the offender may tilt the balance of the mitigation-aggravation scales toward the imposition of the death penalty.

DUE PROCESS ARGUMENT: WHY MENTAL RETARDATION AS A MITIGATING FACTOR WILL NEVER WORK

Thus mental retardation is an "ambiguous mitigating factor." It is possible that the sentencing authority may improperly consider mitigating factors as aggravating, particularly mental retardation, which sometimes may appear to increase a defendant's ongoing threat to the community.[193] This may occur despite the Supreme Court's ruling that defendants have a "constitutional right" to have mitigating factors considered as mitigating.[194]

The Supreme Court has ruled that due process requires that mental illness always be considered as mitigating.[195] By analogy, mental retardation too should be so considered since the basic characteristics of mental retardation always reduce culpability.[196] Mental retardation is a permanent condition, one which can be ameliorated but never cured. Mental illness, how-ever, is not permanent and can be cured.[197] If mental illness, which temporarily destroys a person's ability to think, is always a mitigating factor, then mental retardation which similarly but permanently diminishes thinking capacity, should also be considered as such, and even more so. A mentally ill murderer cannot be executed unless he recovers sufficiently to understand the nature of his wrongdoing. Ironically, the *Penry* decision allows a person with mental retardation who can never recover from his disability and who can never completely understand the legal and moral ramifications of his crime, to be executed. Because the mental and behavioral condition of a murderer who has mental retardation may indicate future dangerousness, the *Penry* decision allows his disabling condition - permanent limited intelligence and deficits in adaptive behaviors - to work against him and to take his life.

In sum, "case-specific" remedies[198] are never sufficient constitutional protection of the due process rights of defendants with mental retardation.[199] They are piecemeal, capricious and arbitrary. They risk that the judge or jury will be influenced by the history of misinformation and discrimination which has plagued the lives of individuals with mental retardation until recent years. Such remedies risk that the sentencing authority will consider mental retardation as aggravating rather than mitigating because of the future dangerousness that may be associated with the mentally retarded person's lack of understanding of the nature and seriousness of his crime. Thus the *Penry* reasoning is fallacious. It leaves the sentencer to consider what to do about a mentally retarded offender's mental retardation, that is, whether or not to consider it as aggravating because of possible future dangerousness, or mitigating because of diminished culpability. Such a universally applied remedy denies a defendant's constitutional due process right to be protected from arbitrariness and capriciousness by having factors which lessen culpability always considered in mitigation.[200]

The Supreme Court's requirements for revision of the death penalty statutes in the 1970s[201] aimed precisely at removing such "arbitrary" and "wanton" discretion from judges and juries.[202] Now, the Supreme Court has abrogated the intent of earlier death penalty reform in its interpretation of state mitigation-aggravation death penalty clauses by returning such arbitrary discretion to judges and juries. The totality of circumstances case-specific approach can never work to safeguard the rights of the mentally retarded when the death sentence is under consideration. It will never prevent at least some mentally retarded persons from being executed. The evidence and circumstances of the executions of Arthur Goode III in 1984 and John Brogdon in 1987 poignantly illustrate this point.[203] When the death penalty is applied in such a manner, it denies a defendant his most basic due process rights. It is cruel and unusual punishment prohibited by the Eighth Amendment.

BEYOND MITIGATION: THE ANTI-CHILD EXECUTION ARGUMENT

A simple Child, That lightly draws its breath, And feels its life in every limb, What should it know of death.
William Wordsworth, *"We Are Seven"*

INTRODUCTION

As argued in the previous section,[204] the functional childhood[205] of the mentally retarded must be treated as a mitigating factor constitutionally and weighted heavily in the mitigation-aggravation balancing formula. Yet such an individualized sentencing process[206] does not suffice theoretically nor practicably for equitable treatment of persons with mental retardation in that it does not universally bar them from execution. This section examines why the functional childhood of the mentally retarded demands, beyond mere mitigation, an all-inclusive forbiddance of their execution.

CHARACTERISTICS OF CHILDREN

Children are the little people aged twelve or under. They aren't teenagers yet. Alas, the wonder, naivete and innocence of childhood end when teenage begins.

Childhood characteristics include less experience, less education, less perception, less responsibility for actions, less aptitude to evaluate actions' consequences, more susceptibility to peer pressure and emotional influences than adults.[207] Children have a lesser ability to constrain their conduct and to plan for the long term.[208] Even though children by tradition are held to know right from wrong by the age of seven,[209] they are incapable of acting with the same degree of culpability as adults or even teenagers. American society's indisputable refusal to execute young children[210] is predicated on these characteristics and the fact that children's "irresponsible conduct is not as morally reprehensible as that of" adults.[211] Thus, it is totally improper to impose the adult penalty of capital punishment on children.

As an advanced and humanitarian civilization grounded in law and constitution, the United States absolutely prohibits[212] strapping a child of twelve or under into the electric chair and sending mega-volts through him until he jerks uncontrollably and dies.

Although the death penalty may be applied to teenagers as young as sixteen at the time of the murder,[213] it is never imposed on children twelve or younger. Minors younger than teens are not executed in this country because it defies common decency and social mores to put children to death, however reprehensible the crime. Society does not want to execute the first grader who drowns his baby sisters in the bathtub, carves them into turkey soup with a kitchen knife, and fiendishly says they deserved it for tormenting him.

THE MENTALLY RETARDED, FUNCTIONAL CHILDREN

> *"He's jes like a kid, ain't he, . . ."*
> *"Sure he's jes' like a kid. There ain't no more harm in him than a kid neither, except he's so strong. . . ."*
>   -- John Steinbeck, *Of Mice and Men*

Similarly, adults with mental retardation are functionally children in fully grown bodies. Mentally retarded persons are childlike "in every morally relevant way."[214] Early case law recognized this factor even in the nineteenth century, long before the concept of "mental age" was developed to describe the phenomenon.[215]

The concept of mental age is used to delineate the level of intellectual development in terms of chronological age. Persons with mental retardation never have a mental age greater than twelve.[216] Their functional childhood is defined precisely like chronological childhood - twelve years old or younger. Like children, the mentally retarded have immature intellects, diminished understanding, and childish behavior patterns. Like children, they have underdeveloped powers to "form criminal intent."[217] Like children, they always lack full intentional abilities.

> ". . . it his birthday, I reckon."
> "How old he?"
> "He thirty-three. . . ."
> "You mean, he been three years old thirty years."
> -- John Steinbeck, *Of Mice and Men*

Because children are ultimately never held criminally responsible nor executed, neither should people with mental retardation be, whatever their chronological age. Whether their developmental age is lesser or greater within the childhood range, that is, whether they are mentally seven or ten or twelve, persons with mental retardation should not be held criminally liable like adults in the capital sentencing process, just as children of these ages are

> IQ: Untested
> Immediately after committing murder, Alton Waye told his companion that he had "killed a woman and put her in the bathtub." He went home and told his father, and then called the police himself to tell them too. In a childlike manner, he didn't try to hide the crime. He was overly anxious to tell everyone what had happened. The statement that I "did it just like . . . on television . . . wiped the knife and everything . . . Man, wait until my friends hear about this" evidences childish naivete.[218] Waye lacked all comprehension that he was in an extremely precarious situation and had committed a very serious crime punishable by death.

not so held. Mentally retarded functional childhood stands in its own right as a reason not to execute persons with mental retardation. To execute a mentally retarded functional child who commits a brutal murder is just as socially intolerable and cruel and unusual punishment as executing the seven or ten or twelve year old.

"You're nuts," she said, "But you're a kinda nice fella. Jus' like a big baby."

--John Steinbeck, *Of Mice and Men*

On May 24, 1990, Senator Joseph R. Biden, Jr. (D-DE), sponsor of the Crime Control Act of 1990, eloquently summarized the arguments against the application of the death penalty to offenders with mental retardation. In an impassioned plea he stated:

> For God's sake, if we acknowledge you should not put children to death, acknowledge that we should not as a nation put to death the mentally retarded. . . .
>
> The Supreme Court says it is all right to put mentally retarded people to death. Just because the Supreme Court said we can, that does not mean we should. . . . My God, what have we come to?[219]

ANTI-RIGHT-FROM-WRONG ARGUMENT

He shook her then, and he was angry with her. "Don't you go yellin'," he said, and he shook her; and her body flopped like a fish. And then she was still, for Lennie had broken her neck.

He looked down at her, and carefully he removed his hand from over her mouth, and she lay still. "I don't want ta hurt you," he said, "but George'll be mad if you yell." When she didn't answer nor move he bent closely over her. He lifted her arm and let it drop. For a moment he seemed bewildered. And then he whispered in fright, "I done a bad thing. I done another bad thing. . . . I done a real bad thing," he said. "I shouldn't of did that. George'll be mad."

-- John Steinbeck, *Of Mice and Men*

Introduction

Whether mentally retarded offenders know right from wrong and can or cannot be held liable for their criminal acts based on this has been at issue for at least two centuries. The way courts have resolved this issue has evolved over time as each successive decision formula has proven to be unsatisfactory. The *Penry* rule which allows for execution if defendants know right from wrong is a retrenchment from an earlier solution based in common law which did not permit such executions. The next section examines the evolution of the right-from-wrong issue in order to come to a humane resolution that will be in keeping with the Eighth Amendment.

EVOLUTION OF THE LEGAL TREATMENT OF THE RIGHT-FROM-WRONG ISSUE[220]

The M'Naghten Rule. The M'Naghten rule, established in nineteenth century English common law, was the first legal resolution of the issue of whether mentally impaired criminal defendants know right from wrong. This test of the competency of defendants with mental retardation was used for more than a century.[221]

The M'Naghten rule stated that, if the *mens rea* element of the crime is lacking, that is, "the accused did not know that his/er actions were wrong, . . ."[222] then he or she cannot be held responsible for criminal actions. The rule was generally stated in terms of "'a defect of reason, from disease of the mind.'" This initially was interpreted to include both the insane and the mentally deficient or mentally retarded.[223] If they could not understand the "nature," "quality," or "wrongfulness" of their actions, then they could not be held criminally responsible.[224]

However, as the M'Naghten Rule evolved over time in the nineteenth century, its usage gradually became limited to the diminished criminal responsibility of the insane. By the early twentieth century, persons with mental retardation were excluded from its aegis.

Lack of adequate accommodation and treatment by the M'Naghten test of persons with mental retardation who cannot distinguish right from wrong led to widespread dissatisfaction with the rule and a search for more equitable interpretations of the issue. By mid-twentieth century, a new rule, the Durham Test, was fashioned and adopted.[225]

The Durham Test. In 1954, the U.S. Court of Appeals for the District of Columbia attempted to address the deficiencies of the M'Naghten rule in dealing with the application of the right-from-wrong issue to persons with mental retardation. In *Durham v. United States*[226] the court distinguished between the terms "mental disease" and "mental defect". The first referred to mental illness, a curable condition, while the second referred to mental retardation, a permanent state of disability. A crime committed as a result or "product"[227] of a mental defect, that is, mental retardation, evidenced diminished criminal responsibility.[228]

However, the same court in the early 1960s retracted from this definitive position.[229] The distinction between mental defect and mental disease was meant only to establish a difference between the two conditions. It remained for juries and judges to determine the definition and content of the term mental defect based on expert testimony. Thus, establishing the fact of mental defect or retardation would not automatically reduce criminal responsibility.[230]

The ALI Test. In 1961, the American Law Institute (ALI), in its formula in the Model Penal Code, reacted to this vacuum in definition of the right-from-wrong issue as applied to persons with mental retardation.[231] The code states that an offender with mental retardation is not criminally responsible if "' . . . as a result of mental . . . defect, he lacks substantial capacity . . . to appreciate the criminality [wrongfulness] of his conduct. . . . '"[232]

Subsequently, some courts and at least several state legislatures adopted a broad interpretation of the ALI test.[233] In 1978 the California Supreme Court held that mental retardation automatically qualifies as a mental defect and reduces culpability. It lessens the mentally retarded person's "capacity to commit crime." Further, the mentally retarded cannot "entertain general criminal intent."[234]

Despite these precedents, some legal experts felt that the ALI rule only allows for consideration of the determination of the offender's ability to appreciate the wrongfulness of his actions,[235] and that it does not require such an interpretation. Therefore, the American Bar Association has offered a more definitive revision of the ALI test.

The ABA Rule. The American Bar Association's (ABA) Criminal Justice Mental Health Standards state that an offender is "not responsible for criminal conduct if . . . as a result of a mental disease or defect, . . . [he or she] was unable to appreciate the wrongfulness of such conduct. . . ." Mental defect includes mental retardation.[236] Here, the mentally retarded are treated precisely the same as the mentally ill, that is, they both have diminished criminal responsibility because of their mental defects, or their mental diseases, respectively. Based on this interpretation, a mentally ill person cannot be executed. By analogy, neither can the mentally retarded.

Similarly, equal protection also prevents a person with mental retardation from being executed.[237] There is some thought that the law will evolve in the future to the point where a person suffering from mental retardation who does not understand right from wrong, like an insane person, is held incompetent to stand trial and not go to trial at all.[238] Currently, however, most defendants with I.Q.s in the mild and moderate ranges of mental retardation are held competent and go to trial.[239]

TREATMENT OF MENTALLY RETARDED OFFENDERS WHO CAN DISTINGUISH RIGHT FROM WRONG

That an individual with mental retardation who does not fully comprehend that his or her actions are morally and legally wrong should not be executed should now be a given. However, the issue of how, in the capital sentencing process, to treat a person with mental retardation who can distinguish between right and wrong is yet to be examined.

The ability of persons with mental retardation to distinguish between right and wrong is always limited. Recall that one of the innate characteristics of mental retardation is incomplete moral development and that people with mental retardation by definition do not attain full comprehension of their own blameworthiness.[240] Even though some mentally retarded offenders may recognize right from wrong in an elemental sought of way, their mental abilities are so curtailed that they have "only the most simplistic understanding of these concepts, and little ability to discern how personal behaviors are linked to the events which produce 'right' or 'wrong' results."[241] In fact, the leading expert in the field points out that persons with mental retardation will "say it is wrong to steal" but will not know why.[242]

In the debate surrounding the passage of the mentally retarded anti-death penalty clause in the federal Crime Control Act of 1990, the U.S. Senate, as representatives of the United States people, thoroughly hashed out the arguments on both sides of this issue. In conclusion, they affirmed that people with mental retardation, even if they have some understanding of right and wrong, should not be executed. The killer with mental retardation can be held accountable for his actions[243] by life imprisonment without parole.

Senator Strom Thurmond (R-S.C.) argued the *Penry* Court's position that mentally retarded offenders who know right from wrong can be executed. He stated that we need a "tougher crime bill" and do not want to weaken the current law. If we favor the death penalty it should include persons with mental retardation who know right from wrong and commit heinous crimes. The Supreme Court and most state legislatures have endorsed this view.[244]

The opposition, led by Senators Joseph R. Biden, Jr. (D-DE) and Edward Kennedy (D-MASS), used an extension of the child argument to rebut these statements. They argued that everyone agrees that we do not execute children of ten or twelve or fourteen, even though they know right from wrong. Even though the Supreme Court has said that teenagers of fifteen, sixteen, and seventeen who know right from wrong can be executed, Congress was herein also proposing to ban these and all executions of minors. The reasons are:

> we collectively in here [the Congress] and in this Nation made a judgment: we will not put children to death, even though they know right from wrong, even though they may commit a heinous crime, even though they may be an axe murderer. . . . [245]

Further, people with mental retardation who know right from wrong "simply do not have enough gray matter to be able to ever in their entirety of their life . . . to achieve an ability to operate beyond that of a 12-year-old." Thus people with mental retardation, like children of twelve or under, and even teenagers, if you need to stretch it that far, should never be executed.[246]

The arguments of Senator Biden were persuasive. The Senate voted by almost a two to one margin (59 to 38) to ban the execution of persons with mental retardation in federal cases.[247]

Thus the Senate, as representatives of the national consensus, argued that persons with mental retardation, like children, should not be executed even though they know right from wrong. The Senate, with its vote for passage of the prohibition of the death penalty for people with mental retardation, has validated the humanity and correctness of the ABA rule in opposition to the *Penry* penalty.

In conclusion, one anecdotal piece of evidence also supports the ban on execution of individuals with mental retardation who know right from wrong. In 1986, Georgia executed Jerome Bowden who knew right from wrong and who had mental retardation. It was this execution that brought the issue forward into the public consciousness and the political arena for discussion and debate. It created an outcry of disgust in Georgia that led to the passage of the first state law in the nation completely banning execution of persons with mental retardation.[248] Clearly, the people of Georgia do not want offenders with mental retardation who know right from wrong executed.

States are litmus paper for the national conscience. Georgia began the national wave of desire to ban executions of people with mental retardation. The *Penry* decision has perpetuated that wave. Like Bowden's execution, the *Penry* decision is unacceptable to the American nation.

Sum

The examination of the congressional debate over offenders with mental retardation who can distinguish between right and wrong and the evolution of the tests for establishing the lack of criminal responsibility of persons with mental retardation who cannot illustrate one point. Political representatives and legal experts have been unhappy with the Supreme Court's failure to grasp and codify the central point that offenders with mental retardation who do not understand right from wrong, and even those who do on some elementary basis, cannot be held fully responsible for their actions and, therefore, cannot be executed under the Eighth Amendment. The *Penry* Court failed to accept the legal evolution of the right-from-wrong issue as evidence of societal consensus. Societal consensus has now been firmly established in the political arena and legal theory. It remains only to be adopted by the Supreme Court, or alternatively, by the remaining state legislatures that have yet to do so.

ANTI-MULTIPLE CLAIMS ARGUMENT

Mental retardation "is a lifetime work. You don't fake mental retardation."

-- Senator Edward Kennedy

Critics of banning the death penalty for people with mental retardation make both a practical and theoretical argument against it. Theoretically they oppose capital punishment for offenders with mental retardation as a "soft liberal approach"[249] that will allow killers who are criminally responsible for murder to avoid the moral and legal punishment - death - with a claim of mental retardation. Practically, they fear that virtually every criminal defendant will claim to have mental retardation and that this will create an enormous taxpayer burden in terms of requiring the State to pay for expensive evaluations by mental retardation specialists.

REPLIES TO THE THEORETICAL ARGUMENT

Two rebuttals can be made to the theoretical argument. First, defendants facing death sentences may claim that they have mental retardation, but the prosecution will argue that they are not. Under the trial advocacy system, facts on both sides of the issue will be brought out, and the jury or judge will make the decision as to whether the defendant does or does not have mental retardation. This is the American system of justice, and it will be applied to this issue as to any other. Thus if the defendant avoids the death penalty, it will be at the time-honored and sacrosanct decision of the jury or judge that he or she fits the mental retardation definition and therefore should not be executed.

The 1990 Crime Control Act[250] presents a second response, that of the federal Senate, to the theoretical multiple claims argument. Essentially the Senate's argument was that mental retardation is such a substantive and identifiable condition that no defendant will be able to get away with a false claim of having mental retardation. Such claims will be self-limited by their *de facto* lack of substantiation.

In unfolding the rationale for banning the death penalty for persons with mental retardation in federal cases, the Senate deliberately did not include a definition of mental retardation. The codification said:

A sentence of death shall not be carried out upon a person who is mentally retarded. A sentence of death shall not be carried out upon a person who, as a result of mental disability-

(1) cannot understand the nature of the pending proceedings, what such person was tried for, the reason for the punishment, or the nature of the punishment, or

(2) lacks the capacity to recognize or understand facts which would make the punishment unjust or unlawful, or lacks the ability to convey such information to counsel or to the court.[251]

During the Senate debate, the straightforward statements of the drafters concisely expressed the argument that the condition is so apparent and distinguishable that it does not have to be defined. Senator Biden explained the lack of a statutory definition with the rationale that has been used to define pornography - "I cannot define it but I know it when I see it."[252]

Later on, Senators Biden, Kennedy and other bill advocates made clear the legislative intent concerning the definition. Generally, someone with an I.Q. of seventy or lower is considered to have mental retardation.[253]

Further, Senator Edward Kennedy (D-Mass) reasoned that:

> . . . I do not come to this debate without strong personal feelings, since I have a sister who is mentally retarded. So I have spent some time learning about the affliction. . . . Anyone who says that, well, you are going to be found guilty and then you are going to say 'mental retardation' does not understand what mental retardation is about, has no idea what it is about.[254]

He also clearly summarized the argument that you can't fake mental retardation. "Faking mental retardation . . . is easily rebuttable . . . . You do not fake mental retardation. You either are or you aren't." Proof must come from "a lifetime of examinations or medical treatment, over a lifetime, that you have these deficiencies."[255]

Thus there are multiple ways to verify mental retardation. Previous testing and school records are important. An offender with mental retardation can be identified by "his schooling, . . . vocabulary, literacy, confusion and signature."[256] In Maryland, the law requires a preponderance of evidence of mental retardation, for example, from witness testimony, previous school and treatment records, as a way to ferret out false claims of mental handicap.[257]

REPLY TO THE PRACTICAL ARGUMENT

Indeed, an evaluation by mental retardation experts of a defendant claiming a defense of mental retardation will be required to establish the fact of mental retardation in capital cases. Such an assessment is expensive because it is made by high-priced specialists with substantial education and experience in dealing with offenders with mental retardation. Nevertheless, the requirement for a mental retardation evaluation would be limited to capital cases and would not apply to lesser felonies or misdemeanors. At the most, the public would bear the cost of evaluations in capital cases.

As the issue of mental retardation comes more to the fore, and understanding increases of its implications for capital sentencing, funding for evaluations and defense of the indigent may more frequently be available from other sources than the public weal. In some instances services may be offered *pro bono* by legal and mental retardation experts. Thus the cost to the state can be ameliorated by other avenues to some extent.

On a more theoretical level, where a person's life is at stake, the price of a mental retardation evaluation is not too much to pay. Defenses in capital cases are always expensive whether the defendant has mental retardation or not. Society as a whole is willing to bear this cost because of the fundamental belief in the constitutional and statutory civil rights of the accused and the gravity of execution. A mistake is final. The expense of eliminating the risk of error to the extent possible is a cost that the American public and legal system have always been willing to bear. This social acceptance is no less where people with mental retardation are concerned.

Thus the argument that the cost to the public is too much to bear is specious. Where life or death issues are concerned, the dollars that it takes to protect the rights of the accused are not too much to expend.

SUM

The multiple claims argument is fallacious on three counts. First, the American trial system will determine the fact of mental retardation so that the veracity of claims of mental retardation will be verified or rejected in this traditional manner. Only the penalty of life or death will be predetermined, once a jury determination of the fact is made.

Second, mental retardation is virtually impossible to feign, so impossible that the U.S. Senate believes the fact of mental retardation to be self-evident and beyond the need for statutory definition. Defendants who do not have mental retardation will nearly never be able to get away with false claims and thereby avoid the death penalty.

Third, the cost of mental retardation evaluations is limited to capital cases, may be funded by private or *pro bono* sources, and is not too much to pay to protect the rights of the accused or to minimize the risk of executing a person whose limited intelligence and understanding prevent full criminal responsibility and culpability.

MAINSTREAMING, INDIVIDUALISM AND THE "RIGHT TO EXECUTION"

Some persons make the argument that persons with mental retardation should be treated as individuals and not lumped into a category or class for any purpose. The intent is to get away from historical stereotyping. It is said that individuals with mental retardation should be treated the same as everyone else. If we allow executions of offenders who do not have mental retardation, then we should also allow it for those who do have mental retardation.

Mainstreaming into American life aims to allow people with mental retardation to share equally in all the benefits and privileges of society that non-handicapped citizens enjoy. In the area of rights, persons with mental retardation should not be treated differently from anyone else. Individual and civil rights accrue to them as to all citizens.

However, normalization of people with mental retardation does not take in the right to negative benefits or costs, deprivations or punishments, especially the worst punishment society can hand out, death. Inclusion in the American Dream and mainstream of American life for persons with mental retardation does not embrace the "right to execution." There is no right to be executed on an individual basis for persons with mental retardation because execution is not a benefit, privilege or right. It is the deprivation of a right, the right to live. There is no individual right to die at the hands of the State for the mentally handicapped and persons with mental retardation.

Treating people with mental retardation like individuals in terms of execution is continuation of the historical discrimination and deprivation of the rights of the mentally handicapped. People with mental retardation have historically been given the worst of treatment. Juries and even judges have considered them more dangerous than others because of their limited intelligence. Persons with mental retardation have disproportionately been sentenced to death because of the public's fear and lack of understanding. Mainstreaming and treating them like every other individual citizen aims to stop this victimization. Mainstreaming means treating persons with mental retardation like individuals on the positive side of rights, not on the deprivation of rights, not with execution.

Americans are a just and fair-minded people. In the last quarter century of so, we as a nation have come to realize that in the past and even to some extent today, we have discriminated against minority classes of all types because of their differences. The Civil Rights Act of 1964 was the first attempt by the nation to allow minorities to enjoy the same benefits as all citizens enjoy and to end discrimination. Minorities began to be treated as classes in order to protect their rights. Thus the non-discrimination clause that states that there will be "no discrimination on the basis of race, religion, color, national origin, sex or handicap" was born. If we are to treat people with mental retardation as individuals in the sense that is being advocated, then we should advocate for removal of the word "handicap" from the non-discrimination clause.

Such a movement to promote individual treatment, although well-meaning, is a dangerous thing. It has unintended negative consequences associated with it. It carries the threat of destroying the hard-won statutory and constitutional protections that identification of minorities as legal classes has come to mean. Without such protections, the floodgates would open for denial of the civil rights of persons with mental retardation and renewed massive discrimination against them.

We cannot allow discrimination against the retarded in the name of individual and case by case treatment. Removing the barriers to such discrimination in the name of individual treatment abrogates the progress that has been made in civil rights for the mentally handicapped. We as a nation and as just citizens interested in the rights of the "least of these" cannot let this happen.

ANTI-GEORGIA ARGUMENT

[The Georgia mentally retarded death penalty] statute reflects a societal consensus against the execution of mentally retarded offenders.... Executing a mentally retarded defendant... constitute(s) cruel and unusual punishment prohibited by the Georgia Constitution. . . . It destroys public confidence in the criminal justice system."
-- Majority Opinion, *Fleming v. Zant*

Some critics contend that the lead of an unsophisticated, Deep South state like Georgia, the first to pass legislation which barred execution of the mentally retarded,[258] should not be followed by other more progressive and advanced states outside the South.

However, this is a specious argument based on prejudice that denigrates a State's integrity, intelligence and capability to respond to social issues because of its geography and past history.

It is no accident that Georgia was the first state to pass legislation prohibiting the death penalty for the mentally retarded. Georgia, in spite of its location in the South and perhaps because of it, is a leader in modernization of correctional policies. This leadership has come from several sources.

First, Georgia has had to be a reformer by necessity, because of the consent decrees of the *Guthrie v. Evans* case.[259] This case required the State to provide appropriate services to all mentally handicapped inmates in order to bring the State into compliance with federal and state handicapped law.[260]

Atlanta and the State are a part of the New South with progressive policies concerning race and equality. The death penalty applied to the mentally retarded falls unequally on minorities, and Georgia has consciously and conscientiously remedied this injustice by its statute and the subsequent state Supreme Court decision which made the legislation retroactive.[261] Other states can well emulate this pioneering effort.

The argument that the rest of the United States should not follow Georgia's lead is in another sense moot since other states and the federal government are now proceeding in this area. The question is not which state was first, but do the merits of the position warrant support? The issue should be decided on the merits, not on where the idea originated.

Finally, the citizens of Georgia were stunned and appalled by the electrocution of Jerome Bowden, the mentally retarded murderer whose

execution   provided   the   initial   stimulus   for   the   universal   legislative   and
judicial ban of the mentally retarded death penalty in Georgia.[262] Georgia
became the trail blazer because it had the inequities of executing a mentally
handicapped person poignantly brought home to it by reality.

Georgia took definitive and progressive steps
to insure that it would never have to deal with the
painful and unjust reality of an execution of a person
with mental retardation again.

The rest of the United States can well learn
from the Georgia experience. Other states can avoid
the same mistake by emulating Georgia's legislative
and judicial remedies before, rather than after, they
must face the chilling reality of a mentally retarded
execution.

> "I HOPE THAT BY MY
> EXECUTION BEING
> CARRIED OUT, I
> HOPE THAT IT WILL
> BRING SOME LIGHT
> TO THIS THING
> THAT IS WRONG."
> *Jerome Bowden's Death
> Chair Statement.263
> June 25, 1986*

SUMMATION: THE MEGA-ARGUMENT

> *Let no one say that I have said nothing new, the arrangement of
> the subject is new.*
>
> -- Henri Pascal, *Pensees*

Offenders with mental retardation should never be sentenced to death
nor executed. There are many reasons why this is so. FIGURE 2.5 and the
following section summarize these reasons.

CULPABILITY AND THE *PER SE* DEFINITION

Their lack of understanding of causality and consequences, their
impairments in general comprehension and cognition, their impulsivity,
deficits in ethical and moral reasoning ability, and diminished degree of
deliberateness in acting, *per se* prevent persons with mental retardation from
being fully culpable for their criminal actions. Without full culpability,
offenders with mental retardation can never merit the full punishment of
death.

DISPROPORTIONALITY

Execution is the utmost of punishments. The Constitution requires
that an offender and the characteristics of the offense be equal to the highest
degree of culpability for death to be a proportionate sanction. Because full
culpability is extremely difficult to assess with certainty, and the penalty is
bitter and final, only about one percent of murderers are sentenced to death.
Only a small portion of these are actually executed.

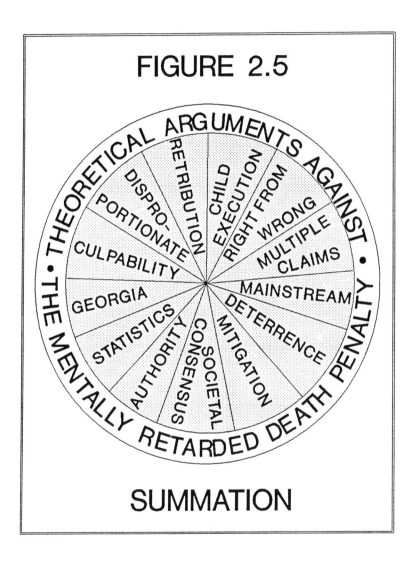

By definition, all persons with mental retardation are in the bottom two percent of the population in intellectual functioning. Because of their limited capabilities, they can never be in the top one percent of defendants who are most culpable and therefore deserving of execution. The most severe punishment is disproportionate to the least functioning citizens. The cleavage between the two is so wide that no individual can simultaneously be in both categories.

DETERRENCE

Punishment is intended to serve the purpose of deterring folks from criminal activity for fear of its consequences. Special deterrence refers to deterrence of specific individuals. Capital punishment of the murderer is the epitome of deterrence because the offender is gone from life and can no longer commit crimes.

On a second level, punishing criminals is said to deter the general public from committing crimes. The death penalty aims to divert both the general public and people with mental retardation from future murders.

Deterrence assumes that human beings act rationally. They see what happens to the murderer and avoid killing to avoid being killed. The general public undoubtedly understands this deterrence relationship, but potential murderers do not universally act on it - and even assuming that deterrence works for the general public, taking persons with mental retardation out of the small pool of those executed would have little effect on it.

Where a potential murderer with mental retardation exists, capital punishment has marginal deterrence value. Persons with mental retardation lack the intellectual capacity to understand the deterrence relationship. They have no conception of whether murderers are or are not executed in their state. Even if deterrence could be fully understood by individuals who have mental retardation, their diminished impulse control prevents them from tailoring their actions to their understanding.

Execution of offenders with mental retardation does not work to deter the general public or other persons with mental retardation. It does deter the murderer with mental retardation who is executed, but life imprisonment better serves other goals of society.

RETRIBUTION

Retribution, the theory of "just desserts," calls for a life for a life. However, because the mentally handicapped are by definition unable to relate fully the consequences of their criminal acts to the commission of the acts themselves, they are not capable of fully forming the criminal intent required for the application of the death penalty. Applying the ultimate retribution, exacting death from the mentally handicapped, serves no real purpose other than the needless infliction of pain upon the incapacitated and bewildered. It is an act of vengeance unworthy of a civilized and humanitarian nation.

SOCIETAL CONSENSUS

The Supreme Court used the methodology of relying on lack of state legislative activity and inconclusive public opinion to refuse to ban the death penalty for persons with mental retardation in the *Penry* case. This method makes the court little more than a mirror of societal and political consensus, while its constitutional and historical role is far greater, that of the final arbitrator of legal principles and the Constitution itself. By relying on societal consensus or lack thereof, it abrogates its substantive constitutional role.

Assuming *arguendo* that the methodology has validity, the Court erred in its assessment of societal consensus. A plethora of objective and convincing evidence exists that the American people do not want offenders with mental retardation to be executed. Sources for this evidence include public opinion polls, the development of habilitative programs for persons with mental retardation, sentencing practices, case law, and federal statutes.

AUTHORITY

All authorities and experts in the field of mental retardation and the law hold that people with mental retardation should never be executed. These distinguished professional authorities include the American Association on Mental Retardation, nine other mental disability support and advocacy groups who joined in filing an *amicus* brief in the *Penry* case, and the American Bar Association. The Supreme Court, a generalist policy-making body with only limited knowledge of mental retardation, ignored the expertise of the proven authorities in the field when it authorized the *Penry* penalty. In doing so, it made a critical policy error.

STATISTICS

People with mental retardation comprise about two percent of the general population in the United States, yet they are far greater proportions of correctional populations, including those given death sentences and those executed. The killer with mental retardation, most frequently African American and poor, is typically defended by inadequate counsel unskilled in the defense of capital cases and untutored in the debilitating characteristics of mental retardation. In a nation based on the protection of minority rights from tyrannical majorities, it is unworthy for a virtually unprotected minority, people with mental retardation, to receive the most severe punishment of a majoritarian society in greater proportion than other criminals.

MITIGATION

Most states' capital sentencing statutes and the Supreme Court have held that the mitigating effects of mental retardation must be elucidated at trial because these effects are relevant and essential to the determination of an equitable and proportionate punishment. Each factor of mitigation associated with the nature of mental retardation must be weighed independently, and the accumulated weight of all such factors creates a preponderance of evidence substantial enough to establish a presumption of life for offenders with mental retardation.

However, aggravating factors can also be introduced to counterbalance mitigation. When such factors as the brutality of a crime or the offender's future dangerousness are vividly portrayed to the court and jury, these factors may outweigh the mitigation of mental retardation. This is especially true if mental retardation is presented and viewed as increasing the defendant's threat to society, that is, as an aggravating rather than mitigating factor. Such an equivocal consideration of the nature of mental retardation, that is, viewing it as aggravating because of future dangerousness, or mitigating because of diminished culpability, is arbitrary and capricious. The Supreme Court's requirements for revision of death penalty statutes in the 1970s were targeted precisely at removing such wanton discretion from sentencing authorities. Under the *Penry* decision, that arbitrary discretion has been restored.

Thus case-specific remedies are never sufficient to guarantee the protection of the rights of defendants with mental retardation because they permit arbitrary discretion in the determination of the mitigating or aggravating quality of mental retardation. When the death penalty is applied in this way, it denies fundamental due process to the defendant and is cruel and unusual punishment prohibited by the Eighth Amendment.

CHILD EXECUTION

Children are less responsible for their actions than adults because of their emotional and intellectual immaturity. Society refuses to execute children twelve or younger, however horrendous their crime, based on this reduced culpability.

Adults with mental retardation are functional children in grown bodies, childlike in all morally relevant aspects. They never have a mental age greater than twelve. Like children, they should never be executed.

RIGHT FROM WRONG

Whether people with mental retardation know right from wrong and can be executed on the basis of this knowledge has been legally debated for at least two centuries. The first legal guideline for judging this issue, the

M'Naghten rule, held that those who cannot distinguish right from wrong cannot be held criminally responsible. Gradually M'Naghten was limited to the criminally insane, and persons with mental retardation were excluded.

In 1954, dissatisfaction with this formula led to the adoption of the Durham test. Durham stated that mental illness, a curable condition, must be distinguished from mental defect, which includes the lifelong condition of mental retardation. Crimes resulting from mental defect have diminished culpability.

However, in 1962 in *McDonald v. United States*,[264] the Durham test was again narrowed, and juries and judges were left to determine the content of mental defect based on expert testimony. Establishing the fact of mental retardation would not automatically validate reduced criminal responsibility.

Disillusioned with judicial interpretation of the right-from-wrong issue, the American Law Institute subsequently adopted a diminished culpability standard as a part of the Model Penal Code. It stated that a person with mental retardation is not criminally culpable if he or she lacks the substantial capacity to appreciate an action's criminality because of mental defect. People with mental retardation cannot entertain general criminal intent.

The American Bar Association's Mental Health Standards carry this interpretation even further. They explicitly state that mental defect refers to mental retardation, and an offender with mental retardation is not criminally responsible if he or she cannot appreciate the wrongfulness of his or her actions. Under the ABA rule, a person with mental retardation is treated precisely the same as a mentally ill person. Neither can be executed because of their diminished capacities and culpability. Thus it seems clear that a person who cannot distinguish right from wrong at all cannot be executed.

The issue then becomes whether those offenders with mental retardation who are believed to understand the lawlessness of their actions can be executed. Mental retardation experts hold that persons with mental retardation never have full understanding of the difference between right and wrong. Even those who do have some elemental comprehension of this moral standard should never be given the death penalty because their understanding is incomplete. The killer with mental retardation can be held responsible for his actions equally as well by life imprisonment, a more humane solution to this dilemma.

Most recently, the U.S. Senate made a clear-cut and decisive determination of the issue in the passage of the Crime Control Act of 1990. Key senators stated the universal premise that children are never executed even though they traditionally can distinguish right from wrong by age seven. Despite the Supreme Court's allowance of the execution of teenagers as young as fifteen, the Senate would not tolerate such cruelty. It supported banning these executions and all those of even younger children in the 1990 Crime Control Act.

Similarly, persons with mental retardation who never have a mental age beyond twelve should never be executed. They are still children in mind and spirit even if they understand the difference between right and wrong as children do.

MULTIPLE CLAIMS

Critics contend that banning the death penalty for offenders with mental retardation will allow killers who are in fact criminally responsible to avoid the death penalty. They say that multiple claims of mental retardation will be made by indigent defendants. This will create an enormous taxpayer burden because public payment of mental retardation evaluations will be required. There are several answers to these multiple claims arguments.

First, although multiple claims may be made, the prosecution will argue against this, and the jury or judge will determine whether the defendant fits the definition of mental retardation, as in all contentions made by the defense in the American system of adjudication.

Further, no one can feign mental retardation. It is a so apparent and distinguishable lifelong condition that the U.S. Senate, in drafting the 1990 Crime Control Act, determined that mental retardation does not even need to be defined.

Practically, even though expensive evaluations will be required when a mental retardation claim is made, these will be limited to capital cases. Funding for evaluations and defense of indigent defendants is increasingly available from *pro bono* sources.

Finally, the contention that the cost to the public is too much to bear is philosophically specious. Where life or death is at issue, the cost of protecting the rights of the accused is never too much to pay.

MAINSTREAMING, INDIVIDUALISM AND THE "RIGHT TO EXECUTION"

Some people who deal with people with mental retardation say they do not want to see them treated differently from anyone else. If we allow execution of the non-mentally retarded, then we should also allow it for individuals with mental retardation.

Inclusion in the American Dream for people with mental retardation does not include the "right to execution." Mainstreaming into American life of individuals with mental retardation is to allow them to enjoy all the benefits and privileges of society that non-handicapped citizens enjoy. It does not include the right to negative benefits or costs, deprivations or punishments, especially the worst punishment society can hand out, execution.

There is no right to be executed for offenders with mental retardation because execution is not a benefit, privilege or right. It is the deprivation of a right, the right to live.

Treating persons with mental retardation like everyone else in terms of execution is continuation of the discrimination and deprivation of the rights of the mentally handicapped that has historically existed. People with mental retardation have long been given the worst of treatment. Mainstreaming and treating them like everyone else is to stop this. It is to treat people with mental retardation like everyone else on the positive side of rights, not on the deprivation of rights.

Such a movement to promote individual treatment, although well-meaning, is a dangerous thing. There are unintended negative consequences associated with it. It carries the threat of destroying the hard-won statutory and constitutional protections that identification of minorities as legal classes has come to mean. Without such protections, the floodgates would open for denial of the civil rights of defendants with mental retardation and renewed massive discrimination against them.

GEORGIA

A final argument made against banning the death penalty holds that the lead of an unsophisticated Deep South state like Georgia, the first to ban the death penalty for persons with mental retardation, should not be followed by more progressive states outside the South.

This is a superficial argument based on prejudice. The issue should be decided on the merits, not on where the concept was first implemented. The death penalty applied to people with mental retardation falls unequally on minorities, and Georgia has deliberately taken steps to remedy this.

The argument is in another sense moot since the federal government and several other states have also banned the death penalty for persons with mental retardation.

Georgia became the trail blazer because its citizens were appalled at the execution of Jerome Bowden in 1986. Other states can avoid the same mistake of having the injustice of an execution of a person with mental retardation poignantly brought home to it. Other states can avoid Georgia's error by emulating its legislative and judicial remedies before, rather than after, they face the chilling reality of an execution of a person with mental retardation.

Notes

[1]Herbert J. Grossman, ed., American Association on Mental Retardation (previously Deficiency), *Classification Mental Retardation* (1983), 11.

[2]*See* Emily F. Reed, "Legal Rights of Mentally Retarded Offenders: Hospice and Habilitation," *Criminal Law Bulletin* 25 (September-October 1989):412.

[3]John Blume and David Bruck, "Sentencing the Mentally Retarded to Death: An Eighth Amendment Analysis," *Arkansas Law Review* 41 (1988):731.

[4]American Association on Mental Retardation Brief for Appellant (hereafter AAMR Brief), 5, Penry v. Lynaugh, 492 U.S. 302, 109 S.Ct. 2934, 106 L.Ed 2d 256 (1989).

[5]Blume and Bruck, 747.

[6]Testimony of James W. Ellis, President, American Association on Mental Retardation, United States Senate, Committee on the Judiciary, 27 September 1989, 4. *See also* Penry v. Lynaugh, 109 S.Ct. 2934, 2961 (Brennan and Marshall, concurring in part and dissenting in part).

[7]H. Grossman, 11, 76, quoted in Penry, 109 S.Ct. 2934, 2960. (Brennan and Marshall, concurring in part and dissenting in part).

[8]AAMR Brief, 6.

[9]Blume and Bruck, 731.

[10]Cleburne v. Cleburne Living Center, Inc. 473 U.S. 432, 442, 87 L.Ed 2d 313, 105 S.Ct. 3249 (1985) quoted in Penry, 109 S.Ct. 2935, 2961 (Brennan and Marshall, concurring in part and dissenting in part).

[11]*See* Reed, "Legal Rights," 412. *See also*, American Bar Association, ABA House of Delegates, "Recommendation," February 1989, 2.

[12]*See* Reed, "Legal Rights," 412.

[13]Blume and Bruck, 732, 734.

[14]Ibid., 734.

[15]Ruth Marcus, "Retarded Killer's Sentence Fuels Death-Penalty Debate," *Washington Post*, 22 June 1987, sec. A.

[16]Richard Burr, "The Death Penalty," paper presented at *A Presidential Forum - Offenders with Mental Retardation and the Criminal Justice System*, President's Commission on Mental Retardation, Washington, D.C., 16 September 1989. *See also* Testimony of Ellis, 4-5. AAMR Brief, 8.

[17]AAMR Brief, 8.

[18]"Sentencing of Retarded Killer Fuels Death Penalty Controversy," *Washington Post*, 22 June 1987, sec. A.

[19]Blume and Bruck, 733.

[20]Carolyn Click, "Attorney Will Ask Court to Halt Execution," United Press International, Dateline: Richmond, VA, 27 June 1985.

[21]AAMR Brief, 8.

[22]Blume and Bruck, 733.

[23]AAMR Brief, 7.

[24]Burr, 2.

[25]Sandra Torry, "High Court to Hear Case on Retarded Killer," *Washington Post*, 11 January 1989, sec. A.

[26]Donald Hermann, Howard Singer, and Mary Roberts, "Sentencing of the Mentally Retarded Criminal Defendant," *Arkansas Law Review* 41 (1988):802.

[27]Penry, 109 S.Ct. 2934, 2954.

[28]Burr, 3.

[29]Ibid. *See also* James W. Ellis and Ruth Luckasson, "Mentally Retarded Criminal Defendants," *George Washington Law Review* 53 (1985):423. Penry, 109 S.Ct. 2934, 2960-2961 (Brennan and Marshall, concurring in part and dissenting in part).

[30]Smith v. State, 290 S.E.2d 47 (1982).

[31]Fleming v. Zant, 386 S.E.2d 339, 347 (1989).

[32]Ibid.

[33]Smith v. Kemp, 664 F.Supp. 500 (M.D. Ga. 1987) quoted in Philip L. Fetzer, "Execution of the Mentally Retarded: A Punishment without Justification," *South Carolina Law Review* 40 (Winter 1989):426.

[34]Ed Carnes, Alabama Attorney General's Office, Capital Punishment Division, quoted in Peter Applebome, "2 States Grapple With Issue of Executing Retarded Men," *New York Times*, 12 July 1989, sec. 1.

[35]Tracy Thompson, "Court Rules Man of 65 IQ Unfit to Confess Crime," *The Atlanta Constitution*, 27 August 1988, sec. B.

[36]John J. Gruttadaurio, "Consistency in the Application of the Death Penalty to Juveniles and the Mentally Impaired: A Suggested Legislative Approach," *Cincinnati Law Review* 58 (1989):233.

[37]Donna M. Praiss, "Constitutional Protection of Confessions Made by Mentally Retarded Defendants," *American Journal of Law & Medicine* 14 (Winter 1989):451.

[38]*See* Testimony of Ellis, 5; Ellis and Luckasson, 426.

[39]Tison v Arizona, 481 U.S. 137, 107 S.Ct. 1676, 95 L.Ed.2d 127 (1987), quoted in Penry, 109 S.Ct. 2934, 2956.

[40]W.S. Gilbert and Arthur Sullivan, "A More Humane Mikado," *The Mikado or the Town of Titipu*, (New York: G. Schirmer, Inc., 1885) 173.

[41]Edmund v. Florida, 458 U.S. 782 (1982), quoted in Booth v. Maryland, 107 S.Ct. 2529, 2533 (1987), quoted in Blume and Bruck, 743.

[42]H.L.A. Hart, *Punishment and Responsibility* 15 (1968), quoted in Ellis and Luckasson, 471-472.

[43]AAMR Brief, 8, 12. *See also* Ellis and Luckasson, 429-430.

[44]Tison v. Arizona, quoted in AAMR Brief, 12.

[45]Thompson v. Oklahoma, 108 S.Ct. 2687 (1988), quoted in AAMR Brief, 12.

[46]AAMR Brief, 6-7.

[47]Ibid., 5, 9. *See also* Ellis and Luckasson, 431.

[48]Testimony of Ellis, 4-5.

[49]AAMR Brief, 7.

[50]AAMR Brief, 8. *See also* Testimony of Ellis, 4-5, 7-8.

[51]AAMR Brief, 12-13.

[52]Thompson v. Oklahoma, 108 S.Ct. 2697 (1988), quoted in AAMR Brief, 13.

[53]AAMR Brief, 15.

[54]Ibid., 4.

[55]Alan Dershowitz, quoted in *Time Magazine*, 10 July 1989, 48.

[56]Blume and Bruck, 729-730.

[57]AAMR Brief, 2.

[58]Furman v. Georgia, 408 U.S. 238 (1972).

[59]Spaziano v. Florida, 468 U.S. 447, 460, n.7 (1984), quoted in AAMR Brief, 11.

[60]Thompson v. Oklahoma, 108 S.Ct. 2687, 2697 (1988).

[61]Testimony of Ellis, 7.

[62]Ibid., 4-5. *See also* Ellis and Luckasson, quoted in Sandra Torry, "High Court to Hear Case on Retarded Slayer," *Washington Post*, 11 January 1989, sec. A.

[63]ABA Standards, 5.

[64]Testimony of Ellis, 7. ABA Standards, 5. *Emphasis added.*

[65]AAMR Brief, 19.

[66]Coker v. Georgia, 433 U.S. 584, 592 (1977).

[67]Spaziano v. Florida, 468 U.S. 447, 460, n. 7 (1984).

[68]Coker v. Georgia, 433 U.S. 584, 592 (1977)(plurality opinion), quoted in Blume and Bruck, 738. Gregg v. Georgia, 428 U.S. 153, 173 (1976).

[69]ABA Standards, 5.

[70]Blume and Bruck, 742.

[71]AAMR Brief, 19. Penry, 109 S.Ct. 2934, 2962 (Brennan and Marshall, concurring in part and dissenting in part).

[72]Penry, 109 S.Ct. 2934, 2962-2963 (Brennan and Marshall, concurring in part and dissenting in part). *See also* ABA Standards, 5.

[73]AAMR Brief, 15.

[74]Blume and Bruck, 742.

[75]Ibid., 743.

[76]*See* Chapter 3. A DEATH ROW DOZEN, ALTON WAYE *infra.*

[77]Blume and Bruck, 743.

[78]American Bar Association, ABA House of Delegates, 6.

[79]Exodus 21:23-25. *See also* Deuteronomy, 19:21.

[80]AAMR Brief, 19. Edmund v. Florida, 458 U.S. 782, 800 (1982), quoted in ABA Standards, 5.

[81]Testimony of Ellis, 8-9.

[82]Blume and Bruck, 744.

[83]Reed, "Legal Rights," 421-430.

[84]Blume and Bruck, 745-746.

[85]Deuteronomy, 32:35.

[86]Ford v. Wainwright, 106 S.Ct. 2595 (1986).

[87]Hermann, Singer, and Roberts, 795, referencing Lockett v. Ohio, 438 U.S. 586, 625.

[88]"Evolving Standards of Decency," *Washington Post*, 28 June 1989, sec. A. It is a shame that the Court did not have access to the evidence of state court pronouncements listed below which are equally representative of the people's voice.

[89]Henry Schwrazschild, director of the American Civil Liberties Union's Capital Punishment Project, and Richard Burr, NAACP Legal Defense Fund, and Justice Brennan, respectively, quoted in Alain L. Sanders, "Bad News for Death Row," *Time Magazine*, 10 July 1989, 49.

[90]Al Kaman, "Death Penalty Upheld For Killers in Mid-Teens,"

Washington Post, 27 June 1989, sec. A.
[91]Hermann, Singer, and Roberts, 765.
[92]Ford v. Wainwright, 106 S.Ct. 2595 (1986); Trop v. Dulles, 356 U.S. 86 (1958) quoted in Praiss, 456.
[93]Praiss, 456. Praiss applies the terminology to the mentally ill, but it is also appropriate for persons with mental retardation.
[94]ABA Standards, 1.
[95]Ibid., 6.
[96]Kaman, A.
[97]Blume and Bruck, 751.
[98]ABA Standards, 5.
[99]Ibid., 3.
[100]Torry, A. *See also* Testimony of Ellis, 3.
[101]Between 1936 and 1953 support ranged from 61-68 %. Between 1960 and 1971 this support dropped to around 50 %. From 1972 to the present support rose from 51 % to its current all-time high of around 80 %. The Gallup Report, Report No. 280, January 1989, 27-29. *See also* I. Groller, "Crime Watch," *Parents*, January 1989, 30.
[102]Sanders, 48.
[103]*See* FIGURE 2.3.
[104]Ronald Tabak and J. Mark Lane, "Execution of Injustice: A Cost and Lack-of-Benefit Analysis," *Loyola of Los Angeles Law Review* 23 (November 1989):93, n. 256.
[105]Blume and Bruck, 759-60. *See also* Penry, 109 S.Ct. 2934, 2955.
[106]Blume and Bruck, 759.
[107]Penry, 109 S.Ct. 2934, 2955.
[108]Blume and Bruck, 760, n. 136.
[109]Tabak and Lane, 93, n. 256.
[110]*See* Reed, "Legal Rights," 417 *et seq.*
[111]29 U.S.C. ss. 707-796 (1973).
[112]20 U.S.C. ss. 1401-1461 (1975). *See also* Blume and Bruck, 752.
[113]Blume and Bruck, 753.
[114]Ibid.
[115]Reed, "Legal Rights," 430-443.
[116]Ibid.
[117]Sandra Garcia and Holly Steele, "Mentally Retarded Offenders in the Criminal Justice and Mental Retardation Services Systems in Florida: Philosophical, Placement, and Treatment Issues," *Arkansas Law Review* 41 (1988):844.
[118]Delaware, for example, under two technical assistance grants from the National Institute of Corrections has developed a comprehensive plan for mentally retarded offender community and prison services. In the summer of 1990 this plan began to be implemented through a Delaware Developmental Disabilities Planning Council, Office of Handicapped Services grant to establish a pilot program in the probation department as an alternative to incarceration for mentally retarded inmates.
[119]Blume and Bruck, 745-746.
[120]Ibid., 754.
[121]Penry, 109 S.Ct. 2934, 2955.
[122]"Evolving Standards of Decency," *Washington Post*, 28 June 1989,

sec. A.
[123]Blume and Bruck, 755.
[124]Ibid.
[125]State v. Thompson, 456 So. 2nd 444, 446 (Fla. 1984); State v. Hall, 176 Neb. 295, 310, 125 N.W. 2d 918, 925 (1964); State v. Stokes, 319 N.C. 1, 352 S.Ed 653 (1987) quoted in Fetzer, 442, and n. 162.
[126]State v. Behler, 65 Idaho 464, 475, 146 P.2d 338, 343 (1944).
[127]State v. Hall, 176 Neb. 295, 310, 125 N.W. 2d 918, 925 (1964). Note that this is a contradiction because an I.Q. of sixty-four is in the high mild range and the term imbecile usually refers to the severely and profoundly retarded with I.Q.s below thirty-five.
[128]State v. Thompson, 456 So. 2nd 444, 446 (Fla. 1984).
[129]State v. Stokes, 319 N.C. 1, 352 S.Ed 653 (1987).
[130]Smith v. Kemp, 664 F.Supp. 500 (M.D. Ga. 1987) quoted in Fetzer, 426.
[131]Blume and Bruck, 757, n. 130.
[132]P.L. 100-690.
[133]Congressional Record - House, H7282-7283, 8 September 1988.
[134]Ibid.
[135]Ibid.
[136]P.L. 100-690, s. 7001(l).
[137]P.L. 101-647.
[138]Congressional Record - Senate, 24 May 1990, S.1970.
[139]Helen Dewar, "Senate Votes to Protect Retarded from Execution," *Washington Post*, 25 May 1990, sec. A.
[140]Richard Wolf, "Senate wrestles with death penalty," *USA Today*, 25 May 1990, sec. A.
[141]"Signing Statement, P.L. 101-647," 26 Weekly Compilation of Presidential Documents 1944, *United States Code, Congressional and Administrative News*, 3 December 1990, 6696-1.
[142]ABA Standards, 4-5.
[143]American Association on Mental Retardation Resolution on Mental Retardation and the Death Penalty, Board Book, (1988), 14. *See also* Testimony of Ellis, 2.
[144]Ibid.
[145]*See* AAMR Brief. Many of the arguments in this chapter have relied on that brief.
[146]Testimony of Ellis, 2. *See also* AAMR Brief, 2-4.
[147]Testimony of Ellis, 2.
[148]ABA Mental Health Standards, Standard 7-5.6(a)(b) (1989) 290.
[149]ABA Mental Health Standards (1984) 291.
[150]Terence McCarthy and Clifford Stromberg, "Report of Criminal Justice Section and Individual Rights and Responsibilities Section," American Bar Association, February 1989.
[151]Tabak and Lane, 93, n. 256.
[152]Praiss, 442.
[153]Ellis and Luckasson, 426. *See also* AAMR Resolution, 14; and McCarthy and Clifford D. Stromberg, ABA Resolution, 3.
[154]Testimony of Fred Krause before the Maryland Senate Judicial Proceedings Committee, *Mental Retardation - The Death Penalty Question*, 2

February 1989, 8.

[155]Praiss, 442.

[156]Edward Kenney, "Speaker: Executions Becoming Less Humane," *(Wilmington, DE) News-Journal*, 23 October 1990, sec. B.

[157]Russell Snyder, "Lawyer-Activists 'Horrified' over Death Penalty Process," Dateline: Washington, D.C., United Press International, 8 November 1990. For additional estimates, *see also* John Blume, "Representing The Mentally Retarded Defendant," *The Champion*, November, 1987, quoted in Blume and Bruck, 725-726, n. 4. *See also* Jo-Ann Armao, "Ban on Md. Death Penalty for Retarded Voted," *Washington Post*, 15 March 1989, sec. C; Jo-Ann Armao, "Executing the Retarded Prompts Debate in Md.," *Washington Post*, 3 February 1989, sec. C.

[158]Alain L. Sanders, "Bad News for Death Row," *Time Magazine*, 10 July 1989, 48.

[159]Al Kaman, "Death Penalty Upheld For Killers in Mid-Teens," *Washington Post*, 27 June 1989, sec. A.

[160]National Coalition to Abolish the Death Penalty, "United States Executions," 1991. This figure is as of September 25, 1991.

[161]Nathaniel Lipscomb was executed in Maryland, June 9, 1961. Arthur Goode III was executed in Florida, April 5, 1984. Ivon Stanley was executed in Georgia, July 12, 1984. Virginia executed Morris Mason on June 25, 1985. Terry Roach was executed by South Carolina on January 10, 1986. Jerome Bowden was executed in Georgia, June 25, 1986. William Celestine and John Brogdon were executed in Louisiana on July 20 and 30, 1987, respectively. Horace Dunkins, Jr. was executed by Alabama July 15, 1989. Alton Waye was electrocuted in Virginia on Aug. 30, 1989. Johnny Anderson, from Texas, was executed on May 17, 1990. Louisiana executed Dalton Prejean on May 18, 1990.

[162]Reed, "Legal Rights," 421-426.

[163]Dr. Stephen M. Mechanick, psychiatrist, in testifying in the suppression of confession hearing of Joseph Shields, 19-years-old, White, with a sixty-eight I.Q., accused of raping and murdering a 7-year-old white girl, stated that information had been furnished to him by the American Academy of Psychiatry and Law that the equivalent of a sixth grade education (mental age of eleven) is needed to understand a Miranda warning. The accused, with an I.Q. of 68, has the learning and understanding of a third grader (mental age of eight), and does not comprehend the meaning of the rights to an attorney and to remain silent without one. *See* State of Delaware v. Shields, IN90-04-0410-0413, 1990 Del.Super. LEXIS 418, 8 January 1991.

[164]Praiss, 432-433.

[165]Clark-Edward Anderson, "Low IQ Murderers," *ABA Journal* (October 1989) 26. *See also* "Death Penalty Defendants in South Get Inadequate Legal Advice, Journal Says," *Atlanta Journal and Constitution*, 4 June 1990, sec. A.

[166]Reed, "Legal Rights," 421-426.

[167]ABA Criminal Justice Mental Health Standards, Standard 7-9.3, 472 (1989) quoted in James W. Ellis, letter to the author, The American University, Washington, D.C., 12 February 1990, 2.

[168]Of the thirty-seven states that allow the death penalty, at least

72   THE *PENRY* PENALTY

twenty have aggravating-mitigating factor clauses in their statutes. Joshua N. Sondheimer, "A Continuing Source of Aggravation: The Improper Consideration of Mitigating Factors in Death Penalty Sentencing," *Hastings Law Journal* 41 (1990):409, 419.

[169]Hermann, Singer, and Roberts, 804. *See for example* Eddings v. Oklahoma, 455 U.S. 104, 110-116 and Lockett v. Ohio, 438 U.S. 586, 606-608 (1978).

[170]Penry v. Lynaugh, 109 S.Ct. 2934, 2946-2947.

[171]Blume and Bruck, 741.

[172]Ellis, letter to the author, 2.

[173]Lockett v. Ohio, 438 U.S. 586, 606-608 (1978) quoted in Hermann, Singer and Roberts, 795. *See also* In re Ramon M., 22 Cal.3d 419, 584 P.2d 524, 149 Cal. Rptr. 387 (1978) quoted in Fetzer, 430.

[174]Lockett v. Ohio, 438 U.S. 586, 606-608 (1978) quoted in Hermann, Singer and Roberts, 795.

[175]Woodson v. North Carolina, 428 U.S. 280, 280 (1976) quoted in Sondheimer, 415; Lockett v. Ohio, 438 U.S. 586, 605, quoted in Sondheimer, 416.

[176]Model Developmentally Disabled Offenders Act, in B. Sales, D. Powell, R. Van Duizend, "Disabled Persons and the Law," *State Legislative Issues* 665 (1982) quoted in Hermann, Singer and Roberts, 802. Although this argument was made in *Penry*, the Court did not accept its validity. *See* Petition for Writ of Certiorari, Joint Appendix at 18, Penry v. Lynaugh, *petition for cert. filed*, 57 U.S.L.W. 3024 (U.S. Jan 4, 1988), cert. granted, 108 S. Ct. 2896 (1988)(No. 87-6177)(testimony of Dr. Jerome Brown) quoted in Gruttadaurio, 217.

[177]Lockett v. Ohio, 438 U.S. 586, 606-8 (1978) quoted in Hermann, Singer and Roberts, 795.

[178]Reed, "Legal Rights," 414.

[179]*See* Thompson v. Oklahoma, 108 S. Ct. 2687 (1988); Stanford v. Kentucky; Wilkens v. Missouri, 492 U.S. 361; 109 S.Ct. 2969; 106 L.Ed. 2d 386 (1989).

[180]Blume and Bruck, 761-762. Interestingly enough, the court's rule runs counter to the actual practice of applying the death penalty to the mentally retarded. The younger a mentally retarded murderer, the more likely he is to be executed.

[181]Gruttadaurio, 213.

[182]Editorial, "Execute a 7-Year-Old?" Washington Post, 9 June 1989, sec. A. *See also* Penry, 109 S.Ct. 2934, 2941. Sandra Torry, "High Court to Hear Case on Retarded Killer," *Washington Post*, 11 January 1989, sec. A.

[183]Blume and Bruck, 761-2.

[184]*See* BEYOND MITIGATION: THE ANTI-CHILD EXECUTION ARGUMENT, *supra*.

[185]Hermann, Singer and Roberts, 794.

[186]Ibid.

[187]Ibid., 793-794. *See also* Roach v. Martin, 757 F.2d 1463, 1467 (4th Cir. 1985).

[188]Gruttadaurio, 211.

[189]Hermann, Singer and Roberts, 788.

[190]Ibid., 793-795.

[191]Ibid., 794-795.

[192]Blume and Bruck, 740.

[193]Sondheimer, 410-411, 425, 431. *See also* Lockett v. Ohio, 438 U.S. 586, 593-94 (1978) quoted in Gruttadaurio, 215, and Brief of Amicus Curiae Harris County Criminal Lawyers Association at 8-9 (citing Penry, 691 S.W.2d at 653) quoted in Gruttadaurio, 219, and 219, n. 75, and Penry v. Lynaugh, *petition for cert. filed,* 57 U.S.L.W. 3024 (U.S. Jan. 4, 1988), *cert. granted,* 108 S.Ct. 289 (1988)(No. 87-6177) quoted in Gruttadaurio, 219.

[194]Lockett v. Ohio, 438 U.S. 586, 604 (1978), quoted in Sondheimer, 410.

[195]Zant v. Stephens, 462 U.S. 862 (1983), quoted in ibid., 411.

[196]*See* CULPABILITY AND THE *PER SE* DEFINITION ARGUMENT, *supra.*

[197]Ellis and Luckasson, 424.

[198]Sondheimer, 411.

[199]Blume and Bruck, 754-759.

[200]Zant v. Stephens, 462 U.S. 862 (1983) and Lockett v. Ohio, 438 U.S. 586 (1978), quoted in Sondheimer, 429-431.

[201]Furman v. Georgia, 408 U.S. 238 (1972); Gregg v. Georgia, 428 U.S. 153, (1976).

[202]Furman v. Georgia, 408 U.S. 238 (1972).

[203]Susan Carx, quoted in J.S. Bainbridge, Jr. and Frances D. Williams, "Goode Executed in Fla. Sex-Slaying," *Baltimore Sun,* 6 April 1984. "Louisiana Executes Murderer of 11-Year-Old Girl," *New York Times,* 30 July 1987, sec. A.

[204]*See* ANTI-MITIGATION ARGUMENT, *supra.*

[205]The term "functional" describing the mentally retarded is Gruttadaurio's. *See* Gruttadaurio, 213.

[206]Ibid., 211. Again, "individualized" is Gruttadaurio's terminology.

[207]Thompson v. Oklahoma, 108 S. Ct. 2687, 2692, 2699 (1988), quoted in Fetzer, 430.

[208]Eddings v. Oklahoma, 455 U.S. 104, 115, n. 11 (1982) quoted in Fetzer, 441.

[209]Testimony of Senator Joseph R. Biden (D-Del), Congressional Record-Senate, S6875, S6881, 24 May 1990.

[210]Blume and Bruck, 759.

[211]Thompson v. Oklahoma, 108 S.Ct. 2687, 2699 (1988) quoted in Fetzer, 443.

[212]Thompson v. Oklahoma, 108 S.Ct. 2687 (1988).

[213]The Supreme Court held in Stanford v. Kentucky; Wilkens v. Missouri, 492 U.S. 361; 109 S.Ct. 2969; 106 L.Ed. 2d 386 (1989), cases decided the same day as *Penry,* that teenagers aged sixteen and seventeen can be executed. However, it had previously held in Thompson v. Oklahoma, 108 S. Ct. 2687 (1988), that fifteen-year-olds could not. Thus the minimum execution age is now sixteen.

[214]Blume and Bruck, 759.

[215]Ibid., 748-749, 759.

[216]*See* Testimony of Ellis, 4. *See also* Penry, 109 S.Ct. 2934, 2961-2962, 2962, n. 2 (Brennan and Marshall, concurring in part and dissenting in part).

[217]Hermann, Singer and Roberts, 766.

[218]Waye v. Virginia, 251 S.E.2d 202, 205 (1979).

[219]Testimony of Biden, S6875, S6881. *See also* Helen Dewar, "Senate Votes to Protect Retarded from Execution," *Washington Post*, 25 May 1990, sec. A.

[220]The argument in this section relies heavily on Ellis and Luckasson, 432-444.

[221]Hermann, Singer and Roberts, 775.

[222]Daniel M'Naghten's Case, 8 Eng. Rep. 718 (H.L. 1843) quoted in Garcia and Steele, 832.

[223]Daniel M'Naghten's Case, 8 Eng. Rep. 718, 722 (H.L. 1843) quoted in Ellis and Luckasson, 433.

[224]Hermann, Singer and Roberts, 775-6.

[225]Ellis and Luckasson, 436.

[226]214 F.2d 847 (D.C. Cir. 1962) quoted in Ellis and Luckasson, 436.

[227]214 F.2d 847, 874-875 (D.C. Cir. 1962) quoted in ibid.

[228]214 F.2d 847, 874 (D.C. Cir. 1962) quoted in ibid.

[229]McDonald v. United States, 312 F.2d 847 (D.C. Cir. 1962) quoted in ibid.

[230]McDonald, 312 F.2d 847, 851 quoted in ibid.

[231]Ellis and Luckasson, 437.

[232]Ibid.

[233]*In re* Ramon M., 22 Cal.3d 419, 427-28, 584 P.2d 524, 529-530, 149 Cal. Rptr. 387, 394 (1978); United States v. Shorter, 343 A.2d 569, 572 (D.C. 1975), quoted in ibid.

[234]*In re* Ramon M., 22 Cal. 3d 419, 584 P.2d 524, 149 Cal.Rptr. 387 (1978) quoted in Fetzer, 429-430.

[235]Hermann, Singer and Roberts, 777.

[236]ABA Criminal Justice Mental Health Standards, Standard 7-6.1(a)(b)(ii)(1984) quoted in Ellis and Luckasson, 437.

[237]Hermann, Singer and Roberts, 777.

[238]Testimony of Senator Edward Kennedy (D-Mass), Congressional Record-Senate, S6878, 24 May 1990.

[239]*See* Chapter 2, n. 172 for a listing of mentally retarded offenders in the mild range who have gone to trial, been sentenced to death and executed.

[240]*See* Delaware v. Shields, IN90-04-0410-0413, 1990 Del.Super. LEXIS 418, 8 January 1991.

[241]Blume and Bruck, 744.

[242]Miles Santamour, quoted in ibid., n. 74.

[243]Torry, A.

[244]Testimony of Senator Strom Thurmond, (R-S.C.) Congressional Record - Senate, 24 May 1990, s 6880.

[245]Testimony of Biden, s 6881.

[246]Ibid.

[247]Dewar, sec. A. Note that this provision did not pass.

[248]Fetzer, 432 and 432, n. 101.

[249]Senator Orrin G. Hatch, (R-Utah), quoted in Steven A. Holmes, "Curbs on Execution Appeals Are Voted," *New York Times*, 25 May 1990, sec. A.

[250]*See* Congressional Record - Senate, 24 May 1990, S.1970.

[251]Ibid.

[252]Ibid., S 6881.

[253]*See* "Senate Agrees to Ban Execution of Mentally Retarded Offenders," *Criminal Justice Newsletter,* 1 June 1990, 3.

[254]*See* Congressional Record, s 6881.

[255]Ibid., s 6878.

[256]Praiss, 452.

[257]HB 675, An Act Concerning Death Penalty - Mentally Retarded, ch.677, 1989 Md. Laws.

[258]GA. CODE ANN. S. 17-7-131(j)(Supp .1988).

[259]Civ. Act. No. 3068 (1981).

[260]*See* Reed, "Legal Rights," 430-436, for a more extended treatment of Georgia's compliance to the Guthrie decrees through mentally retarded prison programs.

[261]Fleming v. Zant, 250 Ga. 687, 386 S.E.2d 339 (1989). *See also* Jeanne Cummings, "Court Extends Ban For Retarded," *Atlanta Journal and Constitution,* 2 December 1989, sec. A.

[262]Jeanne Cummings, "Supreme Court to Review Fleming Case," *Atlanta Constitution,* 27 July 1989, sec. C.

[263]*See* "Retarded Killer Dies in Georgia Chair," *Chicago Tribune,* 25 June 1986.

[264]McDonald v. United States, 312 F.2d 847 (D.C. Cir. 1962).

3

A Death Row Dozen

Any man's death diminishes me, because I am involved in mankind; and therefore never send to know for whom the bell tolls; it tolls for thee.

--John Donne, *Devotions*

INTRODUCTION

This chapter presents the issue of the death penalty for offenders with mental retardation from an empirical perspective. It describes in detail the characteristics, circumstances and court processes surrounding twelve condemned and executed murderers who had mental retardation in order to flesh out the theoretical arguments. The stories of a dozen others who have been spared from execution are summarized in the next chapter to illustrate the breadth of the problem. All analyzed cases and death sentences except the first occurred after 1976 when the Supreme Court reauthorized the use of capital punishment.[1]

It is important to memorialize the least of these who cannot scribe for themselves. The straightforward telling of their tales comes not from any saccharin sympathy for murderers, because as will be seen as the chapter unfolds, the crimes committed by them were truly horrendous and beyond sympathy. Their stories are told as a memorial to the senselessness of the American legal system and the vacuum in understanding upon which court decisions are based. In its formalism and reliance on preservation of the technicalities and letter of the law without regard to substantive issues, the Supreme Court has strayed afar from traditional American decency and the original humanitarian principles upon which the very Constitution it purports to preserve was based.

The chapter, as a monument to an age of disdain for human life, aims to advance to a new humanity. The goal for the future is to look back upon the *Penry* decision as an aberration from our constitutional doctrine of guaranteeing life and of insuring the rights and safety of those who cannot protect themselves from the uninformed usage of the formal power of governmental institutions.

THE EXECUTED

NATHANIAL LIPSCOMB

Nathanial Lipscomb, an African American, was executed in the Maryland gas chamber on June 9, 1961 at the age of thirty-three.[2] He died for the 1959 serial rapes and strangulation murders of three Baltimore, Maryland women, Mae Hall, Lottie Knight, and Pearl Weiss.[3] Lipscomb, whose I.Q. tested between fifty-one and fifty-nine in the moderate range of mental retardation,[4] is the first known mentally retarded person to be executed in the United States and the last person executed in the State of Maryland to date.[5]

In 1959 little was known about the nature of the relationship of mental retardation to guilt and culpability. Lipscomb's defense attorneys argued for a verdict of not guilty by reason of insanity, even though multiple psychiatric examinations clearly showed that he was not insane. The insanity defense was used because there were no other legal remedies available for a person with mental retardation.

Lipscomb also was an alcoholic and his drinking at the time of the crimes was offered as a mitigating factor. However, the nature of alcoholism as a disease was not yet widely known, and the appellate court stated that "it is the general rule that voluntary drunkenness does not relieve an individual of responsibility for his crimes."[6] Thus neither his low mental capabilities nor his disease of alcoholism could prevent Lipscomb from being sentenced to death and executed.

Lipscomb's execution, along with the pending execution of James Trimble[7] have provided the impetus for the passage of Maryland's anti-death penalty statute for offenders with mental retardation.[8]

ARTHUR FREDERICK GOODE, III

Arthur "Freddy" Goode III, a never married, white man with mental retardation, was born in March, 1954,[9] the only brother of three sisters.[10] Goode's I.Q. tested "in the low sixties,"[11] but despite this low intelligence, he was able to read and write to some extent.[12] He had completed the equivalent of the ninth grade in school.[13]

Goode was dually diagnosed as both mentally retarded and mentally ill. His parents noticed abnormal aggressive tendencies in him when he was yet a toddler, and he received psychiatric treatment from the age of three. He was under the jurisdiction of Maryland mental health and probation officials for at least twelve years prior to the murder for which he was executed. He had made multiple threatening phone calls to young boys in the Washington, D.C. area and had committed numerous sexual assaults. According to one psychological report, Goode had been "emotionally disturbed almost from infancy."[14]

Goode was a self-declared pedophile[15] who, in March, 1977,[16] at the age of twenty-three, was convicted of the 1976 sodomy and murder of a nine-year-old white boy, Jason VerDow, in Cape Coral, Florida.[17]

He was also convicted in Virginia of a second murder, this time of an eleven-year-old white boy, Kenneth Dawson, killed ten days after the first. Goode received a sentence of life imprisonment for this crime. Virginia did not have the death penalty at the time.[18]

Goode was on probation at the time of both murders for prior felony sex crimes,[19] and had "walked away" from the non-secure Spring Grove Hospital Center in Catonsville, Maryland where he had been sentenced for treatment for his pedophilia. He had been admitted there at least four times before for deviant sexual behavior, the first time at age fourteen,[20] and had walked away at least one other time.[21]

On the same day of his escape from treatment, Goode kidnapped and sexually assaulted a paperboy, Billy Arthes, in Towson, Maryland. He was never prosecuted for this crime.[22]

Evidence of Goode's mental imbalance abounds. Throughout his years on Death Row he showed no remorse for his killings. In fact, he wrote letters to the victims' parents saying that he was "proud" of what he had done, and that he would rape and kill again, given the opportunity. He wrote abusive letters to his own parents. They believed that he was insane and worked throughout his Death Row stay to prevent his execution on this basis.[23] However, a panel of three psychiatrists appointed by Maryland Governor Robert Graham in 1984 to determine if Goode was mentally competent and could be legally executed judged him to be sane.[24]

While on Death Row, Goode appeared frequently on television as a self-styled expert on pedophilia.[25] He stated that he had committed the murders as a protest against society's discrimination against pedophiles and misunderstanding of pedophilia.[26] He stated that his last wish was to have sex once more with a young boy.[27] Thus by his own admissions Goode showed a high level of future dangerousness, an aggravating factor working against reprieve and favoring his execution.

Goode wrote multiple letters to the media and public officials, sometimes as many as ten or fifteen a day. A major theme of these missives was his demand to be put to death.[28] A few days before he was scheduled to be electrocuted, he said "that he was 'competent to be executed'"[29] and demanded that the execution be carried out.[30]

Arthur Goode was one of the most obnoxious of killers with mental retardation and the least worthy of mitigation or mercy. His crimes were particularly violent and brutal. During his trial, he graphically depicted how he sexually tortured and then strangled his victim.[31] Only at the last did his bravado fade and did he show any remorse at all. He then apologized to the victims' parents and to his own for what he had done.[32]

Thus the aggravating circumstances of his crimes, their violence, the young ages of the victims, Goode's lack of remorse and self-admitted future dangerousness, far outweighed the mitigating factors of his mental retardation and mental illness. Consequently, on April 5, 1984 after seven years on Death Row, and at the age of thirty, with "the eyes of a child" as he approached his death,[33] Goode was electrocuted in the Florida State Prison[34] in Lee County, Florida.[35]

IVON RAY STANLEY

Born in 1957,[36] in Decatur County, Georgia,[37] Ivon Ray Stanley, was a poor African American child with mental retardation. He had a younger brother, Jeffrey, and a sister, Mildred. His father deserted his mother before he was born. His mother "treated him coolly," and he was raised by his maternal grandmother,[38] Eliza Yulee.[39] Stanley's I.Q. measured sixty-two. His reading ability was that of a second grader, and he had difficulty writing intelligently. He dropped out of high school in the eleventh grade.[40]

In 1976, at the age of nineteen, he had a common law wife[41] and was sometimes employed as a sawmill worker[42] in Bainbridge, Georgia.[43]

At this time, he and an accomplice, Joseph Edward Thomas, twenty-eight, who was the perpetrator,[44] plotted to rob and "get rid of"[45] a leading white businessman and insurance collector, Clifford Floyd, forty-six. Floyd was a Baptist Church deacon and an executive in a local civic club.[46]

The circumstances of the crime were particularly brutal. Floyd was kidnapped, hit on the head and arm with a hammer, tied to a tree, beaten and jabbed with a shovel in the chest, throat and head, and finally made to lie down in a shallow grave where he was shot three times and buried alive, all while pleading for his life. An autopsy indicated that he died of suffocation.[47]

In his trial, Stanley's lawyers claimed that Stanley was not the instigator but merely a follower of Thomas. As the assault progressed, Stanley allegedly pled with Thomas not to kill Floyd, but Thomas continued in his deadly attack. Thomas was also sentenced to death for his part in the crime.[48]

Stanley's common law wife testified against him at trial.[49] However, his mother, grandmother, and younger brother supported him throughout his death penalty ordeal. Stanley claimed to the end that Thomas committed the murder and that, although he was at the crime scene, he was innocent.[50]

Stanley's grandmother stated that as a young man, Stanley was particularly mild-mannered. He was "always looking to help someone" and was teased and bullied by his peers, as frequently happens to children with mental retardation, but refused to retaliate. Once when asked by his grandmother to kill a chicken for dinner, he was unable to do it.[51] His brother stated that "We was never bad boys. . . . He was [just] at the wrong place."[52]

Although the mitigating circumstances of his youth, I.Q., low reading ability, and lack of prior criminal convictions were brought out at trial, multiple aggravating factors greatly outweighed them.   The murder was committed during other capital offenses (kidnapping with bodily injury and armed robbery).[53] The crimes were "outrageously and wantonly vile, horrible and inhuman," involved "depravity of mind, . . . torture of the victim," and were committed "for the purpose of receiving money and other things of value."[54]   Thus the death sentence was upheld by the Georgia Supreme Court, and Stanley, at the age of twenty-eight, was electrocuted in Jackson, Georgia on July 12, 1984, eight years after he was sentenced to death.[55]

MORRIS ODELL MASON

Born in March, 1952 in Virginia, Morris Mason was an African American, poorly educated laborer,[56] with an I.Q. in the sixty-two to sixty-six range and the mental age of an eight-year-old.[57] Mason stayed in school until the tenth grade and was never married.[58]

In October, 1978 at the age of twenty-six, Mason was condemned to death for the May 13, 1978 rape, torture and slaying of Margaret K. Hand, a 71-year-old white woman.[59]

Mason was mentally ill with paranoid schizophrenia,[60] and had a record of psychiatric commitments from the age of seventeen.[61] Beginning when he was twenty-one-years-old, he heard voices ordering him to do violent things.[62]   Alcoholic, Mason claimed that his drinking was the dominant factor in his violent and homicidal actions.[63]   Indicative of his mental ability, Mason asked a legal aid what he should wear to his funeral. He was unable to understand that he would not survive his own demise.[64]

Mason's defense attorney argued that he should not be executed because his mental retardation and mental illness were insufficiently brought out and established during his trial,[65] and that they prevented him from comprehending the essence of his crimes and punishment.[66]   However, because of the aggravating circumstances of the crime, these factors in mitigation - mental retardation, mental illness, alcoholism, poor schooling, lack of employment skills - and failure to discover them at trial, were insufficient to save Mason from the death penalty.

The first such factor was the event attributes. Mr. Mason's crime was excessively violent and heinous. He tied his seventy-one-year-old female victim to a chair, nailed one of her hands to it, hit her with an axe several times, left her inside the door, and, while she was still alive, set her, the chair and the house on fire,[67] burning her to death.[68]

Second, Mr. Mason, calling himself the "Killer for the Eastern Shore," had an extensive and violent criminal record. He had been paroled from a ten-year sentence for arson and grand larceny less than a month before he went on the two-week violent rampage which included the death penalty murder. He confessed to committing additional rapes and murders of an eighty-six-year-old woman and a twelve-year-old girl. He admitted shooting and attempting to burn the murdered girl's thirteen-year-old sister in a leaf pile when she resisted his rape attempts.[69] She was left permanently paralyzed from the attack.[70]

On the same day that he was indicted for the old lady's torture and burning death, Mason was charge with fifteen additional felony counts for crimes committed during the previous crime spree.[71]

With this massive amount of violent crime as indicator, Mr. Mason could be considered extremely dangerous in the future and likely to commit more such acts given the opportunity. The trial court found two statutory aggravating factors, first, that his prior criminal history and circumstances of the instant crime made it likely that he would commit additional violent crimes and would be a continuing threat to society, and second, that his actions in committing the instant offense were "outrageously or wantonly vile, horrible and inhuman... [involving] torture, depravity of mind or aggravated battery of the victim."[72] Thus the aggravation of the crime prevented the mitigation of his mental disabilities from staying his execution. Mr. Mason, aged thirty-two, was put to death by electrocution on June 25, 1985 in Northhampton County, Virginia, after seven years on Death Row.[73]

JAMES "TERRY" ROACH

James Terry Roach was born in South Carolina in February, 1960. He was white, unmarried, with a fourth grade education. His mental retardation was in the borderline range.[74]

On October 23, 1977 at the age of seventeen, Roach and two accomplices, Joseph Carl Shaw and Ronald Mahaffey, selected two teenagers at random to rob, rape, and murder in Columbia, South Carolina.[75] The victims were Thomas Taylor, seventeen-years-old, and Carlotta Harkness, age fourteen, both white.

The three assailants had been drinking and taking drugs throughout the morning prior to the homicides. In the afternoon, they decided to seek out "a girl to rape."[76] They came upon the victims in a parked car at a baseball diamond. The three ordered the girl to get in the back seat of their car. They robbed Taylor of his wallet. Roach then shot Taylor three times in the head with a .22 rifle.[77]

Roach, Shaw and Mahaffey drove to a dirt road nearby, forced Harkness to take her clothes off, and all three repeatedly raped her. She was then forced to lie with her face in the dirt, and Roach volunteered to kill her.

He shot her repeatedly in the back of the head. They then returned to Taylor's car and shot him again to make sure that he was dead.[78]

In December, 1977, less than two months later, Roach pled guilty to two counts of murder, kidnapping, armed robbery and criminal sexual assault. The trial judge imposed the death penalty for the two murder counts.[79] Joseph Shaw was also sentenced to death for his part in the murders and was executed on January 11, 1985.[80] Mahaffey turned state's evidence and received a life sentence in return for his cooperation with the prosecution.[81]

Aggravating and mitigating factors were weighed against each other as required by South Carolina statute. Three aggravating factors were enumerated. The murders were committed during the commission of three other major felonies, rape, kidnapping and robbery.[82]

In mitigation were:

The defendant had no significant prior violent criminal activity, although he had been convicted of one prior felony, and was on escape status from a state reformatory at the time of this crime.[83]

He acted under extreme mental disturbance. This factor was related to his being high on drugs and alcohol.

He suffered from mental retardation and was diagnosed as having anti-social personality disorder.

He acted under the duress or domination of another person (as is frequently the case when persons with mental retardation commit criminal acts.)

His abilities to appreciate the wrongfulness of his acts and to conform them to the law were substantially impaired. This again refers to his mental retardation and drug-induced impairment.

He was a minor below the age of eighteen at the time of the crime.[84]

Despite this lengthy list of mitigating factors, the court found that aggravation outweighed mitigation, and Roach was sentenced to death.[85]

Subsequent to his death sentence, Roach developed an hereditary degenerative illness, Huntington's Disease. The disease may have already begun its degenerative process at the time of the murder.[86] Huntington's Disease is "a disorder of movement, personality and thought," that leads to atrophy of the mind and to mental retardation.[87] These facts were stated in Roach's appeals, but the U.S. Supreme Court did not deem them, nor any of the other mitigating factors, to be adequate to overturn his death sentence.[88]

Eight years after the murders, with all appeals exhausted, on January 10, 1986 in Richland County, South Carolina, this young man, aged twenty-five, a juvenile at the time of the murders who already had mental retardation, suffering from a personality disorder and a physical disease that was deteriorating his already limited mental capabilities, was electrocuted.[89] His defense attorney stated later that "People like [Terry] . . . become the classic sidekick for any psychopath whose path [they] happen to cross."[90] He also stated that executing Roach "was like executing a child."[91]

JEROME BOWDEN

On October 11, 1976 in Columbus, Georgia, Jerome Bowden, a twenty-four-years-old, never-married African American with mental retardation,[92] was accused of the robbery and bludgeoning killing of a fifty-five-year-old white woman, Kathryn Strycker, for whom he did yard work. Bowden was also charged with the beating of the seventy-six-year-old, paralyzed and bedridden mother of the victim, Wessie Jenkins, who survived her injuries.[93] An accomplice and the instigator of the crime, a sixteen-year-old juvenile named James Graves, was the next door neighbor of the victims.[94]

Bowden was born in July, 1952.[95] His I.Q. was measured at fifty-nine at the ages of twelve[96] and fourteen.[97] He attended special education classes most of his school years and dropped out of school during the ninth grade after an argument with the principal.

Bowden had several minor brushes with the law as a teenager, but he had committed no other violent crimes. He had two prior burglary convictions[98] and had served three years in prison for these. He had no adult felony convictions, and no charges were pending at the time of the murder.[99] Thus his criminal record was not extensive.

Prior to the crime, Bowden had spent much of his time helping out the elderly by chopping wood, delivering groceries, and doing yard work. He was described by those who knew him as soft-spoken, pleasant, optimistic and always smiling.[100]

Bowden was convicted of murdering Ms. Strycker in December, 1976, less than two months after she died.[101] As the circumstances of the crime for which Bowden was convicted were described, they were violent, but not excessively so when compared to those of other executed killers. The victim was hit in the head twice with the butt of a pellet gun. The blows crushed her skull. Although Bowden could not read,[102] he signed a confession which stated that he then stabbed her in the chest with a butcher knife to "'put her out of her misery.'" The autopsy indicated the victim had already died from the head blows before she was stabbed.[103] The victim was not raped or tortured.

In mitigation, the accomplice, James Graves, sixteen-years-old at the time and younger than Bowden, suggested the robbery and was the instigator of the crime. There was some evidence that Graves himself may have committed the murders. He was arrested first and then implicated Bowden as the principal perpetrator. There was no evidence at the crime scene to tie Bowden to the murder.[104] However, Graves received life imprisonment.[105]

In aggravation of the crime, Bowden also was in the midst of a burglary and robbery, and committed the additional assault on the victim's aged and vulnerable mother.

In sum, the mitigating factors - Bowden's mental retardation, his minor criminal record, the lack of a particularly heinous crime compared to other capital murders, and the instigation of the crime by another - did not seem to be outweighed by aggravating factors. Nonetheless, an all-white jury from which African Americans had systematically been excluded[106] found the existence of two statutory aggravating factors - that the murder was committed during the commission of an armed robbery which is another capital offense, and that it was committed during a burglary. Both these aggravating circumstances enabled them to impose the death sentence despite the evidence of non-statutory mitigation.[107]

In 1986, after ten years on Death Row, and with his execution imminent, Bowden won a ninety day stay of execution from the Georgia Board of Pardons and Parole in order to have his mental competency evaluated.[108]

Bowden's supporters argued that he was so mentally incompetent that he didn't comprehend the meaning of death and what was happening to him,[109] and that he did not know right from wrong.[110]

However, within a few days of the imposition of the stay, a psychologist from Emory University in Atlanta, Dr. Irwin Knopf, measured Bowden's I.Q. at sixty-five. Dr. Knopf indicated in his psychological assessment that Bowden knew the difference between right and wrong.[111] Based on this single mental competency evaluation, the Pardons and Parole Board believed that Bowden's I.Q., which now measured at sixty-five, enabled him to know right from wrong,[112] that he was sufficiently intelligent to know the gravity of what he had done and the meaning of being executed, and that he was therefore qualified to die in the electric chair.[113] Six days after the issuance of the execution suspension, the postponement was lifted, and Bowden was hastily executed the next day.[114] An eleventh hour appeal to the U.S. Supreme Court on the day the stay was withdrawn by Pardons and Parole Board also failed.[115]

Bowden, thirty-three-years-old, was electrocuted on June 23, 1986 in Muscogee County, Georgia.[116] The suddenness of the execution and its justification on the basis of only one psychological assessment caused cries of outrage from the interested public. The execution was described as "a willful lack of decency by the State of Georgia."[117] Members of the Association for Retarded Citizens (ARC), a prominent singer, Lou Reed, and two rock bands, Sting and U2, took up Bowden's cause after his death.[118]   A well-respected ARC attorney and president of the Georgia ARC, Patricia Smith, said that the difference between an I.Q. of fifty-nine and sixty-five is "insignificant" and that it is not professional nor accepted practice to rely on only one I.Q. test as did the Pardons Board.[119]   This is especially true where a man's life is at stake.

The public dismay in Georgia that followed the fact of Bowden's execution and the hasty way in which it was done created the impetus in the Georgia legislature for the passage of the first state law in the nation with a straightforward, comprehensive ban on the death penalty for persons with mental retardation.[120]   Georgia took a definitive legislative step to insure that such a shameful event would never occur again in its borders.

WILLIE CELESTINE

Willie Celestine, an African American, was born in Louisiana in May, 1956. In June, 1981,[121] when he was twenty-five, he was condemned to death for the beating, aggravated rape and murder of an eighty-one-year-old white woman, Marcelianne Richard, in Lafayette, Louisiana.[122]

On September 13, 1981, in the middle of the night Celestine broke into the old woman's home, raped her and beat her badly enough to make her face unrecognizable. She suffered six broken ribs and a fractured neck vertebrae.[123]   The cause of death was strangulation. Celestine had been drinking and taking "speed" throughout the day, and stated that he was high on drugs at the time of the crime.[124]

Celestine had a long and violent criminal history dating back to his early teens. He had five juvenile convictions, including disturbing the peace, theft, auto theft, burglary and possession of stolen property. He had been incarcerated for these crimes for eight months in a juvenile training school. As an adult he had twice been convicted of aggravated rape,[125] and he admitted to two additional burglaries and rapes in the weeks prior to the murder.[126]

Celestine's I.Q. measured an average seventy-seven with a verbal score of sixty-nine and a non-verbal score of eighty-one.[127]   He had left school when he was sixteen, had joined the Army at nineteen, and was "dishonorably discharged" four years later for "disobeying orders."[128]   Afterwards he lived with his parents, a carpenter and domestic, approximately a block from the home of the victim. Celestine was married and divorced[129] and the father of one child to whom he contributed no support.[130]

In his murder trial, three aggravating circumstances were delineated. Celestine had earlier been convicted of aggravated rape, the offense was committed in an unusually "cruel manner" and "during an aggravated rape."[131]

On the eve of his execution, Celestine claimed that he committed the murder because he was "high on drugs" and intoxicated.[132] However, no facts in mitigation were stated.[133] Thus although the fact of his borderline retardation was known, the death penalty was imposed without recognition of it nor the mitigating effects it has on culpability.

Celestine's attorneys argued that the Louisiana death penalty discriminated against African Americans and that Celestine was condemned to death because he killed a white person. However, the Appeals Court saw no merit in this claim.[134] On July 20, 1987, almost six years after the crime, Celestine, at the age of thirty, was executed.[135]

JOHN E. BROGDON

John E. Brogdon, one of the four white men with mental retardation who have been executed, was born in January, 1962 in Louisiana.[136] He had an I.Q. in the sixties and, as a child, was a special education student. He dropped out of school in the sixth grade.[137]

One of five children, Brogdon was badly beaten as a child by his father who was schizophrenic, alcoholic, and a family abuser. His father admitted to beating Brogdon so violently at one time that he broke his ribs.[138] His mother died when he was fourteen. After his mother's death, he was placed in a series of foster homes from which he frequently ran away. Around the age of fourteen as he was shuffled from foster home to foster home, he became an alcoholic and developed a severe drug addiction problem.[139] His father admitted to supplying and smoking marijuana with him.[140]

Brogdon had a series of minor juvenile offenses, four juvenile misdemeanors, one misdemeanor theft conviction as an adult, and six additional adult misdemeanor arrests.[141] He had no adult felony convictions, and no charges pending when he committed the murder for which he was executed.[142] Thus his criminal history was relatively minor, that of a petty repeat offender.

In 1981, when he was a nineteen-year-old unmarried young man,[143] Brogdon and another teenager, Bruce Perritt, were arrested for the torture, rape and slaying of an eleven-year-old girl, in Luling, Louisiana.[144] Brogdon pled innocent by reason of insanity at his trial,[145] and a psychologist testified that he had a "personality disorder" that explained his violence and aggression. His mental retardation, along with his "mental disease," were offered in mitigation.[146]

Brogdon's seventeen-year-old accomplice in the murder was sentenced to life imprisonment because the jury could not agree on the death penalty.[147] In Louisiana, the jury is bound by law to consider both aggravating and mitigating circumstances prescribed by statute, as well as any other mitigating factors in the case. Brogdon offered the sentence of life without parole of Perritt, his co-defendant, as such a mitigating factor, but the district court refused to admit it into evidence.[148] Thus in February, 1982, Brogdon was convicted and sentenced to death.[149]

This first conviction was upheld, but the death penalty sentence was overturned by the Louisiana Supreme Court. The Court held that the trial court had erred in issuing instructions to the jury. In his second penalty hearing held in June, 1983, Brogdon was again sentenced to death.[150]

Brogdon's killing was particularly violent and brutal. He beat the victim with bricks and stabbed her with pointed sticks and broken glass while repeatedly raping her as she fought back.[151] Thus the aggravating circumstances of the crime - that it "was committed in an especially cruel, heinous, and atrocious manner,"[152] and the young age of the female victim - made the jury's sentencing decision easy. Criminal aggravation far outweighed the mitigation of Brogdon's mental retardation, abused childhood, alcoholism, drug addiction, and youth at the time of the crime.

Consequently, at the age of twenty-five and after five years on Death Row, Brogdon was executed on July 30, 1987.[153]

HORACE DUNKINS, JR.

Horace "Ronnie" Dunkins, Jr., African American and Alabama poor, was born in Warrior, Jefferson County, Alabama,[154] in February, 1961.[155] Dunkins' mental retardation was in the mild range. He had an I.Q. between sixty-five and sixty-nine and the mental acuity of a ten to twelve-year-old.[156] He was characterized as a "slow learner" throughout his life. He attended special education programs as a child,[157] and dropped out of school in the eleventh grade.[158] As an adult he was functionally illiterate, but was able to hold a job as a common laborer.[159] He was never married.[160]

Dunkins was nineteen-years-old in October, 1980, when he was arrested for the rape, slaying and torture death of a white, twenty-eight-year old mother of four, Lynn McCurry. The murder occurred during the night of May 26-27, 1980 outside the victim's home in Warrior, Alabama, while her four children slept inside.

A co-defendant, Frank Marie Harris, then seventeen-years-old, pled guilty and received life imprisonment without possibility of parole for his part in the crime.[161]

Another witness testified that on the afternoon of the twenty-sixth, Dunkins and Harris, a fellow employee of the Alabama Wire Company, held the following conversation. Dunkins: "'I'm going to get some pussy from a white lady,' and Harris responded, 'Yeah, I'm with you Horace.'"[162] At Dunkins' request the witness then bought surgical tape to tie up the prospective victim.[163]

The woman randomly selected for the rape was found the next day in her own yard, naked, tied to an oak tree[164] with surgical tape, and with a nightgown over her head. The autopsy revealed sixty-six stab wounds[165] all over her body, including one "which penetrated the vagina vault." So much blood was present that no seminal fluid could be found in here body cavities.[166]

When Dunkins was arrested he waived his right to counsel. Later he didn't know that he had done so.[167] Nevertheless, the appeals court held that "a person functioning in the high mild range of mental retardation [like Dunkins] . . . can intelligently waive their rights" and that "he did in fact understand and voluntarily" do so.[168]

In his appeal, Dunkins' new lawyers contended that his trial counsel was ineffective in several respects, and that the jury was not allowed to consider Dunkins' mental deficiencies in determining its death penalty recommendation.[169] The appeals court dismissed these claims.[170]

Nonetheless, Dunkins was not well-represented at trial. His defense attorney was a court-appointed (in Dunkins' words) "scared young lawyer." He failed to present Dunkins' mental retardation to the jury as a mitigating factor weighing on culpability.[171] Two factors in mitigation were brought out - the defendant's young age (nineteen) and the fact that he had no "significant" prior criminal history.[172]

The trial court, a jury of twelve white women,[173] found two statutory aggravating factors present. The crime was "especially heinous, atrocious or cruel" and the victim was alive when she was "stabbed sixty-six times."[174] The premeditation involved was also a factor.

Thus the aggravation of the crime's circumstances far outweighed the mitigation, and the all-female jury recommended to the sentencing judge that Dunkins be put to death.[175] In May, 1981, Dunkins was convicted of the crime, and sentenced to death by the trial judge.[176]

Dunkins was executed on July 15, 1989 in Holman Prison, Atmore, Alabama, in the notorious "Yellow Mama" electric chair.[177] When the current was first turned on, something went awry. The chair had been connected to the wrong electrical jacks. Doctors examined Dunkins, who was unconscious, but had a strong heartbeat.[178] Ten minutes later, with the connections readjusted, Dunkins was jolted again, and finally expired[179] while his father and two uncles looked on. Observers called this "a grisly scene" in which the bumbling of the execution was "torture," both of Dunkins and his family who watched in horror.[180] The botching of the execution brought home the reality of the inhumanity of government-ordered killing of human beings.

ALTON WAYE

In the borderline range of mental retardation with an untested I.Q.,

Alton Waye was born in Virginia in July, 1955.[181] He was a never-married,[182] "poor black man,"[183] with "a diminished mental capacity"[184] and an eighth grade education. He was also an Army veteran and textile factory worker.[185]

On October 14, 1977, Waye, at the age of twenty-two, murdered a sixty-one year old white "widow of a prominent Lunenburg County [VA] farmer,"[186] Lavergne B. Marshall.[187] The woman lived in an isolated rural spot about a mile from the nearest public road.[188]

On the afternoon of the 14th, Waye and an accomplice, Len Gooden, began drinking beer at a cafe. They left around 8:00 PM to look for "a girl named Queenie," ostensibly a prostitute, who was nowhere to be found. Subsequently, Waye drove around while Gooden mostly slept under the effects of alcohol. Around 10:00 PM, Waye drove up into a yard, got out of the car and went to the house. The victim answered the door in a nightgown, whereupon Waye raped and beat her.[189] He then got a butcher knife from the kitchen and stabbed her repeatedly. Waye dragged the body into the bathtub, attempted unsuccessfully to cover it with water, found a bottle of bleach and poured it over her. He went back to the car and immediately told Gooden that he had "'killed a woman and put her in the bathtub.'"[190]

He went home and told his father, and then called the police himself to tell them too. He readily confessed and voluntarily took the police back to the crime scene, whereupon he was arrested for murder.

Conduct such as this is typical of people with mental retardation. They are very anxious to please authority figures, and are disconcerted by irregular events. Talking about such things is their attempt to understand what happened. Waye's total lack of comprehension that he was in an extremely precarious situation and had committed a very serious crime punishable by death is also evidenced by his complete lack of attempts to hide the crime, his overly anxious desire to tell everyone what had happened, and his statements that I "'did it just like . . . on television . . . wiped the knife and everything. . . . Man, wait until my friends hear about this,'"[191] as if he had just hit a home run.

The autopsy revealed that the victim had been stabbed forty-two times. Her face was pummeled "beyond recognition." The body evidenced bruises and bite marks on the "breasts and buttocks," "defense wounds" on the hands, and sperm in both the vagina and anus. Blood was everywhere.[192]

Waye was tried, convicted and sentenced to death in April, 1978.[193] During the trial, the defense offered several factors in mitigation. The defendant's psychiatrist proposed to testify that Waye did not "deliberate and premeditate" committing the crime, but the testimony was deemed inadmissible. In opposition, photographs of the victim were proffered and received in evidence to illustrate that the killing took place in a "methodical manner" manifesting "premeditation and malice."[194]

Similarly, the defendant's drunkenness, that "he was so intoxicated as to render him incapable of committing a willful, deliberate and premeditated act designed to kill the victim" was offered in mitigation, but the court refused to accept this. The evidence of Waye driving the car, his father's testimony of his actions at home, and his companion's opinion that Waye was drunk, but that he suffered no reservations about riding with Waye, countermanded this defense.[195]

The primary factor offered in mitigation by the defense was the statutory culpability factor. "The capacity of the defendant to appreciate the criminality of his conduct or to conform his conduct to the requirements of the law was significantly impaired" by his "mental condition," "mitigating mental abnormality," and "mental retardation."[196] Waye's youth and lack of prior criminal activity[197] were also offered for consideration.

However, the court stated that it believed that "the atrociousness of the offense resulted from a depraved or evil, rather than a disturbed, mind,"[198] so that the primary factor of mitigation, reduced culpability, was disallowed, and the aggravating circumstances of an extremely brutal crime justified the imposition of the death penalty.[199]

After approximately eleven years on Death Row, all of Waye's seventeen appeals heard by thirty judges were exhausted. A panel of judges of the Fourth Circuit Court of Appeals stated, "'There must be some finality. . . and the final stage has been reached in this case.'"[200] Consequently, at the age of thirty-four, on August 30, 1989, Waye was electrocuted.[201] His mother, brother, two sisters, and numerous nieces and nephews were with him on his last day before he faced death.[202]

JOHNNY RAY ANDERSON

Born in 1959 in Texas, Johnny Ray Anderson, White, was a sixth grade dropout and an unemployed former mechanic[203] with an I.Q. of seventy.[204] He had a permanent personality disorder and suffered irreversible brain damage from sniffing glue and gasoline from the age of five.[205] Inhaling of poisonous fumes over a long period of time may have contributed to his mental retardation.

In 1981 when he was twenty-two-years-old and committed murder,[206] Anderson lived with his mother, Rowena Hayes Anderson, fifty-four, an alleged witch, in Vidor, Texas.[207]

Johnny became involved in a bizarre family scheme with his mother,[208] his sister, Laura Lee Anderson Goode Murphy, twenty-seven, the mother of four children,[209] and his neighbor of a couple of months, Delvin Douglas Johnson, Jr., thirty-nine, an oil worker. The cabal plotted to kill Laura Goode's common law husband, Ronald Gene Goode, a twenty-two-year-old white soft drink salesman from Kountze, Texas, in order to collect $67,000 from an insurance policy on his life.[210] Anderson and Johnson were fingered as the triggermen in the homicide.[211]

Johnson testified in Anderson's trial that in the early hours of October 1, 1981, he and Anderson started out to the deserted wooded area of Loop Road, north of Beaumont, Texas. On the way, Anderson stopped at a phone booth, called Goode and lured him to meet them there under a pretext.[212] When Goode arrived, Anderson shot him with the shotgun. Goode did not die but crawled away into the trees. Anderson went back to the car to retrieve the rifle. The two used a cigarette lighter to find Goode. Anderson shot Goode again in the head, and his body was left where it lay in the woods by the side of the road.[213] Evidence showed that Goode died from a gunshot wound in the head made by a 30.06 rifle. Another wound in the stomach had been made with a .410 shotgun.[214]

The murder plot that culminated in the death of Goode was entirely in character for a family headed by a witch and described as "a violent type . . . always arguing . . . and fighting amongst each other and the other neighbors."[215]

Conflicting testimony was given in the various trials of the participants as to how the scheme evolved. Laura Goode testified that her mother, Mrs. Anderson, was the instigator because she didn't want Laura, her son-in-law, and favored granddaughter, Penny, thirteen, to move away.[216] Laura also stated that her mother, with whom Johnny Anderson lived, had repeatedly threatened to kill Goode herself and had attempted to do so at least four times, using a knife, gun and poison on different occasions. Johnny had offered to do the job for her,[217] both from fear and in an attempt to please her. Rowena Anderson was alleged to control people by casting spells on them and by threatening to kill them.

Laura said she herself gave the others "insurance money because they threatened her." She denied any part in the plot.[218]

Despite her testimony, Laura Anderson was convicted of murder for hiring Anderson and Johnson to perform the killing.[219] Johnson testified in Johnny Anderson's trial that Laura had paid him $5,000 to kill her husband. Rowena Anderson had offered him a sum of $6,000 on the same day to do the deed. The night of the crime, Johnny told him he would receive $10,000.[220]

Laura Anderson was sentenced to life imprisonment and served eight years of her sentence. After her murder conviction was overturned by an appeals court, she pled guilty to a lesser charge and was released on parole.[221]

The first trial of Rowena Anderson, Johnny's mother, was declared a mistrial. She was acquitted in the second trial.[222]

Johnson was convicted of capital murder for his role in the crime. He was sentenced to fifty years in prison,[223] but was paroled after serving eight years.[224]

Only Johnny, the person with mental retardation, was sentenced to death.[225] On February 12, 1983, when the jury imposed this sentence, it considered the aggravating factors of Anderson's crime as indications of future dangerousness and a tendency to commit future violence, and concluded that an alive Anderson was a continuing threat to the safety of the community.[226] Aggravating factors leading to this conclusion included his several prior arrests, his one prior juvenile felony conviction for burglary in 1978 for which he received eight years of probation and was still under supervision when the murder was committed,[227] his reputation for violence in the community, the cold-blooded, calculated and brutal nature of the crime, the fact that the murder was committed for remuneration, the discovery of a "shank" (a homemade knife) in his prison cell after he was arrested, and his threats to harm other inmates.[228]

The mitigating factors of Anderson's low intelligence and mental retardation were not considered by the jury during the penalty phase. Later appeals on the basis of the defense's failure to offer these factors in mitigation were denied.[229]

This case illustrates the prototypic outcome for the unprotected people with mental retardation. Their lack of understanding of the nature of the crime or its consequences makes them susceptible to entrapment in other people's snares. They can easily be taken advantage of and shamefully used by ruthless people, even their own families, because of their great desire to please and gain approval. They lack the means to defend themselves adequately from the criminal schemes of smarter and conscienceless people. They will do as asked or told for big threats or small rewards, or just to please and gain acceptance. Unknowingly and unwittingly, they become the fall guys for the others. When he was on the verge of being executed, Johnny Anderson realized his predicament. In a statement typed by another inmate and signed by Anderson with an unreadable signature, he said that he was "not responsible for the murder" and had become "the excape goat."[230]

Johnny Anderson, according to his attorneys, was just "a poor, dumb, son of a bitch, who should never have been given the death penalty."[231] He was caught in a murder trap devised by his family from whom he received his material support, and for whom he took the ultimate rap.

On May 17, 1990 at the age of thirty and after a little more than seven years on Death Row, Anderson was put to death by lethal injection in the state prison at Huntsville, Texas.[232] By this time all of the rest of the participants in the murder scheme were free persons.[233] Laura Anderson had remarried and become Laura Murphy.[234] It couldn't have worked out better for them.

DALTON PREJEAN

Dalton Prejean was an African American child born in Lafayette, Louisiana in 1959, the second child of four. His I.Q. was between seventy-one and seventy-six, in the borderline range of mental retardation.[235] His intelligence failed to develop beyond the mental age of thirteen,[236] and he had a limited ability to communicate.[237]

When he was two weeks old, Prejean's parents sent him to his alcoholic aunt in Houston, Texas to raise.[238] Throughout his childhood, she beat and otherwise physically abused Prejean. He suffered permanent brain damage either at birth, from these blows, or during a childhood bicycle accident.[239]

Prejean lived with this aunt for his first twelve years[240] without knowing that she was not his mother. In 1971, his parents separated, and his father moved to Houston. The aunt told Prejean about his true parentage before he could learn it from his father.[241]

About the same time, Prejean began to get into a good deal of trouble, and the aunt decided to send him back to his mother in Louisiana. His behavior worsened, and in 1972 his mother had him committed to the Louisiana Training Institute for truancy. He had become incorrigible.[242] He was released seven months later, and shortly after he was arrested for theft and burglary. He was just thirteen. Again committed to reform school, he stayed only a month before running away.[243]

Prejean as a teenager became a double murderer. Soon after his release from the reformatory and at the age of fourteen, he committed his first homicide.[244] While attempting to rob a cab driver with two accomplices, he took a gun from one of them because he thought the boy was too nervous to hold it. He then shot and killed the cabbie and fled from the scene. He later stated that he believed that the driver was reaching for a gun.[245]

For this murder, Prejean was sentenced to an indefinite term at a New Orleans reform school. After serving about two years, he was released on parole. Six months later, when he was seventeen, he shot and killed a white Louisiana state trooper, Donald Cleveland, the crime for which he was executed.[246]

Shortly after 5:00 AM on the morning of July 2, 1977, Trooper Cleveland was on his way to work in his squad car in Lafayette, Louisiana. He stopped the car driven by Prejean because its tail lights were out.[247] Prejean, his brother, Joseph, and two friends, Michael Broussard and Michael George, had just left a nightclub and were a few hundred yards down the street from it. They had been using drugs and drinking all night in various bars in the vicinity.[248] Prejean had smoked marijuana and "angel dust" (PCP), and drunk an unknown quantity of "beer, vodka and white port wine."[249]

When they stopped for the policeman, Prejean's brother attempted to switch places with him because Prejean didn't have a driver's license. Trooper Cleveland saw this and ordered Joseph Prejean out of the car. He held Joseph against the car with his head against the roof while searching him.[250]   Joseph struggled and protested this treatment, causing Prejean to state to the others that "I don't like the way he's doing my brother." He pulled a gun from under the seat, got out of the car with it held against his leg,[251] walked up to Cleveland, took a "shooter's stance"[252] and shot Cleveland twice, once in the jaw and once in the chest. Cleveland was killed outright. All four fled the scene but were captured later.[253]   Cleveland left a widow, Candy, and two small children.[254]

During the first week of May, 1978, Prejean was tried, convicted, and unanimously sentenced to death for this crime by an all-white jury.[255] Four of the nine prosecutor's peremptory challenges of potential jurors were used against African Americans.[256]

In the penalty phase, the prosecution established one statutory aggravating factor, the killing of a peace officer in the performance of his duties.[257]   In mitigation, the defense offered three factors - Prejean's young age, his inability to appreciate the wrongfulness of his conduct and conform his acts to the law because of his "natural mental condition," and exacerbation of these deficiencies by his intoxication.[258]   However, the jury did not find these mitigating factors sufficient to outweigh the aggravating factor. Prejean was condemned to death.[259]

On appeal, Prejean's attorneys bargained for his life on several grounds. They argued that Prejean was a young African American who had been convicted by an all-white jury of killing a white policeman, and that African Americans had been systematically excluded from the jury. Prejean's young age and the *de facto* racial disparity of an exclusively white jury sentencing an African American murderer of a white man should be sufficient to reduce the sentence.[260]

Prejean had not received an adequate psychiatric evaluation prior to trial. The level of his brain damage was never correctly assessed because the examining psychologist failed to administer the appropriate tests.   Thus Prejean's mental retardation and abused childhood were never presented to the jury. If they had known these facts, the death penalty may not have been imposed.[261]

Finally, Prejean showed extreme remorse for the crime.

However, various state appeals courts[262] and the Fifth Circuit Court of Appeals did not accept these arguments. In 1989, the U.S. Supreme Court refused to hear the case.[263]

Prejean remained on Louisiana's Death Row for ten years, and received ten stays of execution. Despite his youth, he was called the "Old Man of Death Row" because of his long wait to be executed.[264]

Although Prejean was never married, he fathered a son during a conjugal visit in the Lafayette County, Louisiana jail when he was twenty-one years old. Dalton, Jr. was born in 1981.[265]

The Louisiana Board of Pardons voted twice, once in 1989 and once in 1990, by a vote of three to two to commute Prejean's sentence to life imprisonment.[266] The three members voting for sentence commutation were African American. The other two were white.[267] The Pardons Board cited multiple reasons for its recommendation for clemency. These included most of those that had been rejected by the courts, including Prejean's childhood physical abuse and brain damage, his ineffective court-appointed trial counsel who never offered his abused childhood, mental retardation, and intoxication at the time of the crime in mitigation at his trial, his "good prison record," and his evidence of remorse.[268] However, Louisiana Governor Buddy Roemer refused to follow the Pardons Board's recommendation for clemency.[269]

Despite an international outcry, after twelve years on Death Row, Prejean, at the age of thirty, was executed on May 18, 1990 at the Louisiana State Penitentiary's Death House in Angola, Louisiana.[270] He is the last known criminal with mental retardation to have been executed in the United States.

SUMMARY

The stories of twelve deceased men with mental retardation have been told in this chapter. All were executed for crimes of murder. One was executed in 1961. The remaining eleven were executed since 1976 when the United States Supreme Court reauthorized the death penalty. These eleven comprise approximately eight percent of those killed by the death penalty since that date, compared to the approximately three percent of the population at large that is inflicted with mental retardation.

Two-thirds (eight) of the men were African American. One-third (four) were white. All of the victims were white.

Louisiana has executed the most persons with mental retardation (three) of any state. Virginia and Georgia have each executed two. One each has been executed by Alabama, Florida, Maryland, South Carolina and Texas. FIGURE 3.1 summarizes the data contained in this chapter.

NEW DIMENSIONS IN DEFENSE

I have a rendezvous with Death, At some disputed barricade, When Spring comes round with rustling shade, And apple blossoms fill the air.
I have a rendezvous with Death, When Spring brings back blue days and fair.

Alan Seeger, *I Have a Rendezvous with Death*

FIGURE 3.1. EXECUTED MENTALLY RETARDED OFFENDERS

Name	State	Age	Date Executed	I.Q.	Race	Race of Victim
1. N. Lipscomb	MD	33	6/9/61	51-59	Black	Unknown
2. A. Goode III	FL	22	4/5/84	62	White	White
3. I. Stanley	GA	19	7/12/84	62	Black	White
4. M. Mason	VA	25	6/25/85	66	Black	White
5. T. Roach	SC	17	1/10/86	70-75	White	White
6. J. Bowden	GA	25	6/25/86	59-65	Black	White
7. W. Celestine	LA	19	7/20/87	69-81	Black	White
8. J. Brogdon	LA	19	7/30/87	60s	White	White
9. H. Dunkins	AL	22	7/15/89	65-69	Black	White
10. A. Waye	VA	17	8/30/89	Untested	Black	White
11. J. Anderson	TX	22	5/17/90	70	White	White
12. D. Prejean	LA	17	5/18/90	71-76	Black	White

Executing States				Race	
Louisiana	-	3	25 %	Black	8 - 67 %
Virginia	-	2	17 %	White	4 - 33 %
Georgia	-	2	17 %	Total	12 100 %
Alabama	-	1	8 %		
Florida	-	1	8 %	Race of	
Maryland	-	1	8 %	Victim	
So.Carolina	-	1	8 %		
Texas	-	1	8 %	Black	0 - 0 %
Total		12	99 %	White	11 - 100 %
				Unknown	1 - -- %

Average Age   21
Average I.Q.   68

ROBERT HARRIS

The case of Robert Alton Harris, an offender with borderline mental retardation,[271] is important enough to be included here because it has a peculiar twist. Improvement is being made in the mental retardation defense, and this defense is evolving in new directions for the nineteen nineties. This case is on point.

Robert Alton Harris, was a thirty-nine-year-old white Californian when he was executed in 1992. Like John Paul Penry,[272] he alleged that he suffered from profound emotional, intellectual and physical disabilities, post-traumatic stress disorder and organic brain dysfunction caused by head trauma from multiple blows to the head, fetal alcohol syndrome, and savage child abuse. Like Penry,[273] Harris contended that his disabilities resulted in poor impulse control and made it extremely difficult for him to bridle his violent tendencies and actions. His claims were supported by "neuropsychological" testing conducted in 1990.[274]

Harris spent his early childhood in the worst of damaging and dysfunctional families. His early life makes that of John Paul Penry look like a convent. His mother was an alcoholic who drank heavily while carrying him in the womb, and he was born three months prematurely with fetal alcohol syndrome. She was regularly kicked by her husband while pregnant.[275]

His preschool days were filled with "physical and psychological terror at the hands of his parents."[276] They beat him with fists and weapons.[277] His father menaced him with guns and sometimes choked him so roughly that he convulsed.[278]

When he was eleven, his father was sentenced to two prison terms for having sex with his sisters. It was about this time that he began his prolonged and violent life of crime. He was first arrested at the age of eleven for burglary and cruelty to animals.[279]

When his father went to prison, his mother took a boyfriend and went on the migrant picker trail. She herself later robbed a bank and was on probation when Harris was arrested for murder.

Harris was expelled from the family at the age of fourteen for not working hard enough. He soon stole a car and was convicted of car theft, for which he served four years in various federal youth camps and prisons. He was also convicted of escape and attempted escape during this sentence. He had other convictions for being a runaway, for burglary, auto theft, and parole violation.[280]

When he was twenty-two, Harris was convicted of voluntary manslaughter of a nineteen-year-old neighbor whom he beat to death with head blows after a "drinking spree" while contemptuously asserting he was teaching him self-defense. He also cut off the victim's hair, threw lighter fluid on him and set him on fire with matches. When arrested for this crime he was on welfare, and his house was so filthy that it was a noteworthy news item.[281]

While in prison for this crime, he terrorized other inmates, threatened to kill another man in full hearing of a guard, committed forcible sodomy, manufactured a "wire garrote" and hand-made knives called "shanks" which constituted "implied threats" for the use of violence. Fortunately they were confiscated before he could use them.[282] When paroled from this sentence he stole firearms and accumulated a small arsenal of guns, all illegally acquired and illicit for a convicted felon to have in his possession.[283] When not incarcerated, and even when he was, Harris was a dangerous, cold-blooded and sadistic one-man violent crime wave.

In the spring of 1978, while Harris was on parole from the manslaughter conviction, he and his brother, Daniel, plotted to rob a bank. They stole guns from a neighbor of Daniel's, and planned to heist a car to use as a getaway vehicle. On July 5, 1978, they spotted a likely car in a grocery store parking lot across the street from the bank they intended to rob. Harris got in the back seat, held a pistol to the occupants, sixteen-year-old Michael Baker and fifteen-year-old John Mayeski, who were eating hamburgers, and ordered them to drive to a remote area where the brothers had been target practicing. Harris assured Daniel and the occupants that no one would be hurt. Daniel followed in his brother's car.[284]

When they reached the target practicing area, Harris ordered the two teenagers to walk up the hill trail. All at once, Harris shot Mayeski in the back, and then executed him with a shot in the head. He hunted down Baker who was crying and hiding in the brush, wounded him with four shots, returned to Mayeski and shot him again, went back to Baker who was conscious and praying, and told him "God can't help you now, boy. You're going to die." He then killed him with a shot to the head.[285] The Harrises returned to the house where they were staying, and Harris ate the rest of the boys' lunch, "giggled and laughed" about what he had done, and bragged that he had "shot the arm off" of one victim. He speculated to his brother how it would be to be a police officer informing the families of the death of the victims. Daniel Harris was sick and mortified.[286] Later, he testified that he had nothing to do with the murders, and as a part of a plea agreement, he was sentenced to only six years in prison.[287]

The brothers continued on their course and robbed the bank. Harris stated to Daniel that he wanted to kill everyone in the bank, but Daniel pled for no more killing.[288]

When they left the bank, someone followed them. Their house was soon surrounded. They were arrested, whereupon Harris confessed to the murders.[289]

Harris' murders were extremely merciless and brutal. He shot the teenagers in cold blood, made the incredible statement that "God can't help you now," and ate the victim's food while bragging about the crime. He continued on his course of robbing the bank as if nothing significant had happened.[290]

Harris had many other uncharged offenses in connection with the murders of the teenagers, including burglary, bank robbery, receiving stolen property, firearms and car theft.[291]

Despite Harris' appalling lifetime of crime, a dozen years after the murders, Harris' defense lawyers put forward the "brain damage" defense.[292] They claimed that fetal alcohol syndrome, severe beatings, mental and physical abuse as a child, all of which led to organic brain damage and post-traumatic stress disorder caused by his violence-filled childhood, had made him unable to control his violent behavior.[293]

On April 3, 1990 just hours before he was to be executed, Harris won a stay of execution from Ninth Circuit Court Judge John T. Noonan which was upheld by the U.S. Supreme Court. The stay was based on the claims of inadequacy of psychiatric testimony in bringing out these facts at trial.[294] At a subsequent hearing on the issues before a three judge panel of the Ninth Circuit Court in August, 1990, the court refused to order a new hearing on the incompetency of psychiatric testimony at Harris' original trial, and the way was cleared for his execution.[295] His execution finally took place in California's gas chamber on April 21, 1992.[296] Like Penry's mental retardation defense, Harris' brain damage defense had proven unsuccessful.

Notes

[1]Gregg v. Georgia, 428 U.S. 153 (1976).
[2]M. Watt Espy and John Oritz Smylka, "Executions in the United States, 1608-1987: The Espy File," [machine-readable data file] Tuscaloosa, Ala. Ann Arbor, MI: Inter-university Consortium for Political and Social Research [distributor], 1987, line 5765.
[3]Lipscomb v. Warden of Maryland Penitentiary, 225 Md. 634, 171 A.2d 247 (1961).
[4]Ibid.
[5]Jo-Ann Armao, "Executing the Retarded Prompts Debate in Md." Washington Post, 3 February 1989, sec. C.
[6]Lipscomb v. Warden, 225 Md. 634, 171 A.2d 247 (1961).
[7]Armao, "Executing the Retarded," sec. C.
[8]MD. CRIM. LAW CODE ANN., ART. 27, S. 412 (revised 1989).
[9]"Capital Punishment in the United States, 1973-1989," United States Department of Justice, Bureau of Justice Statistics, Ann Arbor, MI: Inter-university Consortium for Political and Social Research [distributor], February 1991, Case No. 525.
[10]Charles Fishman, "Repentant Goode Executed in Florida," Washington Post, 6 April 1984, sec. A; "2 Convicted Killers Die in a Single Day in Southern Prisons," New York Times, 6 April 1984, sec. A.
[11]Philip L. Fetzer, "Execution of the Mentally Retarded: A Punishment without Justification," South Carolina Law Review, 40 (Winter 1989): 432.
[12]Fishman, sec. A.
[13]"Capital Punishment in the United States, 1973-1989," Case No. 525.
[14]J.S. Bainbridge, Jr., "System Failed to Prevent the Emergence of a Killer," Baltimore Sun, 6 April 1984.
[15]"2 Convicted Killers," sec. A.
[16]"Capital Punishment in the United States, 1973-1989," Case No. 525.
[17]Bainbridge, 6 April 1984.
[18]Fishman, sec. A.
[19]"Capital Punishment in the United States, 1973-1989," Case No. 525.
[20]Andrea Rowand, "Goode Dreams of Cheating Executioner," (Jacksonville) Florida Union Times, 5 April 1984.
[21]J.S. Bainbridge, Jr. and Frances D. Williams, "Goode Executed in Fla. Sex-Slaying," Baltimore Sun, 6 April 1984.
[22]Bainbridge, 6 April 1984.
[23]Fishman, sec. A.
[24]Rowand, 5 April 1984.
[25]Fishman, sec. A.
[26]Bainbridge and Williams, 6 April 1984.
[27]Fishman, sec. A.
[28]Ibid.
[29]Fetzer, "Execution," 432.
[30]Fishman, sec. A.
[31]"2 Convicted Killers," sec. A.

[32]Fishman, sec. A.

[33]Susan Carx, quoted in Bainbridge and Williams, 6 April 1984.

[34]Bainbridge and Williams, on 6 April 1984.

[35]The Espy File, line 2738.

[36]"Capital Punishment in the United States, 1973-1989," Case No. 627.

[37]Bill Montgomery and Hal Strauss, "Ivon Ray Stanley, 28, Dies in Georgia's Electric Chair," *Atlanta Journal*, 12 July 1984.

[38]G.G. Rigsby, "Stanley Dies; Florida Killers Get Temporary Stays," United Press International, Dateline: Jackson, GA, 12 July 1984.

[39]Montgomery and Strauss, 12 July 1984.

[40]Stanley v. Georgia, 241 S.E.2d 173, 176-178 (1977).

[41]Ibid.

[42]The Espy File, line 2738. See also Montgomery and Strauss, 12 July 1984.

[43]"Domestic News," Reuters Ltd., Dateline: Jackson, GA, 12 July 1984.

[44]Montgomery and Strauss, 12 July 1984.

[45]241 S.E.2d 173, 175.

[46]"New Trial Ordered for Thomas," United Press International, Dateline: Atlanta, GA, 10 September 1986.

[47]241 S.E.2d 173, 175-176.

[48]Montgomery and Strauss, 12 July 1984.

[49]241 S.E.2d 173, 178.

[50]Montgomery and Strauss, 12 July 1984.

[51]Rigsby, "Stanley Dies," UPI, 12 July 1984.

[52]Montgomery and Strauss, 12 July 1984.

[53]241 S.E.2d 173, 176-177, 179-180.

[54]Ibid., 179.

[55]The Espy File, line 2738.

[56]"Capital Punishment in the United States, 1973-1989," Case No. 6875.

[57]Carolyn Click, "Eastern Shore Sex Killer Executed," United Press International, Dateline: Richmond, VA, 26 June 1985.

[58]"Capital Punishment in the United States, 1973-1989," Case No. 6875.

[59]Tom Sherwood, "`Killer for Eastern Shore' Executed After Gov. Robb Denies Final Pleas," *Washington Post,* 26 June 1985, sec. B.

[60]Jeff Shapiro, "Mason to Appeal to Supreme Court," United Press International, Dateline: Richmond, VA, 21 June 1985.

[61]Carolyn Click, "Executed Killer Sends Final Greetings to Fellow Inmates," United Press International, Dateline: Richmond, VA, 26 June 1985.

[62]Mark Lazenby, "Execution Set for Admitted Killer," United Press International, Dateline: Richmond, VA, 16 February 1985.

[63]Tom Sherwood, "Lull Expected in Virginia Executions: None Likely Until Late this Year as 28 Remain on Death Row," United Press International, Dateline: Richmond, VA, 27 June 1985.

[64]Carolyn Click, "Attorney Will Ask Court to Halt Execution," United Press International, Dateline: Richmond, VA, 19 June 1985.

[65]"Two Men Convicted of Murder Are Executed in Virginia and Texas," *New York Times,* 26 June 1985, sec. A.

⁶⁶Fetzer, "Execution," 432. *See also* Sherwood, "`Killer for Eastern Shore,'" 4.

⁶⁷Mason v. Commonwealth of Virginia, 219 Va. 109, 254 S.E.2d 118 (1979); Tom Sherwood, "Execution Set Today for Man Convicted in Va. Rape-Slaying," *Washington Post*, 25 June 1985, sec. D.

⁶⁸Click, "Executed Killer."

⁶⁹Ibid.

⁷⁰"Two Men Convicted," sec. A.

⁷¹Mason, 219 Va. 109, 254 S.E.2d 118, 119.

⁷²Ibid.

⁷³"Two Men Convicted," sec. A. *See also* The Espy File, line 14285.

⁷⁴"Capital Punishment in the United States, 1973-1989," Case No. 1470.

⁷⁵Roach v. Aiken, 474 U.S. 1039, 106 S.Ct. 645, 88 L.Ed. 2d 637 (1986).

⁷⁶Roach v. Martin, 757 F.2d 1463, 1468 (1977).

⁷⁷Ibid. *See also* John Monk, "International Pleas For Mercy Fail as S.C. Executes Terry Roach," *Charlotte Observer*, 11 January 1986.

⁷⁸Ibid., 1468.

⁷⁹Ibid., 1467-1468.

⁸⁰Monk, "International Pleas," *Charlotte Observer*, 11 January 1986.

⁸¹Amnesty International, *The United States of America: The Death Penalty* (New York: Amnesty International Publications, Inc., 1987), 71.

⁸²757 F.2d 1463, 1468.

⁸³"Capital Punishment in the United States, 1973-1989," Case No. 1470. *See also* The Espy File, line 11805; Monk, "International Pleas," *Charlotte Observer*, 11 January 1986.

⁸⁴757 F.2d 1463, 1468-1469.

⁸⁵Ibid., 1469.

⁸⁶Monk, "International Pleas," *Charlotte Observer*, 11 January 1986.

⁸⁷Ibid. *See also* Roach v. Aiken, Justice Thurgood Marshall, joined by Justice William Brennan, dissenting.

⁸⁸"National ARC Seeks to Protect Rights of Inmates with Retardation," *Michigan ARC Focus*, July/August 1987, 7.

⁸⁹National Coalition to Abolish the Death Penalty, "United States Executions," 1991, 3.

⁹⁰David Bruck, "Banality of Evil," in Ian Gray and Moira Stanley, *A Punishment in Search of a Crime* (New York: Avon Books, 1989), 2.

⁹¹David Bruck, quoted in "National ARC," 7.

⁹²"Capital Punishment in the United States, 1973-1989," Case No. 631.

⁹³"Retarded Man, 33, Electrocuted as Plea of High Court is Rejected," *New York Times*, 25 June 1986, sec. A.

⁹⁴"Georgia Halts Execution for Mental Evaluation," *New York Times*, 17 June 1986, sec. A. *See also* "Mentally Retarded Killer Wins Stay of Execution," United Press International, Dateline: Jackson, GA, 17 June 1986.

⁹⁵"Capital Punishment in the United States, 1973-1989," Case No. 631.

⁹⁶Jim Barber, "Bowden Dies in Electric Chair," United Press International, Dateline: Jackson, GA, 25 June 1986.

⁹⁷"Georgia Halts Execution," sec A.

[98]United Press International, Dateline: Jackson, GA, 14 October 1985.
[99]"Capital Punishment in the United States, 1973-1989," Case No. 631.
[100]Robert Perske, *Unequal Justice* (Nashville, TN: Abingdon Press, 1991), 31.
[101]"Capital Punishment in the United States, 1973-1989," Case No. 631.
[102]Perske, 29.
[103]Bowden v. Kemp, 344 S.E.2d 233, 234 (1986).
[104]Perske, 29.
[105]"Retarded Killer Dies in Georgia Chair," *Chicago Tribune*, 25 June 1986, sec. 1.
[106]"State Supreme Court Refuses to Halt Execution of Retarded Man," United Press International, Dateline: Jackson, GA, 16 June 1986.
[107]Bowden v. State, 238 S.E.2d 905, 911 (1977).
[108]Rebecca Rakoczy, "Execution of Bowden 'Outrage,'" *(Lawrenceville, Georgia) Gwinnett Daily News*, 25 June 1986.
[109]"Georgia Halts Execution," sec. A. *See also* UPI, 23 June 1986.
[110]United Press International, Dateline: Jackson, GA, 23 June 1986.
[111]Rakoczy, "Execution of Bowden," 25 June 1986.
[112]UPI, Dateline: Jackson, GA, 23 June 1986.
[113]Fetzer, "Execution," 432.
[114]Rakoczy, "Execution of Bowden," 25 June 1986.
[115]"Retarded Killer Dies," sec. 1.
[116]"Capital Punishment in the United States, 1973-1989," Case No. 631.
[117]Perske, 35.
[118]"Retarded Killer Dies," sec. 1.
[119]United Press International, Dateline: Jackson, GA, 23 June 1986.
[120]"Supreme Court to Review Fleming Case," *Atlanta Constitution*, 27 July 1989, sec. C.
[121]"Capital Punishment in the United States, 1973-1989," Case No. 2562.
[122]Peter Applebome, "Governor of Louisiana To Spare Inmate's Life," *New York Times*, 17 August 1989, sec. A.
[123]Gary Hines, "Domestic News," United Press International, Dateline: Angola, LA, 20 July 1987.
[124]Louisiana v. Celestine, 443 So.2d 1091, 1093 (1983).
[125]Ibid., 1097-1098.
[126]Ibid., 1093.
[127]William F. Buckley, "But Did They Get the Right Man?" *Washington Post*, 16 August 1989, sec. A.
[128]443 So.2d 1091, 1096-1097.
[129]Sister Helen Prejean, "A Pilgrim's Progress," in Gray and Stanley, *A Punishment*, 96.
[130]443 So.2d 1091, 1096.
[131]Ibid., 1097.
[132]"Louisiana Executes 81-Year-Old's Killer," Chicago Tribune, 21 July 1987, sec. 1.
[133]*See generally* Louisiana v. Celestine, 443 So.2d 1091, 1093 (1983).
[134]Ibid., 1097.

135Richard Cohen, "Senseless Execution," *Washington Post*, 24 April 1990, sec. A.

136"Capital Punishment in the United States, 1973-1989," Case No. 2568.

137"Louisiana Executes Murderer of 11-Year-Old Girl," *New York Times*, 30 July 1987, sec. A.

138Louisiana v. Brogdon, 457 S.E.2d 616, 630 (1984). *See also* "Mentally Retarded Killer Executed," *Washington Post*, 30 July 1987, sec. A.

139457 S.E.2d 616, 631.

140"Murderer of Girl Is Put to Death in Louisiana," *New York Times*, 30 July 1987, sec. B.

141457 S.E.2d 616, 631.

142"Capital Punishment in the United States, 1973-1989," Case No. 2568.

143Ibid.

144"Louisiana Executes Murderer," sec. A. Lisa Frazier, "Top Court Lets La. Send Killer to Electric Chair," *New Orleans Times-Picayune*, 30 July 1987, sec. B.

145"Killer Waiting For Judge to Rule on Execution Delay," *New Orleans Times-Picayune*, 14 July 1987, sec. B.

146457 S.E.2d 616, 621-2, 628.

147"Louisiana Executes Murderer," sec. A.

148457 S.E.2d 616, 625.

149"Capital Punishment in the United States, 1973-1989," Case No. 2568.

150Marsha Shuler, "Death Row," *(Baton Rouge, LA) Morning Advocate*, 14 August 1983.

151"Murderer of Girl," sec. B.

152457 S.E.2d 616, 623.

153"Louisiana Executes Murderer," sec. 21. *See also* "Capital Punishment in the United States," Case No. 318.

154John Archibald, "On Second Try, Dunkins Executed for Murder," *Birmingham News*, 14 July 1989.

155"Capital Punishment in the United States, 1973-1989," Case No. 1712.

156John Archibald, "On Second Try, Dunkins Executed for Murder." *Birmingham News*, 14 July 1989.

157Dunkins v. State, 489 So.2d 603, 608 (Ala.Cr.App. 1985)(hereinafter Dunkins II); Dunkin v. State, 437 So.2d 1349,1353 (Ala.Cr.App. 1983)(hereinafter Dunkins I).

158"Capital Punishment in the United States, 1973-1989," Case No. 1712.

159Dunkins I, 1353.

160"Capital Punishment in the United States, 1973-1989," Case No. 1712.

161Dunkins I, 1356. *See also Encyclopedia of World Crime*, 1990 ed., s.v. "Dunkins, Horace Franklin, Jr.," by J. R. Nash; and Archibald, "On Second Try, Dunkins Executed for Murder," *Birmingham News*, 14 July 1989.

162Dunkins I, 1353.

163Ibid.

[164]Archibald, "On Second Try, Dunkins Executed for Murder," *Birmingham News*, 14 July 1989.

[165]Dunkins I, 1353.

[166]Ibid.

[167]Peter Applebome, "2 States Grapple with Issue of Executing Mentally Retarded Men," *New York Times*, 12 July 1989, sec. I.

[168]Dunkins II, 610.

[169]Archibald, "On Second Try, Dunkins Executed for Murder," *Birmingham News*, 14 July 1989.

[170]Dunkins II, 606, 609.

[171]Dale Aukerman, "The Execution of Ronnie Dunkins," *Washington Post*, 22 July 1989, sec. A.

[172]The defendant had been tried and acquitted for a previous rape. *See* Dunkins I, 1356, fn. 1.

[173]Perske, 82.

[174]Dunkins I, 1356.

[175]Archibald, "On Second Try, Dunkins Executed for Murder," *Birmingham News*, 14 July 1989.

[176]Aukerman, "The Execution," sec. A.

[177]Archibald, "On Second Try, Dunkins Executed for Murder," *Birmingham News*, 14 July 1989. "Yellow Mama" had failed at least once before. In 1983, when John Louis Evans III was executed, he had to be given three jolts of electricity before he died.

[178]Ibid.

[179]Aukerman, "The Execution," sec. A.

[180]Archibald, "On Second Try, Dunkins Executed for Murder," *Birmingham News*, 14 July 1989.

[181]"Capital Punishment in the United States, 1973-1989," Case No. 3361.

[182]Ibid.

[183]Pamela Overstreet, "Rapist-Killer Electrocuted in Richmond," *Washington Post*, 31 August 1989, sec. B.

[184]*Encyclopedia of World Crime*, 1990 ed., s.v. "Alton Waye," by J. R. Nash.

[185]Ibid.

[186]"Waye Conviction Overturned," United Press International, Dateline: Richmond, VA., 14 February 1986.

[187]Waye v. Virginia, 251 S.E.2d 202, 205 (1979). *See also* Overstreet, sec. B.

[188]Ibid.

[189]Ibid.

[190]Ibid.

[191]Ibid.

[192]Ibid., 205-206.

[193]"Capital Punishment in the United States, 1973-1989," Case No. 3361.

[194]251 S.E.2d 202, 208-209.

[195]Ibid., 208, 211.

[196]No psychological tests of I.Q. and adaptive behavior were ever administered. Ibid., 210, 212, n. 4.

[164]Archibald, "On Second Try, Dunkins Executed for Murder," *Birmingham News*, 14 July 1989.

[165]Dunkins I, 1353.

[166]Ibid.

[167]Peter Applebome, "2 States Grapple with Issue of Executing Mentally Retarded Men," *New York Times*, 12 July 1989, sec. I.

[168]Dunkins II, 610.

[169]Archibald, "On Second Try, Dunkins Executed for Murder," *Birmingham News*, 14 July 1989.

[170]Dunkins II, 606, 609.

[171]Dale Aukerman, "The Execution of Ronnie Dunkins," *Washington Post*, 22 July 1989, sec. A.

[172]The defendant had been tried and acquitted for a previous rape. *See* Dunkins I, 1356, n. 1.

[173]Perske, 82.

[174]Dunkins I, 1356.

[175]Archibald, "On Second Try, Dunkins Executed for Murder," *Birmingham News*, 14 July 1989.

[176]Aukerman, "The Execution," sec. A.

[177]Archibald, "On Second Try, Dunkins Executed for Murder," *Birmingham News*, 14 July 1989. "Yellow Mama" had failed at least once before. In 1983, when John Louis Evans III was executed, he had to be given three jolts of electricity before he died.

[178]Ibid.

[179]Aukerman, "The Execution," sec. A.

[180]Archibald, "On Second Try, Dunkins Executed for Murder," *Birmingham News*, 14 July 1989.

[181]"Capital Punishment in the United States, 1973-1989," Case No. 3361.

[182]Ibid.

[183]Pamela Overstreet, "Rapist-Killer Electrocuted in Richmond," *Washington Post*, 31 August 1989, sec. B.

[184]*Encyclopedia of World Crime*, 1990 ed., s.v. "Alton Waye," by J. R. Nash.

[185]Ibid.

[186]"Waye Conviction Overturned," United Press International, Dateline: Richmond, VA., 14 February 1986.

[187]Waye v. Virginia, 251 S.E.2d 202, 205 (1979). *See also* Overstreet, sec. B.

[188]Ibid.

[189]Ibid.

[190]Ibid.

[191]Ibid.

[192]Ibid., 205-206.

[193]"Capital Punishment in the United States, 1973-1989," Case No. 3361.

[194]251 S.E.2d 202, 208-209.

[195]Ibid., 208, 211.

[196]No psychological tests of I.Q. and adaptive behavior were ever

administered. Ibid., 210, 212, n. 4.

[197]He had no charges pending when arrested and no prior criminal record. Ibid., 214-215. *See also* "Capital Punishment in the United States, 1973-1989," Case No. 3361.

[198]Ibid., 215.

[199]Ibid.

[200]Overstreet, sec. B.

[201]*Encyclopedia of World Crime*, 1990 ed., s.v. "Alton Waye," by J. R. Nash.

[202]Overstreet, sec. B.

[203]Teleconference with Law Offices of Louis Dugas, Defense Attorney for Johnny Anderson, Orange, TX, 12 August 1991. *See also* United Press International, Dateline: Beaumont, TX, 12 February 1983.

[204]Richard Luna, "Texas Killer Executed," United Press International, Dateline: Huntsville, Texas, 17 May 1990.

[205]"Louisiana Man Put to Death in 1977 Killing of State Trooper," *New York Times*, 18 May 1990, sec. A. *See also* E.J. Dionne, Jr., "Capital Punishment Gaining Favor as Public Seeks Retribution," *Washington Post*, 17 May 1990, sec. A.

[206]Luna, "Texas Killer Executed."

[207]"Soninlaw," United Press International, Dateline: Beaumont, TX, 6 August 1982. *See also* "Convicted Killers Executed in Texas and Missouri," United Press International, 17 May 1990.

[208]Ibid.

[209]UPI, 12 February 1983.

[210]Anderson v. Texas, 717 S.W. 2d 622, 624 (1986).

[211]Ibid., 625.

[212]Ibid.

[213]Ibid.

[214]Ibid. *See also* Luna, "Texas Killer Executed."

[215]Ibid., 627. These are Delvin Johnson's words.

[216]UPI, 6 August 1982.

[217]Goode v. Texas, 740 S.W.2d 453, 455, n. 2 (1987).

[218]"Soninlaw," UPI, Dateline: Beaumont, TX, 6 August 1982.

[219]740 S.W.2d 453, 456.

[220]717 S.W. 2d 622, 625.

[221]Richard Luna, "Texas Killer Executed," United Press International, Dateline: Huntsville, Texas, 17 May 1990.

[222]717 S.W. 2d 622, 625.

[223]UPI, 12 February 1983.

[224]Luna, "Texas Killer Executed."

[225]717 S.W. 2d 622, 634.

[226]Ibid., 625, 634.

[227]Ibid., 633.

[228]Ibid. Anderson stated that if "these people keep messing with me, I stab real easy, and I'll drop one of them." In 1984 Anderson actually did stab a fellow inmate seven times. The man recovered.

[229]Richard Luna, "Court Rejects Death Row Appeal," United Press International, Dateline: Huntsville, Texas, 16 May 1990.

[230]"Louisiana Man Put to Death," sec. A.

New York Times, 18 May 1990, sec. A.

[267]Cohen, sec. A.

[268]"Retarded Slayer," sec. A.

[269]Cohen, sec. A. *See also* "Louisiana Man," sec. A.

[270]"Over World Protests, Louisiana Executes Near-Retarded Killer," *Atlanta Journal and Constitution*, 18 May 1990, sec. A. *See also* Bill McMahon, "Prejean Put to Death," *Morning Advocate*, 18 May 1990.

[271]Jorge Casuso, "Does Death Row Hold a Victim? California Convict Gets Final Appeal," *Chicago Tribune*, 12 April 1992, sec. News.

[272]*See* Chapter 1. THE *PENRY* CASE, *supra*.

[273]Ibid.

[274]Richard Restak, "The Brain on Trial," *Washington Post*, 29 April 1990, sec. D.

[275]Katharine Bishop, "The Man-Made Disasters on Death Row," *New York Times*, 8 April 1990, sec. 4.

[276]Ibid.

[277]Restak, "The Brain on Trial," sec. D.

[278]Bishop, "Man-Made Disasters," sec. 4.

[279]People v. Harris, 71 Cal.Rptr. 679, 685 (1981).

[280]Ibid., 684.

[281]Ibid., 684-5.

[282]Ibid., 688.

[283]Ibid., 683.

[284]Bishop, "Man-Made Disasters," sec. 4.

[285]Harris, 71 Cal.Rptr. 679, 684.

[286]Ibid., 689. *See also* David G. Savage and Kevin Roderick, "Justices Uphold Stay of Execution," *Los Angeles Times*, 3 April 1990, sec. A. William Carlsen, "Top State Court Refuses to Stop Harris Execution," *San Francisco Chronicle*, 17 March 1990, sec. A.

[287]Ibid., 699, (Tobriner concurring).

[288]Ibid., 684.

[289]Bishop, "Man-Made Disasters," sec. 4.

[290]Harris, 71 Cal.Rptr. 690-691.

[291]Kate Callen, "Harris' Lawyers File Opening Round in New Appeal," United Press International, Dateline: San Diego, 13 April 1990. *See also* Pamela MacLean, "State Argues for Harris Execution," United Press International, Dateline: San Francisco, 26 April 1990.

[292]Restak, "The Brain on Trial," sec. D.

[293]Callen, "Harris' Lawyers," UPI, Dateline: San Diego, 13 April 1990.

[294]MacLean, "State Argues," UPI.

[295]Jane Gross, "California Closer to Its Final Execution Since 1967," *New York Times*, 30 August 1990, sec. B.

[296]"Not in Our Names," *Lifelines*, April/May/June 1992, 2.

4

The Survivors

Though they go mad they shall be sane,
Though they sink through the sea they shall rise again:
Though lovers be lost, lovers shall not,
And death shall have no dominion.

--Rom. 6:9

INTRODUCTION

Some murderers with mental retardation who have been sentenced to death have later had their sentences commuted, pardoned or thrown out by the courts. These offenders are similar in many ways to those who have been executed, but different in other ways. This chapter delineates the stories of those murderers suffering from mental retardation who have been spared from execution subsequent to their convictions or death sentences. By so doing, it prepares the foundation for a comparison of the executed and the spared in the next chapter.

THE SPARED

I will ransom them from the power of the grave: I will redeem them from death: Oh death, I will be thy plagues; O grave, I will be thy destruction.

--Hos. 13:14

JOHNNY MACK WESTBROOK

Johnny Mack Westbrook, an African American man in his middle fifties, has an I.Q. that is hard to measure. It falls somewhere between twenty-five and fifty.[1] Westbrook is either severely or moderately retarded, dependent upon whether his actual intellectual acuity is below or above an I.Q. of thirty-five, the dividing line of the severe and moderate categories.[2]

Typically, offenders with mental retardation have inadequate legal representation.[3] Because of their lack of intelligence, they are unable to defend themselves or acquire adequate counsel. They are left at the complete mercy of a hostile legal system which customarily views their retardation as increasing rather than mitigating their dangerousness.[4] Old-fashioned attitudes hold persons with mental retardation to be sub-human, untamed and harmful beasts to be locked away from society forever. Westbrook is a case on point. In Georgia in the fifties he was sentenced to 59-118 years for the theft of property worth $300, a nonviolent misdemeanor ordinarily calling for probation. He spent twenty years of that sentence in prison.[5] A sentence of this severity could never have been imposed for such a minor crime on a person of normal intelligence with adequate legal counsel.

Nonetheless, and perhaps because of his lengthy prison incarceration, Westbrook subsequently became a particularly dangerous criminal. Over a lifetime he accumulated an extensive criminal history of seventeen convictions, including eleven burglaries, one attempted burglary, one simple larceny, three weapons offenses, and two prison escapes. Typical of people with mental retardation who have difficulty in understanding and following prison rules,[6] while incarcerated he had thirty-four prison rule violations.[7]

Also typical, persons with mental retardation are frequently led by more intelligent criminals into illegal acts. In 1977, Westbrook followed another man into the kidnapping and slaying of two elderly white women in Macon, Georgia. Westbrook and his accomplice raped the first woman, forced her to drive to the bank to withdraw cash, kidnapped the second woman when she came to the aid of the first, drove them both to a wooded area where they were tied to trees and beaten to death with a two-by-four.[8]

The trial jury found the presence of one statutory aggravating circumstance. The crime was "outrageously or wantonly vile, horrible or inhuman in that it involved torture, depravity of mind or an aggravated battery to the victim."[9] Westbrook was convicted of both murders, given life for one, and death for the other.

However, in 1987 the Georgia Supreme Court reduced Westbrook's sentence to life imprisonment. Subsequent to this, again typical of what happens to offenders with mental retardation in the legal system, Westbrook was "lost in the [prison] shuffle." He remained on Death Row for another year and one-half. Neither his lawyers nor prison officials made any attempt to carry out the State Supreme Court's orders to move him off of Death Row. Prison officials stated that Westbrook was in no danger of being executed because they knew his sentence had been reduced.[10]

HERBERT WELCOME

The case of Herbert Welcome, an African American man with an I.Q. around sixty and the mental age of an eight-year-old, is one of the most straightforward and uncomplicated of those of murderers with mental retardation. Welcome was twenty-eight years old in 1981 when he shot and killed his aunt, Dorothy Guillory, an African American woman, aged fifty-seven, and her boyfriend, Wallace Maturin, a white man, aged forty-six, in

New Iberia, Louisiana. The murders occurred while Welcome was fighting with Guillory and Maturin over a pocketknife. Welcome shot the man during the argument. He then ran his fleeing aunt down and killed her too.[11] He received a life sentence for the murder of the man, and the death penalty for that of his aunt.[12]

Welcome's crime was moderately brutal and violent as crimes go for which murderers receive the death penalty. It was not premeditated. No rape or torture was involved. In fact, both victims often carried guns, were known to be violent, and frequently fought with each other.

In mitigation, Welcome's defense offered several factors. The murders were committed under the "mental disturbance" caused by the brouhaha. The defendant felt justified in that his aunt assaulted him during the melee by hitting him over the head with her purse. Mr. Maturin had sadistically taken advantage of his limited intelligence many times by teasing and tormenting him. Maturin had withheld Welcome's paycheck and turned his dog lose on Welcome to attack and bite him.[13]

Typical of people with mental retardation, Welcome mimicked what he saw. He took his revenge in the violent way he had learned by example from his tormenters. He had minimal knowledge that social and legal norms did not accept guns and shooting as a solution to being picked on. In the heat of violence he was unable to brake his reaction to the violence of his tormentors.

Welcome suffered from mental retardation, but despite his handicap he had a reasonably stable and responsible work history. He had no significant prior criminal record. He had committed no prior felonies although he had been convicted of multiple misdemeanors, including four weapons charges.[14]

The jury took these mitigating factors into account in sentencing Welcome to life imprisonment for the death of Mr. Maturin.

However, there were two aggravating factors involved in the crime. First, there were two victims, one of whom was "crippled," and, second, the aunt was chased down and "calculatedly executed."[15] That he ran down his aunt to kill her was sufficient aggravation for him to receive the death penalty despite the previous humiliation and provocation he had suffered from her and Mr. Maturin, and his previous good record in life.[16]

In 1987, outgoing Governor of Louisiana Edwin Edwards took cognizance of the mitigation of Welcome's mental retardation and the other circumstances of his crimes. The Governor commuted Welcome's death sentence to life imprisonment.[17] This commutation was one of only a very few in the nation since the 1976 re-authorization of the death penalty.[18] It provides additional evidence "that the death penalty is no longer an appropriate punishment for persons with mental retardation."[19]

LARRY "CATFISH" JONES

In Mississippi in 1974, two black teenagers, Larry "Catfish" Jones, aged seventeen, and Willie N. Reddix, Jr., aged eighteen, plotted to rob a dry goods shop, Art's Levi Store, in uptown Biloxi.[20] They planned to get Willie's brother, J.D., to drive them to town from the Reddix home. J.D. was not in on the scheme.[21]

The plot was that Willie would enter the store first and distract the elderly white owner, Arthur Weinburger, aged seventy-seven. Catfish would sneak in unseen a few minutes later and shoplift clothing and whatever else he could take in a few minutes time, escaping unnoticed.[22]

On December 2, 1974, the three proceeded as planned. However, when Larry and Willie entered the store around 11:15 AM,[23] something went awry. Instead of distracting Weinburger, Larry grabbed him from behind and hit him over the head three or four times with a "Stilson" wrench, crushing his skull. He dragged Mr. Weinberger into the back room. Weinberger lay there dying while the pair looted the store.[24] Larry stuffed a footlocker full of shirts, hats and trousers. Willie took a black imitation leather coat and threw it over his shoulder.[25] They rifled the cash register. Reddix later stated that he had netted fifty dollars in bills and a silver dollar.[26]

Larry and Willie exited the store. Larry carried the footlocker to J.D.'s waiting white Cadillac in a parking lot several blocks away. The three then drove back to the Reddix house where they left the footlocker and clothing.[27] Mr. Weinberger was discovered shortly afterward and rushed to the hospital. He died about four-thirty that afternoon.[28]

In mid-day in Biloxi in the pre-Christmas shopping season, many persons were around and about in uptown Biloxi. Several witnesses spotted the three black men drive into the parking lot in the distinctive Cadillac. They saw Jones and Reddix leave the car and walk toward Art's store. Several people saw them return fifteen minutes later, one carrying the footlocker and the other with a coat over his shoulder. They saw the car drive away.[29]

Multiple witnesses described Jones as wearing combat boots with fringed tops, a camouflage Army jacket, and military pants.[30] The bloodstained boots were found with the stolen loot in the Reddix house.[31]

Several days after the murder of Arthur Weinburger, Willie Reddix was in jail under arrest on charges of armed robbery and kidnapping arising from another incident.[32] Under interrogation he admitted to the Art's Levi Store robbery, and implicated Larry Jones as the perpetrator of the killing of Arthur Weinburger.[33]

The question arises as to what kind of persons these young men were, who as African Americans in Mississippi, would do such a foolish thing as to rob a white-owned store in the center of town in broad daylight.

The answer is that they were uneducated, mentally retarded juveniles. Larry "Catfish" Jones has an I.Q. of forty-one or lower,[34] in the lowest range of mild retardation. He was "emotionally disturbed, . . . severely limited in his capacity to think," and had limited ability to "understand what was happening around him."[35]

Willie Reddix's I.Q. is eighty-four,[36] in the upper range of borderline retardation. There is no evidence of "Catfish's" educational level, but Reddix's mother testified that Willie Reddix attended school to the eighth grade.[37] Others described him as being "barely literate" and as having "a history of drug abuse."[38]

In March, 1975, both Willie Reddix and Larry Jones were tried, convicted of capital murder, and sentenced to death.[39] Reddix went to trial first and was sentenced to death on March 14.[40] Jones' trial followed a week later. His death sentence was meted out on March 19, 1975.[41]

J.D. Reddix turned state's evidence and testified in Jones' trial against him.[42] Willie Reddix confessed to his role in the crime, implicated Jones as the principle offender, but did not testify against Jones at trial. Thus no evidence was admitted to show who actually delivered the fatal blows to Weinburger.[43] Nor were the limited mental capabilities of the perpetrators offered as mitigating factors. The juvenile status of Jones at the time of the crime was not offered in mitigation,[44] even though the death penalty law then in effect listed youth as a statutory mitigating factor.[45]

Jones and Reddix were no strangers to strong-armed attempts. Aggravating factors in Jones' trial included a previous juvenile felony conviction for armed robbery.[46]

Both Reddix's and Jones' initial convictions and death sentences were later overturned by appeals courts. Jones' conviction was vacated by the Mississippi Supreme Court based on two technicalities. First, a map of the downtown Biloxi area with red and black arrows superimposed allegedly showing the routes of the perpetrators to and from the crime scene was improperly admitted as evidence because there was no direct testimony as to these routes. Second, the trial court improperly denied a defense motion to admit into evidence a taped statement made by Jones to police a week after the crime. Because the prosecution had used a part of the tape as evidence against Jones, all of it should have been admitted despite its "exculpatory" nature.[47]

Both Jones and Reddix were tried a second time in 1977. Both were convicted and sentenced to death again.[48] Three aggravating circumstances were introduced in the penalty phase of Jones' second trial: the murder was committed during the commission of another felony, namely, robbery; the crime was particularly heinous and vile; and Jones had a previous conviction for a felony involving violence or the threat of violence to a person.[49] Again, no mitigating evidence was offered to counteract these aggravating factors. Jones received a second death sentence on December 15, 1977.[50]

In 1980 the Mississippi Supreme Court affirmed Jones' second conviction and death sentence. The Court refused to entertain a contention that the death penalty statute then in effect was invalid because of the U.S. Supreme Court's *Furman v. Georgia*[51] decision. It upheld the outcome based on the "hand of one is the hand of all" common law principle.[52] The court stated that despite the fact that no evidence had been admitted in the guilt-innocence phase of the trial to show who actually committed the murder, this proof was unnecessary. That both were placed at the crime scene and that a death resulted from the crime were enough to convict and sentence both of them to death.[53]

The appeal of the second conviction and sentence then shifted to the federal system. On February 3, 1983,[54] the federal District Court for the Southern District of Mississippi overturned Jones' death sentence, based on counsel's ineffective assistance in the penalty phase of the trial.[55] Jones' attorney had failed to offer his age, mental retardation and lack of proof of "any intent or role in [the] homicide" as mitigating evidence.[56]

Jones' lawyer also made no closing argument but left this to Jones to do himself.[57] The transcript of Jones' *pro se* words illustrates the ludicrous attempts of a eighteen-year-old person with extremely limited intelligence and the mental age of a three- to five-year-old to defend himself in a court of law.[58]

Jones' comments did not constitute an argument. They centered on how many persons were involved in the crime. He seemed unable to decide if there were three or four. Over the continuous objections of the prosecution that he was "testifying" and that the testimony was not subject to cross-examination, Jones seemed more concerned with trying to understand the relationship of the numbers "three" and "four" to the number of persons involved in the crimes than with providing himself with a defense. It was highly apparent that he could not count, nonetheless understand the nature of the legal process.[59]

The State appealed the District Court's remand of the case to the Fifth Circuit Court of Appeals. It upheld the decision. The Circuit Court again remanded the case and ordered that a new sentencing hearing be held within a set time period according to the District Court's order and Mississippi's "180 Day" rule. The rule required that new trials be held within this predetermined time frame.[60]

When the State failed to hold the resentencing hearing in the allotted time, the Federal District Court in June, 1988 reduced Jones' sentence to life imprisonment.[61]

In one of the most telling comments on the legal processes surrounding death penalty cases and the more than decade long lengths of stay on Death Row of some inmates, Judge Dan Russell showed his frustration with a legal system that toys with the lives of these inmates. He stated:

On March 19, 1975, Larry Jones . . . was found guilty of capital murder. . . . Today, over thirteen years later, [his] fate remains undetermined. . . . Like a revolving door, this case has been circulated in and out of the courts of this State since 1975, and although I may not live to see its return, the following is my earnest attempt to adequately effect its demise.[62]

With that he ordered the death sentence of Larry Jones to be vacated. He sentenced Jones, now thirty-one years old, to life in prison.[63]

GEORGE ELDER DUNGEE

George Elder Dungee, an African American man now in his fifties, has an I.Q. of approximately sixty-eight.[64] On May 14, 1973[65] Dungee participated in the murders of six members of the white Alday family in Seminole County, Georgia. Killed in the mass murder melee were Ned Alday, sixty-two, his sons Jerry, thirty-three, Jimmy and Chester Alday, thirty-two, Ned's brother, Aubrey, fifty-eight, and Jerry's wife, Mary Alday, twenty-five. One of Ned Alday's sons, Bud, survived because he was not at the mobile home during the murders.[66]

Dungee, then thirty-six, and two other men, Carl Isaacs, then nineteen, and his half-brother, Wayne Coleman, then twenty-five, both Whites, were incarcerated at the minimum security prison in Towson, Maryland.[67] Coleman, the mastermind and leader of the gang,[68] engineered an escape, inviting anyone who wanted to go with them.

George Dungee accepted the offer despite the fact that he had only one month left to do on his sentence for failure to pay child support.[69]

The three men stole a car belonging to a murdered college student,[70] picked up Isaacs' younger brother, Billy, fifteen, and fled south.

They were almost out of gas in Georgia when they spotted what they thought was a gas pump behind the Jerry Alday mobile home. After investigating and finding no gas, Carl Isaacs and Coleman entered the trailer to burglarize it, leaving Dungee and Billy Isaacs in the car as lookouts. Ned and Jerry Alday returned home and were shot in the head (Ned seven times, Jerry four times) by Coleman and Isaacs, respectively, each in separate bedrooms. One by one as the remaining family members returned, each was also shot and killed by Coleman and Isaacs.[71]

Mary Alday was the last to come. She was gang raped by Coleman and Isaacs in the kitchen, tied, blindfolded, and driven to a nearby wooded area where she was raped again, her breasts were mutilated, and she was shot twice by George Dungee, once in the spine. Mary Alday's murder was the only one directly committed by Dungee.[72]

The Aldays were respected, teetotaling, "good honest . . . country" folk with roots in Seminole County that dated back at least a hundred years.[73] Although some might call it a "redneck" community, the small county was comprised of what the residents consider to be two thousand "good Christian" families, most of whom were "born and raised" in the community.[74]

At their initial trials, attorneys for the defendants petitioned for a change of venue on the grounds that pre-trial publicity had created an atmosphere in which impartial jurors could not be found. It was impossible for the defendants to receive a fair trial.[75]

The trial judge refused to grant the change. Later, it was speculated that the judge refused the removal of the trial to another jurisdiction because he "lived down there, had to run for office, . . . didn't have the strength to do what was right -- change the venue."[76] At the trials themselves, jurors were seated after precursory questioning and despite the fact that some knew the victims and had attended their mass funeral.[77]

All three adult defendants were given the death penalty. Billy Isaacs received a life sentence. The juries found three statutory aggravating circumstances which allowed the death penalty to be imposed - that the murders were committed during the commission of armed robbery and burglary on five counts, that one murder was committed during an armed robbery, burglary, rape and kidnapping,[78] and that all murders were committed by escapees "from lawful confinement."[79]

In Dungee's case, conflict existed over whether he was a direct participant in the five murders of the Alday males. In one instance he was described as remaining in the car during the shootings.[80] However, Billy Isaacs testified that he participated in all the murders, and his fingerprints were found on a beer can in the yard of the trailer.[81] Dungee did, however, participate in killing Mary Alday. Although he did not rape her, he fired the death-delivering shots.[82]

Factors in mitigation for Dungee that were not considered at his trial were his mental retardation, the fact that he went along for the ride with more intelligent, scheming and violent criminals, and that he got caught up in a situation of their making and not his. Only after following their example did he kill Mary Alday. He did not rape her like the others. He had no serious prior convictions as did Coleman and Isaacs.[83]

The cases were first appealed to the Georgia Supreme Court in 1976. That court upheld the verdicts and sentences.[84] The cases eventually went to a three-man panel of the 11th Circuit Court of Appeals. On December 9, 1985, this panel, led by Judge Frank Johnson, Jr.,[85] ordered new trials for the three death row defendants. Relying on the "presumed prejudice" principle of *Rideau v. Louisiana*,[86] the Court held that "pretrial publicity had so saturated the community that selecting an impartial jury was made impossible."[87]

In their second trials, Coleman again was sentenced to death on six counts of murder. Isaacs automatically received a life sentence because his history of "neglect and abuse" was considered by some jurors to mitigate the crime, and the jury could not reach a decision on the sentence.[88]

In 1988, fifteen years after the mass murder, George Dungee received a reprieve from Death Row. The prosecutor in the case decided that he would not seek the death penalty again for Dungee because the passage of Georgia's ban on execution of persons with mental retardation was applicable. Thus Georgia's law worked to save George Dungee, with an I.Q. of sixty-eight, from execution.[89]

JEROME HOLLOWAY

Jerome Holloway is a poor, illiterate African American man[90] in his mid-thirties from Pembroke, Bryan County, south Georgia. He was born in 1957 or 1958. No one is sure which year, because he doesn't know his own birth date.[91] Holloway is unable to relate any of his life history because of his acute degree of mental retardation.

Until his death sentence was thrown out in 1988, Holloway was known as "the most retarded man on Death Row anywhere in the nation."[92] He has the mental age of a seven-year-old.[93] His I.Q. is forty-nine, in the moderate range of mental retardation. His intellectual capabilities are in the bottom .01[94] to .03 percent (.0001 to .0003) of the U.S. population.[95] His intelligence is so low that he does not know the alphabet, cannot read or write,[96] cannot count,[97] make change for a dollar,[98] or tell time.[99] He does not know what country he lives in[100] and confessed in court to having assassinated Presidents Lincoln, Kennedy, and even President Reagan.[101] His appeals attorney states that he "can get Jerome to say anything." Psychiatric reports describe Jerome as an "easily led, manipulated individual operating within a limited range of intelligence . . . [with minimal] . . . social skills and . . . trouble dealing with anything less than concrete issues."[102]

The one skill that Holloway does have is the ability to sign his name.[103] He used this know-how to sign a confession to the murder of Corabelle Berry, a sixty-five year old black woman.

On March 5, 1986 when Holloway was in his late twenties, he allegedly went to the home of an elderly neighbor and friend of his mother to borrow a cup of sugar. Holloway was convicted of beating Ms. Berry to death with a stick and kerosene lamp. The purpose of the murder was robbery. A few hundred dollars were stolen from her home.

After the robbery, the murderer threw away the victim's bloodied clothes, dragged her body to a ditch and buried it in a shallow grave. Holloway confessed to using the money he stole to buy stereo equipment. Ms. Berry's food stamps were found in his car.[104]

In January, 1987, Holloway was tried and convicted of the murder of Ms. Berry. He was sentenced to death. Prior to the trial, Holloway attempted to plead guilty. However, the trial judge refused to accept the plea because he felt that Holloway had no understanding of what waiving the right to trial would mean.[105] Despite the fact that he "does not have the capability to understand the court process and what attorneys are arguing and how it all relates to his own future,"[106] no competency hearing was ever held. The primary evidence against Holloway was the signed confession that he could not read or comprehend.

In November, 1987, only hours before he was to die,[107] the Georgia Supreme Court overturned Holloway's death sentence and remanded his case for a new penalty hearing. The court held that there was substantial evidence that Holloway did not understand the nature of the proceedings against him.[108] Holloway's low intelligence "was not merely a 'significant' issue, it was virtually the only issue."[109] Despite this he was never given a competency hearing and was denied public funding for a psychiatric evaluation to which he was legally entitled.[110]

Subsequently, in August, 1988 the prosecution agreed to reduce Holloway's sentence to two life terms in order to bypass the need for a new penalty hearing and in return for a guilty plea.[111]

WILLIAM ALVIN SMITH

William A. Smith, a twenty-one-year old African American man with a sixty-five I.Q. and the mental age of a ten to twelve-year-old, was convicted in September, 1981[112] of the June 8, 1981 robbery and murder of an eighty-two-year-old white male grocery store owner, Daniel Lee Turner, in Lexington, Georgia. Smith had known the victim all his life and by his own admission the victim had "been good to him."

Smith attempted the robbery in order to get money to buy a new car.[113]

Smith described the crime in this way. "He [the victim] was still scuffling and he fall at the back of store. . . . He had a hammer. I kept stabbing him until he dropped hammer. I picked up hammer and hit him twice with it."[114] After he was arrested, he said, "'I didn't mean to kill Mr. Dan.'"[115] Smith received the death penalty for this act.

Smith's crime was violent, but not particularly so. Smith contended that "the numerous stab wounds and head injuries received by the victim, . . . cannot be said to be repetitious and cumulative,"[116] compared to others in which the death penalty has been imposed. There was only one male victim who was, however, vulnerable because of age. Yet the victim was strong enough to try to resist and to defend himself with a hammer.[117] The crime was committed in the midst of a robbery and was not planned or premeditated. Smith "just went berserk" when attacked by the victim.[118]

Nonetheless, the jury found that one statutory aggravating circumstance was present. The crime was "outrageously and wantonly vile, horrible and inhumane, in that the murder involved torture, depravity of mind and aggravated battery to the victim."[119] This aggravating factor justified the imposition of the death penalty. Although Smith contended that the court erred in not charging the jury to consider the mitigation of his mental retardation, the Georgia Supreme Court held that the Georgia death penalty statute does not require such a jury charge.[120] Thus no balancing of aggravation and mitigation occurred.

The death penalty was appealed to the 11th Circuit Court of Appeals. In August, 1988, that court, in a clear and comprehensive understanding of the limitations of mental retardation, held that Smith, because of his condition, could not knowingly and intelligently waive his Miranda rights. It reasoned that Smith was incapable of voluntarily confessing, and that his confession was therefore inadmissible evidence. The court set aside the conviction and death penalty sentence on these bases.[121] At the age of twenty-eight, Smith was removed from Death Row, thanks to an enlightened and knowledgeable court. Although the court did not reference the recent passage of the Georgia law banning executions of persons with mental retardation, its ruling was in keeping with that legislation.

The 11th Circuit created a partial foundation at the federal level for a complete ban on the death penalty for people with mental retardation by its recognition of the special circumstances of pretrial evidence-taking when persons with mental retardation are accused of crimes. By its recognition that persons with mental retardation lack the mental capacity to voluntarily confess, it established the legal principle of diminished capacity or persons with mental retardation. It wove one thread of the evolving legal principle of diminished capacity of persons with mental retardation that supports the universal ban on capital punishment for persons with mental retardation. Unfortunately, the *Penry* reasoning some ten months later did not refer to this legal precedent.

LIMMIE ARTHUR

Limmie Arthur, African American, thirty-one-years-old, is a prototypic offender with mental retardation. He was raised in a three-room tarpaper shack with broken windows and no running water in Duford, South Carolina. The seventeenth of eighteen children, he was the offspring of poverty-stricken rural sharecroppers. When the trial judge was taken to view where Limmie grew up, he said that the family would have been better off in slavery. At least then someone would have taken care of them.[122]

According to the testimony of many persons at trial, Limmie's mental retardation was a lifelong condition. Even among her eighteen children, his mother recognized early on that he was different and slower than the others.[123] His I.Q. measured consistently at sixty-five from grade school throughout his imprisonment. At the age of twelve he was socially promoted from the third grade. His teacher recalled that he couldn't write his name, even though he had devoted himself to learning how to do so.[124] He dropped out of school at age sixteen. As an adult, Limmie had the mental ability of a child ten to twelve years old. He couldn't say the alphabet. He believed that he was given the death sentence because he couldn't read.[125]

After one court appearance Arthur was happy because he thought everything had gone in his favor. He did not understand that the judge had refused his plea for a new trial or for a reduction of his sentence. When asked what went on, he replied that, "'I don't understand a whole lot of what was going on. . . . I had to listen real close . . . and I get lost very quick. , . . It's bad. It's bad to be retarded.'"[126]

Limmie Arthur received the death penalty for the murder of his neighbor on New Year's Eve, 1984. The victim was a sixty-five-year old physically handicapped African American named "Cripple Jack." Limmie murdered him with an axe for money after they had cashed his social security check and drunk together. After the crime, he was found hiding in an attic because his feet were sticking out. He had left his bloodied shirt at the scene of the crime. In his trial, the prosecution cited the fact that he knew enough to hide as evidence that he knew right from wrong. The defense countered that leaving his bloody shirt at the crime scene and hiding with his feet protruding were hardly acts of an intelligent criminal.[127]

Arthur also had an extensive and violent criminal history. He had been convicted of five burglaries and the manslaughter death of his brother, who had attacked him with a board.[128]

The fact that there was evidence that Limmie knew right from wrong, and the aggravating factors of the brutality of the crime, the vulnerability (elderly age and physical handicap) of the victim, and an extensive and violent criminal history, outweighed the mitigation of Limmie's mental retardation. In May, 1987, the trial judge sentenced him to death after he waived his right to trial by jury.[129]

Subsequently in 1988, the Supreme Court of the State of South Carolina ruled that Arthur had not "knowingly and intelligently" waived his right to trial by jury. The defendant himself must be thoroughly questioned as to his intent to waive his right to a jury trial. In this case, there was a "patently insufficient inquiry,"[130] and the trial judge himself questioned whether Arthur understood what he was doing. The court reversed the sentence and remanded it to be determined by jury.[131] Following this decision, the prosecutor in the case determined not to try the case again.[132]

EDDIE LEE SPRAGGINS

Eddie Lee Spraggins is a never married[133] white man from the poverty-stricken rural town of Manchester, Georgia. Manchester is located in the western Georgia county of Meriwether, about sixty-five miles southwest of Atlanta, and midway between Atlanta and the state capital of Columbus.[134]

Spraggins was born in August, 1942. He has an I.Q. which has been variously measured at fifty-one (in 1956), sixty-one (in 1971 and 1977), and sixty-five (in 1983).[135] His average I.Q. for these test scores is sixty.

Spraggins cannot read or write, make change, nor count. In commenting about his childhood, a sister of his described him as always having "mental problems." She stated that he could not learn in school. The family had sought help for him when he was a child in several places,[136] apparently without much success. Evidently, no one in his home town knew what to do with a mentally retarded child who could not learn in normal classrooms.

There is no record that Spraggins ever attended special education classes, which presumably were not available in the rural area where he lived in the late 1940s or early 1950s when he was growing up. A second grade teacher described Spraggins as "sweet and affectionate," and "not exactly feebleminded," but nevertheless, a child who could not keep "anything in his mind."[137]

After he had completed the sixth grade and was about to turn fifteen, the school authorized him to withdraw from classes because of his "age and inability to learn." His school records stated that he had reached the maximum of his learning capacity and that he could "only be given something to occupy his time."[138]

It has been said that Spraggins' adaptive behaviors, along with his mental abilities, are "very low."[139] In 1987 when he was forty-five years old, his language and communication skills were measured at the level of a child aged three years and ten months. His writing abilities equalled those of a five-year-old kindergartner.[140] His understanding level was that of a child aged seven years and ten months.[141]

In 1977 when Spraggins was thirty-four-years-old, the Manchester, Georgia police knew him as a person who was prone to fights and who occasionally got in trouble with them.[142] Spraggins had at least one prior felony conviction of an unknown type.[143] This can be classified as a moderately severe criminal history.

Like so many other persons with mental retardation, Spraggins became involved in a capital crime under the influence of another person who is much smarter than he.[144] On the evening of January 30, 1977, according to later testimony at trial, Spraggins, then thirty-four-years-old, and a white teenager named Freddie Davis, then aged nineteen, broke into the home of a white woman, Frances Coe, aged fifty-five, in Manchester, Georgia. They were bent on robbery.[145] Mrs. Coe lived by herself in the neighborhood where Spraggins lived. Davis and Spraggins had been planning the event for some time. They knew that Ms. Coe lived alone and believed that she had thirty or forty thousand dollars hidden in her home.[146]

Before going to the scene, the pair had fortified themselves by drinking heavily and taking drugs.[147] Spraggins was intoxicated when he barged his way into Mrs. Coe's home on the pretext of using the telephone. He ordered her to go to the back door where Davis was waiting to be let in. According to testimony, Mrs. Coe then began to scream, and Spraggins grabbed her around the neck and dragged her to the bedroom. Davis handed Spraggins his knife and told him he had to silence her. Spraggins opened the knife and "stabbed her and cut her throat." Ms. Coe would not die, and Spraggins continued to stab her until she was quiet. She eventually bled to death.[148]

Spraggins and Davis then took Ms. Coe's flashlight and ransacked the house. It is unknown whether they found any money or not. Afterwards, Spraggins went home and burned his bloody clothes, a towel he had used to wipe the knife and himself, and the flashlight in his own backyard. They were later recovered there. He was arrested a few days later hiding in the trunk of a car.[149]

Although the defendants denied raping Ms. Coe, circumstantial evidence surrounding the crime suggested that she had been raped. Her body was found in her bedroom the next day with her underwear and panty hose around her knees. She had bruises around the vagina and on her thigh. Testimony of experts indicated that "there had been manipulation of the victim's sexual organs."[150]

Spraggins was tried three times for the rape and murder of Mrs. Coe. He was convicted and sentenced to death each time. After each trial, appeals courts vacated Spraggins' convictions and sentences. Freddie Davis was tried twice and sentenced to death both times. Both of his death sentences were also vacated.[151]

Spraggins first trial was held in the first week of March, 1977, a little more than a month after the event. In that trial, in the closing argument during the guilt/innocence phase, Spraggins' defense lawyer stated to the jury that "I think he went in the house and I think he committed the crime of murder."[152] On March 2, 1977, the jury convicted Spraggins and sentenced him to death.[153]

On appeal to the Georgia Supreme Court, the conviction was upheld but the sentence was vacated because of defects in the jury instructions made by the trial court. The court had failed to instruct the jury that the defendant could be sentenced to life imprisonment even though they had found the existence of an aggravating factor, namely, that the murder had been committed during the commission of another capital offense (rape).[154] The trial judge also failed to instruct the jury that they could consider whether mitigating factors outweighed the aggravating circumstance.[155]

A second penalty trial was held, and Spraggins was sentenced to death a second time. This time, the jury found two aggravating factors involved in the crime. In addition to the original factor of commission during a second capital offense, the jury found that the crime was "outrageously and wantonly vile, horrible, and inhuman" because it involved "depravity of mind on the part of the defendant, or an aggravated battery of the victim."[156]

On appeal to the United States Supreme Court, the case was remanded back to the Supreme Court of Georgia for review. It affirmed the death sentence.[157]

Subsequently, the U.S. District Court in the northern district of Georgia vacated the conviction and second death sentence based on a contention of ineffective assistance of trial counsel.[158] The court held that the defense's admission of Spraggins' guilt was "irrational and rendered his assistance at trial ineffective." Counsel may not "concede the issue of guilt. . . ."[159]

Spraggins third trial and conviction occurred on November 12, 1986. The Georgia Supreme Court reviewed an appeal of this sentence in November, 1987, just a week after it had vacated the death sentence of Jerome Holloway based on Holloway's extremely low mental capacity.[160]

In January, 1988, after Spraggins' third vacated sentence and prior to the issuance of the Georgia Supreme Court's decision in the appeal of the third death sentence, Georgia passed the first statute in the nation barring the death penalty for persons with mental retardation.[161]

A month later in February, 1988, the Georgia Supreme Court again vacated Spraggins' conviction and death sentence. The reasoning this time centered on the trial court's failure to instruct the jury that it could consider a verdict of "guilty but mentally ill" based on testimony of a psychologist that Spraggins had mental retardation. The case was remanded for retrial a fourth time.[162]

In December, 1988, the prosecutor decided not to go through with another trial and agreed to accept a plea of "guilty but mentally retarded" under the new law. Finally, after three death sentences and innumerable appeals, Spraggins' lack of culpability sufficient for his life to be taken was legally recognized. Spraggins was sentenced to life in prison.[163]

RONALD S. MONROE

Ronald Monroe is a poor, indigent, frequently unemployed, African American with the mental age of a thirteen-year-old, and an I.Q. of seventy-three to seventy-seven. This is in the borderline range of mental retardation.

Monroe dropped out of school after the sixth grade.[164] At the age of twenty-two, Monroe allegedly murdered his "next door neighbor" and landlady, Lenora E. Collins, also an African American.[165] Monroe lived with his mother, wife and three-year-old daughter on one side of a "shotgun" duplex house in New Orleans, Louisiana. Collins lived on the other side of the double house.[166]

At 3:00 AM on September 10, 1977, Lenora Collins was asleep in her bed with her two children, Theodise, eleven, and Joseph, twelve. She was awakened by someone crawling through the window and switched on the light. She began to scuffle with her assailant while calling for Joseph to go for help. He ran outside and hid behind a car to escape the assailant who threatened to kill him.[167] Theodise tried to hit the attacker but fell down. He then stabbed her in the back and said that he would kill her too. She escaped to the bathroom and locked herself in. When her mother called out for help Theodise came back to the bedroom. The assailant was gone, and Lenora was struggling to reach the phone. She had been stabbed seven times and died shortly after. The cause of death was three, eight inch deep wounds[168] and the loss of more than two quarts of blood. Her lungs had been pierced and one rib was completely cut through.[169]

Both Theodise and Joseph who had known Monroe for several years positively identified him as the murderer. The alleged motive for the crime was that Lenora Collins' mother had purchased the house, and Monroe was angry that he and his family were being evicted. He had received the eviction notice the day before.[170]

When police searched Monroe's home an hour after the crime, they found Monroe asleep in his bed with fresh blood on his bedspread and a bloody kitchen towel in a trash can. These were seized as evidence.[171] Monroe's alibi for the time of the crime was that he was intoxicated and in bed "sleeping it off."[172]

Monroe was tried twice for the crime and sentenced to death both times. The first conviction in 1980 was overturned because an assistant district attorney from the office that was trying the case served on the jury.[173]

In the second trial, the jury found three statutory aggravating factors. The crime was committed during an aggravated robbery, the risk of death or serious injury was knowingly created for more than one person, and the crime was "especially heinous, atrocious or cruel." Louisiana law required the finding of only one such factor in order for the death penalty to be imposed. Monroe's alleged intoxication which caused his "impaired mental state" was offered in mitigation.[174] Nothing was said in any legal procedure about his near mental retardation. Based on the finding of at least one factor in aggravation, the jury imposed the death sentence.

Subsequent to the trial outcome, in reviewing alleged trial errors, the Supreme Court of Louisiana ruled that the crime was not particularly heinous, atrocious or cruel, and disallowed this aggravating factor. Nonetheless, the sentence was upheld because of the other two aggravating conditions.[175]

Monroe had nothing more than petty prior criminal offenses. He had several "run-ins" with legal authorities as a juvenile and one adult arrest for a fight on a bus. He received a $10 fine for this incident.[176] He had committed no previous "crimes against persons" and had no history of violence.[177]

Shortly after Monroe's second trial and death sentence in 1980, new evidence surfaced which suggested that he might be innocent. Lenora Collins had previously lived with a common law husband, one George Stinson. Stinson was arrested and jailed in Pontiac, Michigan for the stabbing death of his new common law wife, Erma Jean Lofton.[178] While there he bragged to his cell mate that he had killed his previous wife in New Orleans (Lenora Collins) by stabbing her in the neck and chest "in the same way" as he killed this one.[179]

The confidant told Michigan detectives and passed a lie detector test. A Michigan detective contacted New Orleans police with this new evidence of Monroe's possible innocence. The New Orleans police made two attempts to contact Lenora Collins' relatives with the information, and when they initially failed, the incident was forgotten.[180]

The information did not surface again until 1983 when death penalty legal defense experts entered the appeals process on behalf of Monroe. In their investigation of Stinson they also discovered that he had stabbed another wife, Marie Lendo Lee, in 1959. She survived, although he had left her for dead. About this time, he had also attacked a stranger with a club and tried to kill him.[181] Stinson had also been seen in the neighborhood on the night of the murder on Lenora Collins.[182]

Moreover, doubt was cast on Theodise Collins' identification of Monroe as the murderer. A former friend of hers testified that Stinson was forcing Theodise to have sexual relations with him, and that he intimidated and threatened her with harm over these incidents. Her fear of Stinson may have influenced her to identify another man as her mother's murderer.[183] Stinson had a history of intimidating potential witnesses against him.[184]

The Louisiana Board of Pardon heard all this new evidence and found a reasonable doubt in Monroe's guilt. On August 24,1988, it made a unanimous recommendation to the Governor that Monroe's death sentence be commuted to life.[185]

On August 24, 1989, just after the *Penry* decision, Louisiana Governor Buddy Roemer commuted Monroe's death sentence to life imprisonment without probation or parole because of the reasonable doubt that existed concerning his guilt and despite the fact that he personally believed Monroe to be guilty.[186]

Son H. Fleming

Son H. Fleming is a sixty-year-old African American with an I.Q. of sixty-four. He is also organically brain-damaged.[187]

Fleming was sentenced to death for killing a small town, white, Georgia police chief in 1977. Mr. Fleming was forty-six at the time of the crime.[188] He had two accomplices, his nephew, a teenager, who received a life sentence, and another black man, Henry Willis III, who was executed in May, 1989.[189]

Fleming was the first of nine children who were abandoned by their father at an early age. He spent many of his young years tending the other children, and didn't go to school until he was twelve. He never learned to read and write.

When he grew up, he married, had two children, and lived normally until 1966. At that time, another employee where he worked fired shotgun pellets into his hip and face, leaving him badly disfigured. He also seemed to lose virtually all mental capacity and could not remember the simplest of instructions. The shooting resulted in his filing for permanent social security disability benefits, which were granted on the basis that he was "mentally retarded, organically brain damaged and psychotic."[190] He had one heart attack prior to the 1977 murder, and three more afterwards on Death Row. The shooting and first heart attack left him weak, and in the prosecutor's words in his accomplice's trial, "[t]his old man . . . [who] stumbled around and couldn't breathe good,"[191] couldn't possibly have been the instigator and leader of the murderers. Fleming had no prior convictions for violent or serious crimes and had a steady employment record for more than two decades.[192]

Fleming's crime was violent, although not excessively so compared to other crimes for which men are executed. The three criminals took the police chief into the swamps, wounded him, chased him down, and shot him in the face at point blank range. It is unclear as to how many shots were fired by Fleming, but it is clear that not all of them were.[193] In mitigation, there was only one victim, a grown man. However, he was a police officer killed in the line of duty, which the jury considered to be an aggravating circumstance. The crime was also committed during the commission of kidnapping, another capital offense and aggravating factor.[194]

No evidence of Fleming's mental retardation was submitted to the trial court,[195] and his low intellectual capacities were only discovered later from social security records dating back to 1967. Fleming was tested at that time to see if he qualified for disability income.[196] A doctor who examined him stated that he acted like he had "been lobotomized."[197]

After Fleming was sentenced to death, his case was appealed to the Georgia Supreme Court. That Court remanded the case to the trial court to examine whether there was sufficient evidence of mental retardation for Fleming to fall under the recently enacted Georgia ban on capital punishment for persons with mental retardation.[198] Fleming was subsequently spared from execution under the new law.[199]

LEONARD JENKINS

Leonard Jenkins is an African American, mentally retarded man with an I.Q. of about sixty-two[200] or sixty-three.[201] He has a mental age between nine and ten years. Jenkins was born on December 5, 1954,[202] into a large, poor family headed by an abusive, alcoholic father who was gone from the home a great deal during his childhood.[203] In his own words, when his father was home, he "was drinking too much . . . and beating on me. . . . and was no father at all."[204]

Jenkins is considered to be in the "educable" range of mental retardation.[205] He has a reading level between the fourth and fifth grade[206] and reads in a "halting, child-like manner."[207] He was placed in special classes in the Cleveland, Ohio public schools which were designed for slow learners.[208] He attended school through the junior high level.[209]

While he was hospitalized and in pretrial detention for the crime for which he was later sentenced to death, he married his common-law wife, Loretta Taylor.[210]

Leonard Jenkins was the first person to be given the death penalty in Ohio[211] subsequent to its reinstatement on October 19, 1981,[212] after the U.S. Supreme Court required revision of Ohio's death penalty statute three years earlier.[213]

On October 21, 1981, Jenkins, at the age of twenty-six, was involved with another man, Lester Jordon, then fifty-six, in the attempted robbery of a branch of the National City Bank on the east side of Cleveland, Ohio.[214] The two men entered the bank shortly after 9:00 AM. Both carried handguns.[215] Armed with a .357 magnum,[216] Jenkins ordered the bank's customers to the back of the room and proceeded to disarm the bank's security guard by holding his gun to his head.[217] He then had weapons in both hands.

Jordon and Jenkins proceeded from one teller to the next. While Jenkins held each at gunpoint, Jordon took the money from the teller's drawer and stuffed it into a bag. In the meantime, bank personnel succeeded in activating a silent alarm connected directly to the police department.[218]

Two squad cars heard the call of a robbery in process at the bank and hastened toward the scene. A pair of policemen manned the first car to arrive. One man, Andrew Johnson, was a twenty-two-year-old, married African American rookie patrolman, the father of a seven-month-old baby boy.[219] He had been a Cleveland police officer for approximately four months, having graduated from an accelerated training course the previous July.[220] The second officer, John Myhand, aged forty-four, was an eleven year veteran of the police force.[221]

Myhand approached the front door of the bank first. Johnson was several paces behind him.[222] Myhand looked through the bank's double glass doors and saw Jenkins on the other side. He yelled at Officer Johnson to take cover and turned to run away.[223]

From inside the bank, Jenkins saw the police officers arrive. He called at Jordon "that they would have to shoot their way out." He shot a single bullet through the doors at the police. This bullet was apparently the one which eventually killed Officer Johnson.[224]

As he fled, Myhand heard this single shot, and then several more in quick succession. About this time he felt a sharp pain in the back of his knee. He thought he had been hit by one of the bullets and continued to stumble away until he eventually fell down.[225]

In the meantime, Jenkins had run out the front door and exchanged several more shots with Officer Johnson. Jenkins was hit by gunshots in the chest and the back.[226] One bullet severed his spinal cord.[227] His wounds left him a paraplegic, paralyzed from the waist down and confined to a wheelchair.[228]

As Officer Myhand lay on the ground, he was able to turn around and to see his partner, Officer Johnson, lying on the ground with "blood on his face." He also saw another man (Jenkins) lying on the ground near Officer Johnson.[229]

Almost simultaneously, Myhand spotted a red car in the bank's parking lot slowly backing and approaching him. Believing that the driver was attempting to run him over, he fired a single shot at it as he struggled to get to his feet and out of its way.[230]

Officers Gregory L. Henderson and Jerome Howard had just arrived at the scene in a second squad car. They saw the red car backing toward Officer Myhand and opened fire on it, flattening its tires and shattering the passenger's side window. The car was stopped.[231] Later, it was learned that the driver of the car was not involved in the robbery. He had been waiting in his car for a neighbor whom he had driven to the bank. The car was in reverse and the engine was running. When he heard gunfire he flattened himself on the floor of the car, and it started to roll away. He received a scalp wound in the head but was able to escape from the car and leave the scene.[232]

When the gunfire stopped, Lester Jordon came out of the bank holding his gun and the money bag. Officer Henderson disarmed him and made him lie down next to Johnson. Ambulances arrived immediately and transported the wounded to the hospital. Officer Johnson died in the hospital a few hours later from the gunshot wound to the head.[233]

On March 26, 1982[234] a jury of eight women and four men convicted Jenkins of aggravated murder with five aggravating circumstances.[235] These were: the defendant committed the crime to escape prosecution for aggravated robbery; the crime was a part of an attempt to kill more than one person (Officers Myhand and Johnson); the victim was a police officer acting in the line of duty; the offense was committed while the defendant was committing or fleeing from an aggravated robbery; and, the offense was committed while the defendant was committing or fleeing from an aggravated kidnapping.[236] Jenkins was also convicted of fifteen other charges, including one count each of attempted murder and possession of criminal tools, and multiple counts of aggravated robbery and kidnapping.[237]

Jenkins had a moderately severe criminal history prior to the instant offense. He had been convicted of at least two felonies, aggravated robbery and carrying a concealed deadly weapon.[238]

No evidence of mitigation was presented to the jury during the trial phase.[239] However, during the penalty hearing, the defense offered Leonard Jenkins' mental retardation as a mitigating factor.[240] The jury was not persuaded by this evidence. On April 7, 1982, the jury recommended that Jenkins be sentenced to death. The judge imposed the death sentence a week later on April 16, 1982.[241]

How Leonard Jenkins came to be a part of the bank robbery and murder of a police officer is significant of how people with mental retardation invariably become involved in crime. Lester Jordan, the major perpetrator of the robbery, was a man twice Jenkins' age, a sort of father figure and caretaker. Jordon "led" Jenkins[242] into the crime and pressured him into attempting the bank robbery. Jenkins testified at trial that Jordon threatened to kill his common law wife, Loretta, if he did not help with the holdup. Jenkins was afraid for her and did as he was pressured to do.[243] He did not tell his wife this until he was hospitalized after the bank robbery.[244]

Once Jenkins was convicted and sentenced to death, lawyers estimated that it would be three to five years before all appeals were exhausted and Jenkins would be executed. However, in January, 1991, Jenkins was still on Death Row. Outgoing Governor Richard Celeste, an opponent of the death penalty, was barred from running for a third term by state law. On January 11, three days before leaving office, Celeste commuted the death sentence of eight murderers, for women and four men, to life imprisonment. Leonard Jenkins was one of these. All of the pardoned were either offenders who had mental retardation or who suffered from other "mental disorders."[245] The Governor gave the condition of their mental health as the primary factor in his decision to spare their lives.[246]

Besides the factor of their mental handicaps, Governor Celeste cited the racially discriminatory way in which the death penalty had been applied in Ohio. All four women and more than half of the 101 men on Death Row were African Americans.[247]

GARY L. EDGINGTON

Gary L. Edgington is a white, illiterate man with an I.Q. of sixty-four, in the mild range of mental retardation.[248] He was born in 1954 and raised in the productive farm country of central Illinois near Springfield, the state's capital. He attended special education classes, and dropped out of school prior to completing the eighth grade.[249]

In 1989 when he was thirty-three, he resided in the small rural town of Scottville, southwest of Springfield.[250]

Edgington's early life lacked the viability of the land on which he lived. The oldest of thirteen children,[251] he was raised in the extreme emotional and material deprivation of a large, poverty-stricken, dysfunctional and violent family. His alcoholic father "brutally" abused both Gary and his mother when he was a child.[252] As an adult, Edgington suffered long term negative psychic effects from the depravity and destructiveness of his early childhood environment.[253]

At the age of fourteen, Gary was first arrested and subsequently convicted of auto theft and burglary.[254] His juvenile offenses resulted largely for stealing his father's cars.[255] His adult convictions were limited to misdemeanors, including two counts of criminal damage to property, disorderly conduct, attempted theft and reckless driving. On a scale with other murderers with mental retardation, this constitutes a relatively low level criminal history.[256]

As an adult and in his thirties, Edgington is dually diagnosed as both having mental retardation and being mentally ill. He suffers from a "memory defect" and a "schizoid personality," although he is able to distinguish between right and wrong.[257]

One side of Edgington's personality is illustrated by his relationships with women. A woman Edgington intended to marry in 1991 and who had been a long-time consort,[258] asserted that he is "honest, kind and loving."[259] Prior to his engagement to her, Edgington was married once. He has seven children who have three different mothers,[260] including this woman.[261]

Edgington generally relates well to women and is amiable and pleasant when conversing with them. With men, he is frequently sullen and silent.[262] This is perhaps a legacy of his early childhood abuse at his father's hands and his resultant distrust of male authority figures.

Edgington's work record also illustrates the amiable facet of his personality. Throughout his adult life, he was capable of holding menial jobs and had an acceptable employment record as a sawmill worker. One employer described him as a "good, dependable and honest" laborer.[263]

Nonetheless, this ostensibly mild-mannered man, satisfactory to employers and loved by women, was one of three men charged in the murder of Melissa "Missy" Koontz, an eighteen-year-old white college student.[264] Koontz had been an honor student and athlete in volleyball and track for four years at Waverly (Illinois) High School. She was named 1988 "Student of the Year" there in her senior year. After completion of her first year of college at Culver-Stockton College in Canton, Missouri, she was a straight A student.[265] In short, Ms Koontz, strong, attractive, intelligent, athletic and well-liked by her peers, typified "the All-American girl."[266]

During the summer after her college freshman year, Ms. Koontz was employed by the Cub Foods grocery store in Springfield, Illinois, earning money to return to college in the fall. On Saturday evening, June 24, 1989, Ms. Koontz left the grocery about 10:10 PM. She had worked a double shift that day.[267]

Koontz headed her black Ford Escort southwest down the Waverly-New Berlin Blacktop towards her family home in Waverly, approximately twenty miles away, where she was living for the summer.[268]

At about 10:00 PM that same evening, Edgington, Thomas McMillan, forty, of Gillespie, Illinois, Donald "Goose" Johnston, twenty-nine, of Carlinville, Illinois, and a juvenile, aged thirteen, left the country home of Edgington's fiancee. She is the mother of the juvenile,[269] and purportedly the lover of all three men.[270]

The men decided to "cruise around." McMillan suggested that they stop a car and rob the occupants in order to get money for beer, gas and cigarettes. They parked on the Waverly-New Berlin blacktop to await an unsuspecting victim.[271]

About this time Ms. Koontz's car approached the stopped vehicle on her way home. She was flagged down by McMillan, the leader of the group. McMillan dragged Miss Koontz from the car and demanded her money while Edgington held her from behind by her arms.[272] They robbed her of a silver necklace given to her by her mother and later handed over to the police by Edgington's fiancee.[273]

According to Edgington's testimony, as Koontz struggled to free herself from Edgington's grasp, McMillan "went nuts and stabbed her" with "a big butcher knife."[274] Edgington also testified that he had no knowledge that McMillan was going to kill his victim, and that he was surprised at this action. He stated that "we were just going to take the money and leave."[275]

Koontz suffered eighteen stab wounds, four of which were "exit wounds" made by the knife passing completely through her hand and wrist. She was stabbed multiple times in the chest and back. Her heart was pierced three times. Two of these heart wounds killed her.[276]

The group of men stuffed Ms. Koontz's body into the trunk of their car. They drove northwest about fifteen miles from the murder scene and disposed of the body in "a corn field west of Springfield."[277]

Later, around 10:50 PM that night, a farmer driving down the Waverly-New Berlin blacktop stopped to investigate Ms. Koontz's abandoned car. The lights were on, the keys were in the ignition, and her purse was on the front seat. He called police.[278]

The vanishing of "Missy" Koontz set off a massive search by lawmen and volunteers. On foot and horseback, in car, helicopter and airplane, they combed the area of her disappearance for a week without success. Finally, her decomposed body was found by a "passerby" on July 1, 1989 where it had been dumped a week earlier.[279]

The juvenile and all three adults, McMillan, Johnston and Edgington, were eventually arrested for the armed robbery, attempted aggravated kidnapping, and first degree murder of Koontz.[280] The twelve-year-old, who, like Edgington, has mental retardation, and who has an I.Q. of sixty-two, was found incompetent to stand trial. He is being held indefinitely in the Chester County [IL] Mental Health Center.[281]

Donald "Goose" Johnston was the first to be arrested for the crimes. He was instrumental in the arrest of Edgington by cooperating with police in a ruse to gain a confession from him.[282]

Edgington was subpoenaed to appear to testify in the trial of Johnston on May 14, 1990. Johnston was not actually scheduled to be tried that day. The two were left alone to speak to each other in a "bugged" room, and Johnston told Edgington that he was going to testify that Edgington had done the actual stabbing and murder. Detectives taped this conversation and presented it to Edgington afterwards in order to get a confession. Edgington, of course, fell for the ruse, and made a confession of his role in the crime. He was arrested the same day and incarcerated in the county jail.[283]

Two additional incidences from Edgington's history further illustrate the vulnerability of the offender with mental retardation faced with the complexities of court proceedings and the legal system. First, Edgington can neither read nor write, and legal papers had to be read to him throughout trial preparation.[284] A second incident suggests that even when such documents are read to him, it is likely that he understands little. The usual round of motions and reschedulings that occur in capital cases were a part of the preparation for Edgington's trial. Towards the end of 1990, Edgington was told that his trial had been postponed from an upcoming trial date. He replied to this news by saying, "Does it mean I get to go home for Christmas?"[285]

Finally, in April, 1991, Edgington was the first of the three to be tried. His court-appointed defense attorney,[286] Jon Gray Noll, relied heavily on statistical theory in order to pick a jury for the trial. He used a team of experts to prepare for trial. It was comprised of a psychiatrist, psychologist, paralegal, investigator, the Capital Punishment Resource Center, the state appellate defender's office, and local groups opposing the death penalty. Relying on a survey done by the National Legal Aid and Defense Association in 1985, the team developed a questionnaire to present to the jury pool which would help them select jurors least likely to impose the death penalty. That survey suggested that women, minorities, those without a high school diploma, those younger than thirty, manual laborers, liberals, Democrats and Catholics fit this profile.[287] The result was that Noll succeeded in using his fourteen allowable peremptory challenges to select a largely Catholic[288] and all woman (although White) jury panel. The judge was also female.[289]

Illinois law provides for a three-staged determination of the penalty once guilt has been determined.[290] In the first stage of a capital trial, the jury determines whether the defendant is eligible for the death penalty. To qualify, the crime must have been committed during the commission of another felony,[291] and the defendant must have inflicted injuries on the victim, which, if they did not actually cause death, were inflicted "substantially contemporaneously with physical injuries . . . [that] . . . caused the death of the murdered individual."[292]

On April 16, the jury found that Edgington was qualified for the death penalty under these provisions. They believed that he must have used great force to hold Ms. Koontz who was a strong athlete struggling for her life, and that it was likely that she suffered injuries from his grasp.[293]

In the second stage of the penalty hearing, the jury determines whether the death penalty should actually be imposed.[294] On April 17, 1991, the jury spared the life of Gary L. Edgington. They determined not to sentence him to death because he did not actually do the killing and because of his abused childhood and mental retardation.[295]

In the final stage of the penalty imposition, if death is not recommended by the jury, the judge determines the length of the prison sentence within the indeterminate range of twenty years-to-life.[296]

Edgington's sentencing was originally scheduled for June 5, 1991.[297] However, this was postponed to allow for the trial of McMillan, the primary perpetrator, to take place.[298] McMillan was convicted in July, 1991. The jury in his trial also refused to recommend the death sentence.[299]

As of this writing, Judge Susan Myerscough has yet to determine Edgington's sentence.[300]

In sum, Gary L. Edgington became the first known murderer with mental retardation not to receive a death sentence from a jury because of his mental retardation, along with other mitigating factors.

The question arises as to how a generally well-liked and mild-mannered man like Edgington could end up in a situation where he is involved in and convicted of murder, and narrowly escapes the death sentence. The explanation lies in his mental retardation.

Often, persons with mental retardation who have grown up in less than supportive environments have suffered years of mental humiliation, and sometimes physical abuse from those who do not understand their condition and who enjoy tormenting them out of sheer meanness or simply because people with mental retardation are intellectually defenseless. Such was Edgington's lot.

Many persons with mental retardation, because they have experienced years of rejection and ridicule as a result of their slow mentality, have an inordinate need for ordinary human companionship and a desperate desire to belong to a social group. If the companions they fall in with happen to be criminally minded, they become involved in crime themselves. They lack the wit and will to abandon the safety of a group that is virtually their sole source of emotional (and frequently material) support for getting along in a world which is beyond their ability to understand and cope with on their own. Because they are slow-witted, they are under the direction and control of the more intelligent persons of their association. They are also at their mercy both because of their low intelligence and because of how they have been treated for it over a lifetime.

Edgington is such a person. Emotionally deprived and abused as a youngster, he was described as "a follower" who would do "whatever he needs to [do] to be accepted by his group."[301] Thus he followed the stronger-minded and more volatile McMillan into a violent crime and helped him to accomplish it. He had no prior inkling that the purported robbery victim would be killed, but held her while she was stabbed to death in order to assist McMillan who was his leader and protector. But for the skill of trial counsel in selecting a jury and in constantly reminding it of Edgington's mental retardation and abused childhood, and for the jury that was selected and heard the message that a person with mental retardation should not be executed,[302] Edgington too would be awaiting death on Death Row today.

SUMMARY

The stories of twelve men with mental retardation who murdered, who were sentenced to death, (or in the case of Edgington, almost sentenced to death) and whose lives have then been spared, have been told here in order to compare their characteristics to those of the men who have been executed. Are their significant differences in the executed and those who are allowed to live? If so, then it is important to identify the differences in attributes. If offenders with mental retardation with similar features are treated differently, for example, one of two mentally retarded murderers with multiple mitigating factors is executed and one is not, then the sentencing and executions of persons with mental retardation are inequitable. Similarly, if those with different characteristics, for example, instigators and supporters, leaders and followers, are both pardoned or both executed, then these unequally applied outcomes present another argument for the banning of executions of offenders with mental retardation.

The next table summarizes the major characteristics of the twelve men with mental retardation who have been given a reprieve from death sentences. The table lays the foundation for the statistical comparisons made in the next chapter.

FIGURE 4.1. REPRIEVED MENTALLY RETARDED OFFENDERS

Name	State	Age	Date of Reprieve	I.Q.	Race	Race of Victim
1. J. Westbrook	GA	41	03/12/87	35	Black	White
2. H. Welcome	LA	28	1987	60	Black	Bl/Wh
3. L. Jones	MS	17	06/01/88	41	Black	White
4. G.E. Dungee	GA	36	07/12/88	68	Black	White
5. J. Holloway	GA	28	08/15/88	49	Black	Black
6. W.A. Smith	GA	21	08/27/88	65	Black	White
7. L. Arthur	SC	25	1988	65	Black	White
8. E. Spraggins	GA	34	12/05/88	63	White	White
9. R. Monroe	LA	22	08/24/89	73-77	Black	Black
10. S. Fleming	GA	46	12/01/89	64	Black	White
11. L. Jenkins	OH	22	01/10/91	63	Black	Black
12. G. Edgington	IL	33	05/17/91	64	White	White

Pardoning States

Georgia	6 - 50 %
Louisiana	2 - 17 %
Illinois	1 - 8 %
Mississippi	1 - 8 %
Ohio	1 - 8 %
S.Carolina	1 - 8 %
Total	12 - 100%

Average Age 30
Average I.Q. 59

Race

Black	10 - 83 %
White	2 - 17 %
Total	12 100 %

Race of Victim

Black	4 - 33 %
White	6 - 50 %
Both	1 - 8 %
Unknown	1 - 8 %
Total	12 - 100 %

Notes

[1]W. Stevens Ricks, "Death Row Inmate With Mind of Child Is Lost in the Shuffle," *Atlanta Constitution,* 28 September 1988, sec A.

[2]Emily A. Reed, "Legal Rights of Mentally Retarded Offenders: Hospice and Habilitation," 25 *Criminal Law Bulletin* (September-October 1989): 412-413.

[3]"Defense of the Poor Seen Lacking," *Washington Post,* 4 June 1990, sec. A. "Death Penalty Defendants in South Get Inadequate Legal Advice, Journal Says," *Atlanta Constitution,* 4 June 1990, sec. A.

[4]Penry, 109 S.Ct. 2934, 2955 (1989).

[5]Ricks, "Death Row Inmate," sec. A.

[6]Reed, "Legal Rights," 416-417.

[7]Westbrook v. State, 249 S.E.2d 524, 529 (1987).

[8]Ibid., 526.

[9]GA. CODE ANN. s.27-2534.1 (b)(7), as quoted in Westbrook v. State, 353 S.E. 2d 504, 519 (1987).

[10]Westbrook v. State, 353 S.E. 2d 504 (1987). *See also* Ricks, "Death Row Inmate," sec. A.

[11]State v. Welcome, 458 S.E.2d 1235 (1984).

[12]"Killer Waiting for Judge to Rule on Execution Delay," *New Orleans Times-Picayune,* 14 July 1987, sec. B.

[13]Welcome, 458 So.2d 1235, 1243.

[14]Ibid., 1255.

[15]Ibid., 1244, 1255.

[16]Ibid.

[17]John Blume and David Bruck, "Sentencing the Mentally Retarded to Death: An Eighth Amendment Analysis," 41 *Arkansas Law Review* (1988): 757-8, n.130.

[18]*See* Gregg v. Georgia, 428 U.S. 153 (1976). In this case the Supreme Court upheld state statutes that allowed the death penalty to be imposed if aggravating and mitigating factors are weighed against each other.

[19]Blume and Bruck, 757-8, n.130.

[20]"Reddix," United Press International, Dateline: Biloxi, MS, 10 April 1981. *See also* "Death Row Inmate Gets New Hearing," United Press International, Dateline: Washington, D.C., 23 February 1987.

[21]Jones v. Mississippi, 381 So. 2d 988, 987 (1980) (hereinafter Jones II). *See also* Jones v. Thigpen, 741 F.2d 805, 807 (1984)(hereinafter Thigpen I).

[22]Reddix v. Mississippi, 547 So.2d 792, 794 (1989) (hereinafter Reddix IV).

[23]Reddix v. Mississippi, 381 So.2d 999, 1002 (1980)(hereinafter Reddix II).

[24]"Reddix," United Press International, Dateline: Greenville, MS, 31 March 1981.

[25]Reddix II, 1002. *See also* Thigpen I, 807.

[26]Reddix II, 1003.

[27]Jones II, 988.

[28]Reddix II, 1002.

[29]Jones v. Mississippi, 342 So.2d 735, 736 (1977) (hereinafter Jones I).

³⁰Jones II, 988-989.
³¹Ibid., 989.
³²Reddix II, 1005.
³³Ibid., 1008.
³⁴Jones v. Thigpen, 788 F.2d 1101 (1986)(hereinafter Thigpen II).
³⁵Ibid., 1103.
³⁶"Reddix," United Press International, Dateline: Greenville, MS, 31 March 1981.
³⁷Reddix II, 1010.
³⁸"Reddix," United Press International, Dateline: Biloxi, MS, 10 April 1981.
³⁹Jones v. Mississippi, 555 F. Supp. 870, 872 (1983) (hereinafter Jones III).
⁴⁰Jones I, 736.
⁴¹Jones v. Smith, 685 F.Supp. 604, 605 (1988).
⁴²Jones II, 987.
⁴³Thigpen I, 813.
⁴⁴Jones II, 984.
⁴⁵MISS. CODE ANN. s. 99-19-101(g)(Supp. 1979) quoted in Jones II at 998-999, Chief Justice Patterson dissenting.
⁴⁶Jones v. Smith, 340 So.2d 17 (Miss. 1976)(hereinafter Smith I).
⁴⁷Jones I, 736.
⁴⁸See Reddix v. Mississippi, 342 So.2d 1306 (Miss. 1977) (hereinafter Reddix I); and Jones I.
⁴⁹Jones II, 994.
⁵⁰Jones v. Smith, 685 F.Supp. 604, 605 (1988)(hereinafter Smith II).
⁵¹Furman v. Georgia, 408 U.S. 238 (1972).
⁵²William Blackstone, Commentaries on the Laws of England, Of Public Wrongs, (Boston: Beacon Press, 1962), 35.
⁵³Jones II, 989.
⁵⁴Smith II, 606.
⁵⁵Thigpen II, 1101.
⁵⁶Ibid., 1101. See also "Death Row Inmate Gets New Hearing," United Press International, Dateline: Washington, DC, 23 February 1987.
⁵⁷Jones I, 735. See also Jones III, 878.
⁵⁸Jones II, 997.
⁵⁹Ibid., 997-998.
⁶⁰Thigpen II, 1103. See also Smith II, 606.
⁶¹Smith II, 606. See also "Reddix," United Press International, Dateline: Jackson, MS, 2 September 1988.
⁶²Ibid., 605.
⁶³Ibid., 606.
⁶⁴Tom Teepen, "Georgia's Decision Not to Execute the Mentally Retarded is Working," Atlanta Constitution, 14 July 1988, sec. A.
⁶⁵Coleman v. State, 226 S.E.2d 911, 913 (1976).
⁶⁶Barry Siegel, "Anguish in Georgia: Ruling Cast Shadow on Jury System," Los Angeles Times, 20 March 1986, sec. 1.
⁶⁷Ibid.
⁶⁸Teepen, "Georgia's Decision," sec. A.
⁶⁹Encyclopedia of World Crime, 1990 ed., s.v. "Dungee, George, and

Coleman, Wayne, and Isaacs, Carl, and Isaacs, Billy," by J. R. Nash.
⁷⁰Ibid.
⁷¹Coleman, 226 S.E.2d 911, 913; Isaacs v. State, 386 S.E.2d 317, 320 (1989).
⁷²Isaacs, 386 S.E.2d 317, 320.
⁷³Siegel, "Anguish in Georgia," sec. 1.
⁷⁴Ibid.
⁷⁵Ibid.
⁷⁶Ibid.
⁷⁷Ibid.
⁷⁸Dungee v. State, 227 S.E.2d 746, 748 (1976).
⁷⁹Isaacs, 386 S.E.2d 317, 333.
⁸⁰Ibid., 320.
⁸¹Dungee, 227 S.E.2d 746, 748.
⁸²Isaacs, 386 S.E.2d 317, 320.
⁸³Siegel, "Anguish in Georgia," sec. 1.
⁸⁴Ibid.
⁸⁵Judge Johnson had supported one of the first integration efforts, Rosa Clark's claim not to give her bus seat up to a white man, and had ordered George Wallace to desegregate Alabama schools. *See* "Alday Lawyers File Appeal to Disqualify Judge," United Press International, Dateline: Savannah, GA, 4 November 1986.
⁸⁶Rideau v. Louisiana, 83 U.S. 1417 (1962) as quoted in Siegel, "Anguish in Georgia," sec. 1.
⁸⁷Siegel, "Anguish in Georgia," sec. 1.
⁸⁸Teepen, "Georgia's Decision," sec. A.
⁸⁹Ibid.
⁹⁰Joe Parham, "Condemned Man Called 'Most Retarded Man on Death Row," United Press International, Dateline: Atlanta, GA, 12 October 1987.
⁹¹Joe Parham, "Georgia Death Row Inmate 'Most Retarded Man on Death Row Anywhere,'" United Press International, Dateline: Atlanta, 11 October 1987.
⁹²Joe Parham, "Condemned Man," 12 October 1987.
⁹³"Georgia News Briefs," United Press International, Dateline: Pembroke, GA, 3 March 1988.
⁹⁴Holloway v. State, 257 GA 620, 621, 361 S.E.2d 794, 795 (1987).
⁹⁵Joe Parham, "Georgia Death Row," 11 October 1987.
⁹⁶Ibid.
⁹⁷Rhonda Cook, "Attorneys Argue Competency of Mentally Retarded Death Row Inmate," Dateline: Atlanta, GA, United Press International, 13 October 1987.
⁹⁸Joe Parham, "Condemned Man," 12 October 1987.
⁹⁹"Holloway," United Press International, Dateline: Atlanta, GA, 5 November 1987.
¹⁰⁰Rhonda Cook, "Attorneys Argue," 13 October 1987.
¹⁰¹Robert Perske, *Unequal Justice* (Nashville, TN: Abingdon Press, 1991), 17-18.
¹⁰²Rhonda Cook, "Attorneys Argue," 13 October 1987.
¹⁰³Joe Parham, "Condemned Man," 12 October 1987.

[104]Joseph B. Frazier, "Too Retarded to Die for Crimes? Laws say No," *Los Angeles Times*, 17 April 1988, part 1.

[105]Rhonda Cook, "Attorneys Argue," 13 October 1987.

[106]Joe Parham, "Georgia Death Row," 11 October 1987.

[107]Frazier, sec. 1.

[108]Holloway v. State, 257 GA 620, 621, 361 S.E.2d 794, 795 (1987).

[109]Ibid., 796. *See also* "Holloway," United Press International, Dateline: Atlanta, GA, 5 November 1987.

[110]Ibid.

[111]"Georgia News Briefs," United Press International, Dateline: Pembroke, GA, 16 August 1988.

[112]Justice is swift in Georgia. The trial was completed two months after the commission of the crime.

[113]Smith v. State, 290 S.E.2d 44, 47 (1982).

[114]"Court Says Retarded Man Unfit To Confess," United Press International, Dateline: Atlanta, GA, 27 August 1988. *See also* Tracy Thompson, "Court Rules Man of 65 IQ Unfit to Confess Crime," *Atlanta Constitution*, 27 August 1988, sec. B.

[115]"Supreme Court Turns Down Appeal by Norman Baxter," United Press International, Dateline: Jackson, GA, 21 October 1985.

[116]Smith, 290 S.E.2d 44.

[117]Ibid., 47.

[118]"Court Says Retarded Man Unfit", 27 August 1988.

[119]Smith, 290 S.E.2d 44, 48.

[120]Smith v. Francis, 325 S.E.2d 362, 366 (1985). *See also* Smith, 290 S.E.2d 44, 46.

[121]Thompson, "Court Rules," sec. B. *See also* "Court Says Retarded Man Unfit", 27 August 1988.

[122]Ruth Marcus, "Retarded Killer's Sentence Fuels Death-Penalty Debate," *Washington Post*, 22 June 1987, sec. A.

[123]John Blume and David Bruck, "Sentencing the Mentally Retarded to Death: An Eighth Amendment Analysis," 41 *Arkansas Law Review* (1988): 726.

[124]Ibid.

[125]Marcus, "Retarded Killer's," sec. A.

[126]Ibid.

[127]Ibid.

[128]Ibid.

[129]Ibid. *See also* South Carolina v. Arthur, 374 S.E.2d 291 (1988).

[130]Ibid.

[131]Ibid.

[132]Perske, 85.

[133]"Capital Punishment in the United States, 1973-1989," United States Department of Justice, Bureau of Justice Statistics, Ann Arbor, MI: Inter-university Consortium for Political and Social Research [distributor], February 1991, Case No. 620.

[134]"Ohio Woman Stands by Inmate Pen Pal Spared from Execution during New Probe," *Columbus (OH)*, 27 June 1988, sec. D.

[135]Amy Wallace, "Retardation Defense Used in Capital Case," *Atlanta Constitution*, 10 November 1987, sec. A.

[136]Spraggins v. State, 243 S.E.2d 20 (1978).
[137]Prentice Palmer, "High Court to Hear Case on Retarded Death-Row Inmate," *Atlanta Journal and Constitution*, 7 November 1987, sec. B.
[138]Amy Wallace, "Retardation Defense Used In Capital Case, *Atlanta Constitution*, 10 November 1987, sec. C.
[139]Joe Parham, "Attorneys Disagree Over Capabilities of death Row Inmate," United Press International, Dateline: Atlanta, GA, 9 November 1987.
[140]Palmer, "High Court," sec. B.
[141]Parham, "Attorneys Disagree," 9 November 1987.
[142]Spraggins v. State, 243 S.E.2d 22 (1978).
[143]"Capital Punishment in the United States, 1973-1989," United States Department of Justice, Bureau of Justice Statistics, Ann Arbor, MI: Inter-university Consortium for Political and Social Research [distributor], February 1991, Case No. 620.
[144]"Spraggins," United Press International, Dateline: Jackson, GA, 6 December 1988.
[145]Parham, "Attorneys Disagree," 9 November 1987.
[146]Ken Sugar, "Davis Set To Die Next Week in Elderly Woman's Slaying," United Press International, Dateline: Atlanta, GA, 2 December 1988.
[147]Francis v. Spraggins, 720 F.2d 1190, 1193 (1983).
[148]Spraggins v. State, 243 S.E.2d 20 (1978).
[149]Ibid.
[150]Ibid., 21.
[151]Davis v. State, 243 S.E.2d 12 (1978). Davis v. Georgia, 446 U.S. 961, 100 S.Ct. 2935, 64 L.Ed.2d 820 (1980). *See also* "Spraggins," United Press International, Dateline: Jackson, GA, 6 December 1988.
[152]Francis v. Spraggins, 720 F.2d 1190, 1194.
[153]Ken Sugar, "Davis Set to Die Next Week in Elderly Woman's Slaying," United Press International, Dateline: Atlanta, GA, 2 December 1988.
[154]Spraggins v. State, 243 S.E. 2d 20, 22 (1978).
[155]Ibid., 23.
[156]Spraggins v. State, 252 S.E. 2d 620 (1979).
[157]Spraggins v. Georgia, 446 U.S. 961, 100 S.Ct. 2935, 64 L.Ed 820 (1980).
[158]Francis v. Spraggins, 720 F.2d 1190, 1191.
[159]Ibid.
[160]Spraggins v. Georgia, 364 S.E.2d 861 (1988). *See also* Palmer, "High Court," sec. 1.
[161]GA. CODE ANN. s. 17-7-131(j)(Supp. 1988).
[162]Spraggins v. Georgia, 364 S.E.2d 861, 864 (1988).
[163]"One Defendant Gets Life, Other to be Executed," United Press International, Dateline: Greenville, GA, 6 December 1988.
[164]Louisiana v. Monroe, 397 So.2nd 1258, 1269, 1273, 1277 (1981); Peter Applebome, "Death Row Takes On a Higher Profile," *New York Times*, 21 August 1989, sec. A; Tom Wicker, "Injustice at Midnight," *New York Times*, 14 August 1989, sec. A; Ginny Carroll and Eric Press, "Only Two Weeks to Live," *Newsweek*, 21 August 1989, 83.

[165]Louisiana v. Monroe, 397 So.2nd 1258, 1263, 1277. *See also* Carroll and Press, "Only Two Weeks," 83.

[166]Louisiana v. Monroe, 397 So.2nd 1258, 1263-1264. *See also* Carroll and Press, "Only Two Weeks," 83.

[167]Ibid., 1263-1264.

[168]Ibid., 1264.

[169]Ibid., 1275.

[170]Ibid., 1264, 1267, n. 2, 1277.

[171]Ibid., 1265.

[172]Ibid., 1264, 1268.

[173]Ibid., 1277.

[174]Ibid., 1273-1274, 1277.

[175]Ibid., 1274-1276.

[176]Ibid., 1277. *See also* William F. Buckley, "But Did They Get the Right Man?" *Washington Post*, 16 August 1989, sec. A.

[177]Louisiana v. Monroe, 397 So.2d 1258, 1278-1279.

[178]Wicker, "Injustice at Midnight," sec. A.

[179]Buckley, "But Did They?" sec. A.

[180]Carroll and Press, "Only Two Weeks," 83.

[181]Ibid.

[182]Wicker, "Injustice at Midnight," sec. A.

[183]Buckley, "But Did They?" sec. A.

[184]Applebome, "Death Row," sec. A.

[185]Carroll and Press, "Only Two Weeks," 83.

[186]Applebome, "Death Row," sec. A.

[187]Jeanne Cummings, "Supreme Court to Review Fleming Case," *Atlanta Constitution*, 27 July 1989, sec. C.

[188]"Get the Retarded Off Death Row," *Atlanta Constitution*, 18 July 1989, sec. A.

[189]"Retarded, or a Criminal Leader?" *Atlanta Constitution*, 27 July 1989, sec. C.

[190]Fleming v. Zant, 386 S.E.2d 339, 340 (Ga. 1989).

[191]Willis v. State, 243 Ga. 185, 253 S.E.2d 70 (1979). *See also* "Retarded, or a Criminal Leader?" sec. 1.

[192]Fleming v. State, 240 S.E.2d 37, 39 (Ga. 1985).

[193]Willis, 253 S.E.2d 70, 72 (1979).

[194]Fleming, 240 S.E.2d 37, 40.

[195]"Get the Retarded Off," sec. A

[196]Zant, 386 S.E.2d 339, 340. *See also* "Supreme Court to Review," sec. C.

[197]"Retarded, or a Criminal Leader?" sec. C.

[198]Fleming v. Zant, 386 S.E.2d 339 (1989).

[199]*See* Chapter 6. LEGISLATIVE INITIATIVES TO ABOLISH THE DEATH PENALTY FOR THE MENTALLY RETARDED, FLEMING V. ZANT, *infra*, for an elaboration of this decision.

[200]Mike Casey, "Jenkins Begs 'Don't Kill Me,'" United Press International," Dateline: Cleveland, OH, 6 April 1982. *See also* "Sentencing Hearing Monday for Convicted Cop-Killer," United Press International, Dateline: Cleveland, OH, 4 April 1982.

[201]Mike Casey, "Judge in Jenkins' Case Voted Against Repealing

Capital Punishment," United Press International, Dateline: Cleveland, OH, 13 April 1982.
[202]State v. Jenkins, 1984 WL 14150, 42 (Ohio App.)(1984)(hereinafter Jenkins III).
[203]Ibid., 39.
[204]Casey, "Jenkins Begs," 6 April 1982.
[205]Ohio v. Jenkins, 473 N.E.2d 264, 299 (1984)(hereinafter Jenkins I).
[206]Jenkins III, 38.
[207]Casey, "Jenkins Begs," 6 April 1982.
[208]Jenkins III, 39.
[209]Jenkins I, 321.
[210]"Man Facing Trial in Cop Slaying Gets Permission to Marry," United Press International, Dateline: Cleveland, OH, 25 December 1981.
[211]Jenkins I, 272.
[212]Ibid., 269.
[213]Ibid., 272. See also Lockett v. Ohio, 438 U.S. 586, 98 S.Ct. 2954 (1978).
[214]State v. Jenkins, 536 N.E. 2d 667, 670 (1987)(hereinafter Jenkins II). See also "Clevelanders to Face Death Penalty In Police Slaying," United Press International, Dateline: Cleveland, OH, 22 October 1981.
[215]Jenkins III, 1.
[216]Mike Casey, "Jenkins Begs," 6 April 1982.
[217]Jenkins I, 270-271.
[218]Ibid., 271.
[219]Jenkins III, 16.
[220]"Copshot," United Press International, Dateline: Cleveland, OH, 26 October 1981.
[221]"Clevelanders to Face Death Penalty In Police Slaying," United Press International, Dateline: Cleveland, OH, 22 October 1981.
[222]"Copshot," 26 October 1981.
[223]Jenkins I, 271.
[224]Ibid.
[225]Ibid.
[226]Ibid. Actually, Officer Myhand had not been shot but had suffered a compound fracture of his leg bone in his haste to avoid being shot.
[227]Jenkins I, 319.
[228]"Jury Starts Deliberations in Police Killing Trial," United Press International, Dateline: Cleveland, OH, 25 March 1982.
[229]Ibid.
[230]Jenkins III, 1.
[231]Jenkins I, 271.
[232]Ibid., n. 1.
[233]Jenkins III, 2.
[234]Jenkins II, 667.
[235]"Sentencing Hearing Monday for Convicted Cop-Killer," United Press International, Dateline: Cleveland, OH, 4 April 1982.
[236]Jenkins I, 293.
[237]Jenkins III, 1.
[238]"Sentencing Hearing Monday," 4 April 1982.
[239]Jenkins II, 669.

[240]Casey, "Judge in Jenkins' Case," 13 April 1982.

[241]Jenkins II, 668.

[242]"Sentencing Hearing Monday," 4 April 1982.

[243]Casey, "Jenkins Begs," 6 April 1982.

[244]Jenkins I, 289.

[245]"At End of Term, Ohio's Governor Commutes Death Sentences for 8," *New York Times*, 12 January 1991, sec. 1.

[246]Ibid.

[247]"Celeste Commutes Death Sentences of Eight Murderers," United Press International, Dateline: Columbus, OH, 11 January 1991.

[248]Pat England, "Edgington's Life Spared," *The (Springfield, Illinois) State Journal-Register*, 18 April 1991, sec. 1.

[249]Margaret Blair, Paralegal, Noll & Associates, Attorneys for the Defense, Springfield, Illinois, telephone conversation with author, 26 August 1991.

[250]"Bond Set at $1 Million Each for Men Accused of Koontz Killing," Dateline: Springfield, Illinois, United Press International, 15 May 1990.

[251]Margaret Blair, telephone conversation with author, 26 August 1991.

[252]Ibid.

[253]England, "Edgington's Life Spared," sec. 1. *See also* Pat England, "Jurors Find Edgington Eligible for Death Penalty," *The State Journal*, 17 April 1991, sec. 1.

[254]Ibid.

[255]Margaret Blair, telephone conversation with the author, 26 August 1991.

[256]England, "Jurors Find Edgington," 1.

[257]Pat England, "Edgington Jury Hears His Taped Confession," *The State Journal-Register*," 18 April 1991, sec. 1.

[258]Pat England, Reporter, *The State Journal-Register*, telephone conversation with author, 23 August 1991.

[259]Ms. Pocklington also created an alibi for Edgington by saying that he was with her at the time of the crime. England, "Jurors Find Edgington," 1.

[260]Ibid.

[261]Pat England, telephone conversation with the author, 23 August 1991.

[262]Margaret Blair, telephone conversation with the author, 26 August 1991.

[263]England, "Jurors Find Edgington," 8.

[264]"Deliberations Begin in Koontz Trial," Dateline: Springfield, Illinois, United Press International, 22 July 1991. *See also* Pat England, "Parents: Trial 'brings it all back,'" *The State Journal-Register*, 18 April 1991, sec. 1.

[265]Pat England, "Jury Selection To Start in Koontz Murder Case," *The State Journal-Register*, 8 April 1991, sec. 3.

[266]"McMillan Spared Death Penalty," United Press International, Dateline: Peoria, Illinois, 23 July 1991.

[267]England, "Jury Selection," sec. 1.

[268]Ibid.

[269]Pat England, telephone conversation with the author, 23 August 1991.

[270]Margaret Blair, telephone conversation with the author, 26 August 1991.

[271]England, "Edgington Jury," sec. 1.

[272]Ibid. *See also* "McMillan Spared Death Penalty," Dateline: Peoria, Illinois, United Press International, 23 July 1991. Although some believe that Ms. Koontz was raped at this point, none of the perpetrators was ever charged with the crime. None testified to this effect, nor was any evidence ever introduced at trial to support this contention.

[273]England, "Edgington Jury," sec. 1.

[274]Ibid.

[275]Ibid.

[276]Ibid.

[277]Ibid.

[278]England, "Jury Selection To Start," sec. 3.

[279]Ibid.

[280]Ibid.

[281]Ibid.

[282]England, "Edgington Jury," sec. 1.

[283]England, "Jury Selection To Start," sec. 3.

[284]Margaret Blair, telephone conversation with the author, 26 August 1991.

[285]Ibid.

[286]Ibid.

[287]Pat England, "Death Penalty Avoidance Prompted All-Female Jury," *The State Journal,* 8 April 1991, sec. 3.

[288]Ibid.

[289]Pat England, "Death Penalty Avoidance," sec. 3.

[290]*See generally* ILL. REV. STAT. ch. 38, ss 9-1, 1005-5-3.

[291]Ill. Rev. Stat. ch. 38, s 9-1(a)(6). *See also* Pat England, "Jurors Find Edgington, sec. 1.

[292]ILL. REV. STAT. ch. 38, ss 9-1(a)(6)(a)(ii), 9-1(d). *See also* Pat England, "Edgington Convicted," *The State Journal-Register,* 16 April 1991, sec. 1.

[293]Pat England, "Jurors Find Edgington", sec. 1.

[294]ILL.REV. STAT. ch. 38, s 9-1(g).

[295]Pat England, "Edgington's Life Spared," *The State Journal-Register,* 18 April 1991, sec. 1.

[296]ILL.REV. STAT. ch. 38, ss 9-1(g), 1005-5-3(c)(1), 1005-8-1.

[297]England, "Edgington's Life Spared," 1.

[298]Pat England, telephone conversation with the author, 23 August 1991.

[299]"McMillan Spared," 23 July 1991.

[300]Margaret Blair, telephone conversation with the author, 26 August 1991. *See also* Pat England, telephone conversation with author, 23 August 1991.

[301]England, "Jurors Find Edgington," sec. 1.

[302]England, "Edgington Convicted," sec. 1.

5

Who Dies?
Characteristics of the
Pardoned
and the
Executed

Must we kill to prevent there being any wicked? This is to make both parties wicked instead of one.

--Henri Pascal, *Pensees*

THE "3-D'S" OF DEATH PENALTY SENTENCING

The preceding case studies and delineation of the stories of twenty-four mentally retarded persons who have been given the death penalty since 1976,[1] the descriptions of the circumstances of their crimes, and the analysis of their court proceedings and legal appeals point to a simple explanatory notion - the "3-D's" of mentally retarded death penalty sentencing. These three D's or dimensions are: disparity, discretion and discrimination.

Disparity or dissimilarity in state death penalty statutes combined with the discretion of sentencers to impose or not to impose the death penalty on offenders suffering from mental retardation result in inconsistent outcomes for mentally retarded murderers, even though they have similar characteristics and crime circumstances. The following summary of the disparity, discretion and discrimination surrounding the sentencing of persons suffering from mental retardation who are convicted of capital crimes clarifies how the many enumerated characteristics influence their life or death situations.

SENTENCE OUTCOME

> . . . *a tiny .016 percent of those convicted for murder and 1.5 percent of those sentenced to death [between 1975 and 1985] were actually executed.*
> --Ian Gray and Moira Stanley, *A Punishment in Search of a Crime*[2]

The first evidence of the 3-D's of death penalty sentencing is the final outcome of the death sentences that have been imposed on mentally retarded murderers. Twelve persons[3] with mental retardation have been executed, and twelve have been spared.

Of those who have had their sentences reduced to life, governors have commuted the sentences of four (Jenkins, Monroe, Smith, and Welcome). In four cases (those of Arthur, Dungee, Holloway and Spraggins), after a first or subsequent conviction was thrown out, the prosecutor decided not to seek the death penalty again.   The sentences of three (Fleming, Jones, and Westbrook) have been reduced to life imprisonment by the courts. In a final case (Edgington's), the trial jury refused to impose the death sentence after the defense attorney continually placed the fact of the defendant's mental retardation and associated limitations before it. FIGURE 5.1 graphs these numbers.

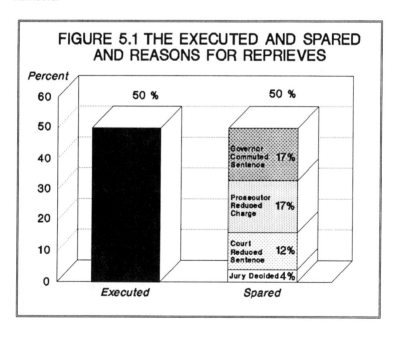

FIGURE 5.1 THE EXECUTED AND SPARED AND REASONS FOR REPRIEVES

Without looking at any of the other characteristics or circumstances of the crimes of the twenty-four persons with mental retardation who have had a final determination made, these facts indicate that the odds of being executed or spared are exactly even. Individualized determination and the discretion of the sentencing process end in unexplained disparity. It is impossible to discern from this minimal information why some murderers who suffer from mental retardation are executed and why some are not.

Other characteristics that are ordinarily associated with the severity of sentences need to be examined to find a rational explanation for this execution-survival ratio. Three categories of factors require scrutiny.

First, the offender's characteristics may be pertinent to outcome. These characteristics include race, I.Q., educational level, marital status, age at the time the crime was committed, age at execution or reprieve, years on Death Row, criminal history, and social history. Courts use the term "social history" in a broad scene. It includes such factors as childhood experiences and upbringing, mental health, and organic brain damage.

The second category of characteristics contains the circumstances of the crime. Included here are the geographic locus of the crime, the year it was committed, the crime's violence quotient, whether the offender was the principal offender or merely an accomplice, whether the person acted alone or with others, and what weapon was used.

Last, victim characteristics relevant to the outcome include the number of victims, their race, age, gender, whether a sexual assault occurred or not, and vulnerability because of handicap.

FIGURE 5.2 summarizes the characteristics to be analyzed in this chapter. The next section examines each characteristic one by one in search of a rationale for the apparent randomness of who lives or who dies.

FIGURE 5.2
SUMMARY OF CHARACTERISTICS

Offender Characteristics	Crime Circumstances	Victim Characteristics
Race	Crime's Location	Number
IQ		
Education	Year of the Crime	Age Vulnerability
Marital Status	Violence Quotient	Race
Age at Crime	Principal Offender/	Gender
Age at Outcome	Accessory	
Years on Death Row	Number of	Sexual Assault
Criminal History	Accomplices	Handicapped
Social History	Weapon	Vulnerability

OFFENDER CHARACTERISTICS

RACE

> *We have used the death penalty almost genocidally against blacks, especially . . . in the South.*
>
> Watt Espy, *American Gothic*

The concentration of mentally retarded capital punishment in the South casts a suspicion that death penalty sentencings and executions are related to race. In fact, the mentally retarded who have been condemned to death are disproportionately Black.

As FIGURE 5.3 depicts, eighteen (75 %) of those with finalized sentences were Blacks, and six (25 %) were Whites. The percentage of Blacks is far greater than it is of Death Row inmates nationally (40 %)[4] and than in the general United States population (12.1 %).[5]

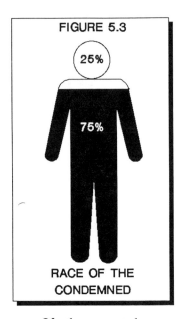

FIGURE 5.3

25%

75%

RACE OF THE CONDEMNED

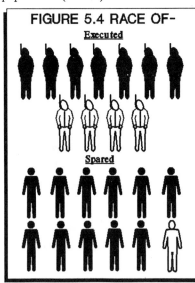

FIGURE 5.4 RACE OF-

Executed

Spared

Of the executed, seven (two-thirds) were black, and four (one-fourth) were white. Of the twelve spared, ten (83 %) were black and two (17 %) were white. FIGURE 5.4 depicts these proportions.

As the figure suggests, there are no significant differences in the race distribution of the executed and the spared.[6] Differences in race cannot be shown to be related to outcome.

I.Q. AND OUTCOME

> *Look at death row, look who's there. Retarded people. . . .*
> --Reverend Joseph Ingle, *Strange Fruit*

The I.Q.s of the mentally retarded murderers are distributed across three ranges (moderate - 36-50, mild - 51-70, and low borderline - 70-79).[7] The lowest I.Q., that of Johnny Westbrook, may be as low as twenty-five (severe) or as high as fifty (moderate), but cannot be accurately measured because it is so low. Willie Celestine, who has tested between sixty-nine and eighty-one, and Ronald Monroe, who has tested between seventy-three and seventy-seven, have the highest I.Q.s. The largest group in the sample are in the middle sixties and clustered around the average of sixty-three.

The range of the I.Q.s of the executed varied between a bottom of sixty-two and a top of seventy-seven. The average was sixty-eight. The range of I.Q.s of the reprieved was slightly lower, between a minimum of twenty-five to fifty and a maximum of seventy-five. The average for the reprieved was fifty-nine. FIGURE 5.5 shows the distribution of I.Q.s.

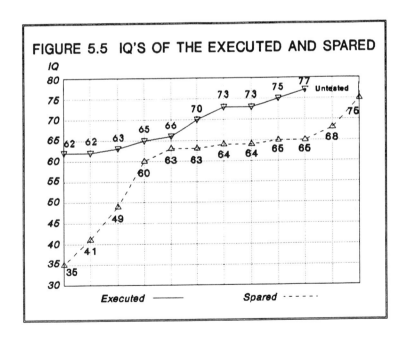

FIGURE 5.5 IQ'S OF THE EXECUTED AND SPARED

As the graph suggests, there is a solid relationship between I.Q, and execution. The I.Q.s of the spared are significantly lower than those of the executed. A reasonable pattern in discretionary and individualized death penalty outcomes is evident. The higher the I.Q. of a person with mental retardation, the more likely is he to be executed.[8] Theoretically, persons with lower I.Q.s are able to comprehend less, are less culpable, and should not be held accountable for their actions by execution. It is a hopeful sign that decision makers in some instances recognize the disabilities of the more seriously retarded and do not execute them.

Nonetheless, persons with I.Q.s in the borderline or upper range of mild retardation still lack complete comprehension and culpability. They too should not be subjected to the death penalty.

EDUCATIONAL LEVEL AND EXECUTION

> *A sixth grade educational level is required to comprehend the meaning of Miranda rights.*
> Dr. Stephen Mechanick, *Delaware v. Joseph Shields*

The educational level of the murderers with mental retardation is understandably low. Many were African American children growing up in the South where special education programs were sparse for white children, and non-existent for minorities in segregated school systems. Many children with mental retardation dropped out of regular schools in the early grades because teachers found them impossible to teach in full classrooms of normal children. Thus two offenders in the sample (Fleming and Westbrook) had no formal education. None of the persons in the sample group achieved high school diplomas. The highest grade completed by any person was the eleventh. The average years in school was 7.2 years.

The average level of education, like the average I.Q., is a statistically important factor in why persons with mental retardation are executed or spared. The higher the educational level, the more likely the person was to be executed. The average years in school of persons who were spared was five years; of the executed, 8.4 years.[9] FIGURE 5.6 compares the average grades completed of the two groups.

Lack of education seems to be taken into account in the determination of final outcome. Persons with more education are apparently held more responsible and accountable because they are better able to understand the implications of their crimes. Those with little formal education are presumably spared in greater proportions because it is more apparent to prosecutors, judges and juries that they are not able to understand Miranda warnings, court proceedings, the seriousness and implications of their crimes, and the meaning of execution. The relationship between education and outcome makes sense.

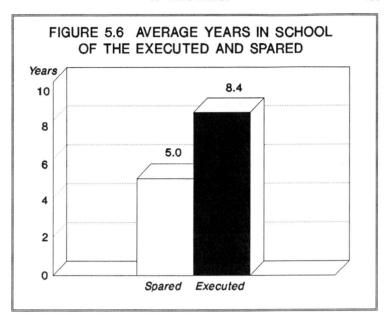

FIGURE 5.6 AVERAGE YEARS IN SCHOOL OF THE EXECUTED AND SPARED

MARITAL STATUS

The marital status of mentally retarded murderers is related to whether they are executed or not. Those who were married at the time of the crime or had been previously married were less likely to be executed than those who were not married or had never been married.[10] Six of the men in the sample had been or were married at the time of the crime. Two of these were killed. The other four were spared. Of the sixteen unmarried, nine were executed, and seven were spared.[11] Thus the chances for execution of the married are one in three (thirty-three percent), but the chances of the unmarried are more than one in two (fifty-three percent).

THE "FEAR AND SYMPATHY" SYNDROME: AGE AND EXECUTION

> . . . it degrades society . . . . the United States is one of the few places that executes children.
>
> --Darryl Bell, *Checkmate*

The age at which a mentally retarded offender commits a crime is strongly predictive of whether he is spared, or whether he dies at the hands of the executioner. The younger the mentally retarded person is at the time of the crime, the more likely he or she is to be executed.

A significant difference exists between the average ages at the time of the crimes of those mentally retarded persons who were executed and the average ages of those who were not.[12] The executed were seventeen to twenty-five years old, with an average age of twenty-one when they murdered. Those who were reprieved ranged from seventeen to forty-six years old when they committed their crimes. They were an average thirty years old at the time of the crimes, nine years more than the executed. FIGURE 5.7 graphs the difference in the ages at the time of the crime of the executed and surviving.

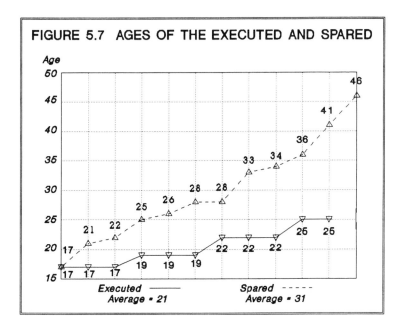

FIGURE 5.7 AGES OF THE EXECUTED AND SPARED

A possible theoretical explanation for the relationship between the murderer's age at the time the crime was committed and whether he is executed or not is the "fear and sympathy syndrome." Younger men are to be feared, while older men garner sympathy.

A young, wild-eyed man with little understanding of societal norms and few brakes on his violent behavior seems more dangerous and likely to commit additional murders or violent crimes if he is allowed to live, even in prison. Such a person was Dalton Prejean, fourteen when he committed his first homicide, and seventeen when he cold-bloodedly murdered a policeman for which he was executed. The young man seems more virile and has a longer life expectancy in which to anticipate additional violent offenses.

Similarly, the ages of older men with mental retardation may work in their favor. They do not elicit fear, so much as sympathy. A generally accepted phenomenon of criminal offenders is that they tend to "burn out" with age. The older they get, the fewer crimes they commit. An older murderer with mental retardation has this factor working in his favor.

Further, someone who obviously has already spent a lifetime of retardation without hope for a future cure looks pathetic. A statement such as that made by Limmie Arthur in relation to his inability to understand court proceedings is on point.[13] Arthur was twenty-five at the time of the crime. Such a person is more likely to gain compassion when it comes time for decision makers to determine the last chance, life or death decision.

Nonetheless, executing the young and sparing the mature is a sort of reverse age discrimination. Age, like race, should not be a determinant of life and death decisions. Young African Americans with very limited intelligence should not be the primary recipients of the death penalty and execution. Such disparity evidences racial discrimination.

AGE AND DEATH ROW LENGTH OF STAY

> *Justice without speed is undesirable.   Speed without justice, however, is unthinkable.*
>
> John Curtain[14]

The ages at the time of the sentence outcome (executed, or given reprieve) of murderers with mental retardation differ according to their ages when they committed the crime and their length of stay on Death Row.

The average executed man with mental retardation was 29.7 years old when he died, having spent 8.6 years on Death Row. The average man with mental retardation who was spared from execution was 38.5 years old when told of the pardon, having spent 8.0 years on Death Row. However, this slight difference in length of stay is not statistically significant.[15]

The age differences at outcome, nevertheless, are not random.[16] Because both the executed and the spared spend about the same time on Death Row (8.3 years), the differences between the two groups' average ages at the time of determination are related to their average age at the time the crime was committed.[17] The younger a person was when the crime was committed, the younger he was likely to be when his life or death future was determined.

The average length of stay of all the executed in the U. S. is eight years.[18] This is slightly less than that of the executed murderer with mental retardation (8.3 years). That it takes a bit longer on the average to execute those with mental retardation than the average may reflect that the decision concerning the intellectually handicapped is more carefully pondered and more warily implemented, although the outcome is the same in the end.

Although the average length of stay on Death Row of an executed man with mental retardation is 8.3 years, this number covers a wide variation in times ranging from no time (Edgington) to fourteen years (Jones).

Crimes committed between 1976 and 1978 during the first three years after the reinstatement of the death penalty by the Supreme Court took longer to resolve than those crimes committed in 1981 or thereafter. This difference is probably a function of the uncertainty in the early years that surrounds implementation of any new policy of serious consequences. The final outcomes of persons with mental retardation sentenced early in the death penalty reinstatement period were decided with more hesitation than were those of men who committed their crimes four or more years later. FIGURE 5.8 shows the number of years spent on Death Row of those offenders with mental retardation who were executed and spared.

CRIMINAL HISTORY AND OUTCOME

Did you know that a third of Florida's death row is there for its first offense? First offense, and they are on death row.
Reverend Joseph Ingle, *Strange Fruit*

Criminal history, that is, the number and severity of crimes committed prior to the instant crime, is ordinarily one of the most significant factors that influences sentencing. Where sentencing guidelines have been adopted,[19] criminal history, usually measured as prior convictions, incarcerations or probations, along with the severity of the current offense, are the major factors determining whether the offender receives prison or probation, and for how long.

Comparably, criminal history should be jurisprudentially related to whether an offender with mental retardation, first, receives the death penalty, and second, is eventually executed.

Many states which have the death penalty use criminal history or lack thereof as a statutory aggravating and mitigating factor in the sentencing process.[20]

However, the actual execution/reprieval experience does not confirm the first hypothesis. Two of the men with mental retardation (Stanley and Waye) who were condemned to death had no prior criminal activity. Some had only a few minor or petty crimes in their past. Some had more serious records with several non-violent and/or violent felony convictions. Finally, some had very severe criminal histories, including six men with previous killings and other numerous violent crimes. Despite this diversity of criminal histories, all of the men were sentenced to death, so that criminal history does not seem to be related to the sentence. FIGURE 5.9 pictures the distribution of the prior records of the persons with mental retardation studied here. Note that the criminal histories of two persons (Anderson and Holloway) are unknown.

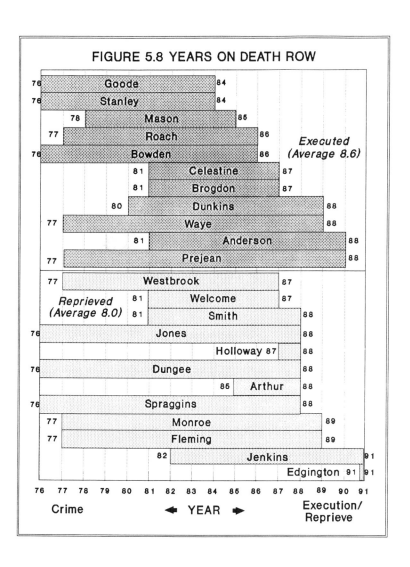

FIGURE 5.8 YEARS ON DEATH ROW

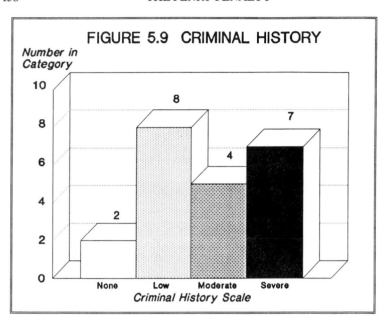

FIGURE 5.9 CRIMINAL HISTORY

Some rationality exists in the fact that only one of eight persons with minor records was executed. That four of the six men with prior homicides and the one person (Celestine) with a long, violent criminal history were executed makes sense. That two men with prior homicides were spared does not. That half of the four persons with moderately severe records were executed, and half were spared is inexplicable. Similarly, there is little reasonableness in the execution of the two men with no prior criminal records.

In sum, FIGURE 5.10 illustrates that although the beginnings of a reasonable pattern in the outcomes of mentally retarded murderers exists based on the degree of prior criminal activity,[21] disparity in outcomes continues to exist.

The lack of a significantly proportionate pattern in outcome based on a mentally retarded offender's prior record again illustrates the inequitable disparity that occurs when discretion is allowed in the determination of the sentence. A murderer who has previously killed should be more likely to get the death penalty than one who has never been convicted of a crime before. But this is not the case.

Unfortunately, when different governors, different prosecutors, different appellate courts, and different juries in different states determine the outcome, the mentally retarded offender's prior criminal record has

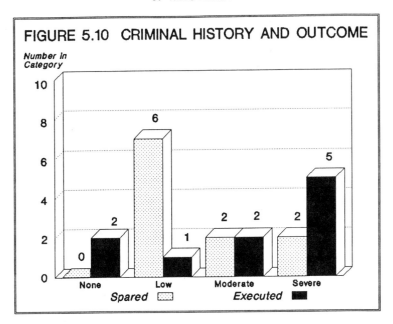

FIGURE 5.10 CRIMINAL HISTORY AND OUTCOME

virtually no rational relationship to the result. Since prior records are not used in any consistent way in the determination of the outcome, factors other than criminal history are unquestionably the final determinants of life or death.

MENTAL ILLNESS, CHILD ABUSE, BRAIN DAMAGE, AND OUTCOME

> . . . the people who are accused of these heinous crimes are victims of . . . broken homes and broken communities and neglect--they've been kicked around and brutalized.
>
> --Byron E. Eshelman, *Death Row Chaplain*

Mental illness, physical and psychological abuse in childhood, and brain damage, are factors which occur with some frequency in the life histories of mentally retarded murderers. Since they bear on the culpability of the perpetrator, they should also be factors in the determination of final outcome.

Mental Illness. Ample evidence of their mental illness was presented in the trials of eight of the mentally retarded murderers (Brogdon, Edgington, Fleming, Goode, Jones, Mason, Prejean and Spraggins) in this study. Four of these (Brogdon, Goode, Mason and Prejean) were executed.

The executions of two, Brogdon and Prejean, occurred in 1987 and 1990, respectively, without regard to the U.S. Supreme Court's 1986 dictum in *Ford v. Wainwright*[22] which made such executions constitutionally suspect. Thus evidence of mental illness did not mitigate the outcome in two of the determined cases despite *Wainwright*.

Four of the mentally ill persons were spared from execution. The jury refused to sentence Edgington to death; appeals courts overturned the sentence of Fleming and Jones; and, after Spraggins' death sentence was remanded for the third time, the prosecutor decided not try the case again and to accept a plea bargain.

Thus half of those dually diagnosed with mental illness and retardation were executed. Slightly less than half (forty-four percent) of the persons with mental retardation who were not mentally ill met this fate. The differences in outcome rates between the mentally ill and those who were not are not great enough to show a definitive pattern.[23]

The lack of a significant difference in the rates of execution of persons with mental retardation who were also mentally ill and those who were not mentally ill reflects the disparity of executions. Mental illness does not mitigate the execution rate as mitigating circumstances generally should and as *Wainwright* suggests mental illness ought. If anything, mental illness increases rather than lessens the rate of execution of offenders with mental retardation, further exacerbating the irrationality of the application of capital punishment.

Childhood Abuse and Brain Damage. Child abuse and brain damage, like mental illness are mitigating factors. A child who is abused learns from parents or other authority figures that physical violence and degradation are the way that others should be treated. Without intervention, the abused frequently grow up to be abusers.[24] An abused mentally retarded person has little if any capability to sort out the propriety, morality, and legality of learned physical violence and abusive behavior. Thus child abuse becomes a mitigating factor because it lessens culpability.

Similarly, physical damage to the brain impinges on its normal functioning. Brain damage, an organic correlate of mental retardation, interferes with intelligence, impulse control, and other factors that influence behavior. To the extent that a damaged brain causes erratic behavior, a person's guilt and culpability are lessened. Thus brain damage should also be treated as a mitigating factor in sentencing.

Seven of the offenders in the sample were known to have been abused as children and suffered brain damage either as a result of this childhood abuse or from some other factor. Three of these (Brogdon, Anderson and Prejean) were executed despite the evidence that child abuse and brain damage were significant factors in their behavior and that they were not totally responsible for their actions.

Four of the men in the sample (Edgington, Fleming, Jenkins and Welcome) were spared. The defense for Son Fleming presented evidence of his brain damage which resulted from shotgun wounds to the face and head as a adult. This evidence was vital to the Georgia Supreme Court's vacating of his sentence.[25] The fact that Herbert Welcome was tormented and abused by his aunt and her lover whom he murdered was important in the decision of Louisiana Governor Edwin Edwards to commute Welcome's sentence to life. The mental condition of Leonard Jenkins who was abused by an alcoholic father as a child was given as the reason for a similar commutation of the death penalty by Ohio Governor Richard Celeste. Similarly, Gary Edgington was also abused by an alcoholic father. Edgington's defense lawyer continually placed this factor and Edgington's mental retardation before the jury which subsequently refused to order his execution.

Thus child abuse and brain damage have worked to prevent the execution of some few murderers with mental retardation. But it has failed to influence the outcome of others, as it should. This lack of universality results in sentencing disparity and inequitably, that is, treatment of similar offenders differently.

Sum. To summarize, mental illness, brain damage and child abuse have no consistent effect on the outcome of the death sentences of offenders with mental retardation. These factors should mitigate the crime and reduce the penalty. Yet they do not consistently have that effect. If anything, like mental retardation itself, they increase rather than decrease the chances of execution.

When discretion and individualized sentencing occur in death penalty cases, rationally determined, equitable outcomes are lost. Execution is inconsistently applied.

CIRCUMSTANCES OF THE CRIME

The circumstances surrounding the crime, like the criminal's characteristics should be determinants of the severity of the punishment and the life or death outcome. Crime characteristics that are ordinarily considered as sentencing factors include the violence of the crime and whether the offender was the principal offender or not.

Some characteristics should not influence sentencing, but do. Geographic location and the time period in which the crime was committed are such factors. This section examples these crime circumstances in detail.

STATES AND THE DEATH PENALTY

In the states of Virginia, Alabama and Louisiana blacks account for 85% of all executions through history.
--Watt Espy, *American Gothic*

The two dozen condemned men whose stories are told in the previous chapters were tried, convicted and condemned predominantly in eight southern "Death Belt"[26] states. Georgia was the locus of more than one-third (eight) of the cases. Five cases (22 %) originated in Louisiana. Two each came from Texas (9 %) and Virginia (9 %). Alabama, Florida, Illinois, Mississippi, Ohio and South Carolina each sentenced one man (4 %). Only two cases (9 %) derived from states outside the South (Illinois and Ohio). In both of these cases, the defendants' lives were spared. No person with mental retardation has been executed outside of the South. FIGURE 5.11 displays the states in which the murderers with mental retardation were executed or spared.

Although Georgia has condemned the most murderers with mental retardation who have had a final decision made, it has executed only two (25 %) of them - Ivon Stanley in 1984 and Jerome Bowden, in 1986. The public outcry at Bowden's execution brought almost immediate results in the form of the original state statute[27] to ban the execution of all persons with mental retardation. Public opinion and the law prevented any of the other six from meeting the same fate. After 1986, the remaining murderers with mental retardation on Georgia's Death Row (Westbrook in 1987, William Smith, Dungee, Holloway and Spraggins in 1988, and Fleming in 1989) were all spared.

Of the five killers with mental retardation in Louisiana who have been condemned to death and whose outcome has been determined, the executioner has taken three (60 %)(Celestine, Brogdon, Prejean). In raw numbers, Louisiana leads in these executions.

South Carolina has condemned two men with definitive outcomes. One was executed (Roach), and one was spared (Arthur).

Virginia has electrocuted both (100 %) of its condemned men (Mason and Waye). Alabama (Dunkins), Florida (Goode) and Texas (Anderson) have each killed the only condemned man (100 %) in their states whose outcome has been finalized. Ohio (Jenkins) and Illinois (Edgington), the two states outside of the South in the sample, have both spared their only murderers with mental retardation whose outcomes have been determined. FIGURE 5.12 shows the death penalty states' sentencing and execution decisions regarding persons with mental retardation.

Where a killer with mental retardation commits a murder is important in whether he lives or dies. Based on past experience, he or she has the best chances of being spared in Illinois and Ohio, the two northern states that have faced the issue. Both have spared 100 % of their murderers with mental retardation whose outcomes have been determined.

In the South, Mississippi (100 %), Georgia (60 %), South Carolina and Louisiana (40 %) have the best rates of sparing persons with mental retardation. Even though Alabama, Florida and Texas have executed only

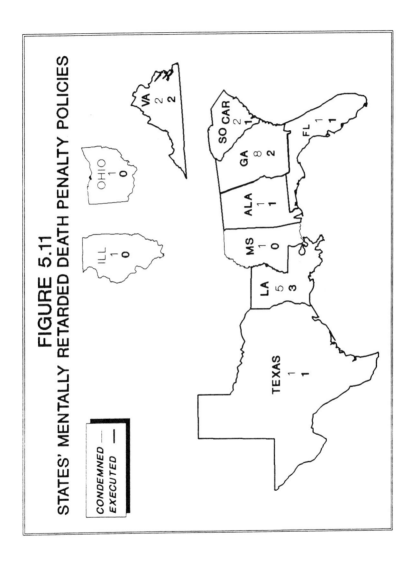

FIGURE 5.11
STATES' MENTALLY RETARDED DEATH PENALTY POLICIES

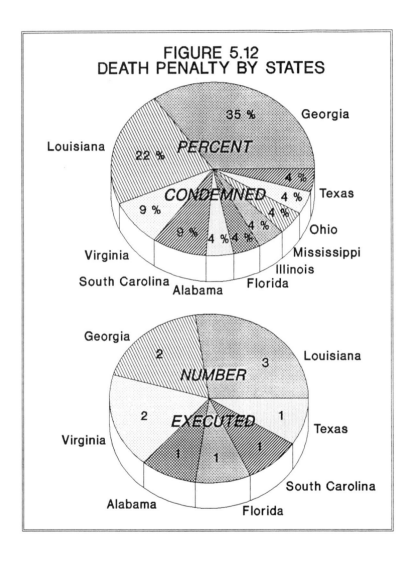

FIGURE 5.12
DEATH PENALTY BY STATES

one each, chances for survival in those states are poor to none. They have pardoned no murderers with mental retardation.

Since no evidence can be found of capital punishment inflicted on any person with mental retardation in any of the other twenty-six death penalty states, inside[28] or outside the South,[29] the unmistakable conclusion is that murderers with mental retardation elsewhere than in the seven punitive southern states have virtually no chance of being executed. This penalty is limited exclusively to the South.

Discrepancy in the outcome is related to geography. If a person with mental retardation by accident of birth or residence happens to commit a capital crime in the executing Death Belt states, he or she has a far greater chance of dying for the crime than if the crime is committed in any of the other states with or without the death penalty. Virtually no chance exists of actual execution outside these few southern states.

YEAR OF THE CRIME

> *People now . . . are upset about killing retarded people . . . . And*
> *that is something that is different from five years ago.*
> --Clive Stafford Smith, *An Englishman Abroad*

The intellectually disabling effects of mental retardation were unknown in the late 1970s and early 1980s and only recently have begun to be disseminated. Thus one would expect that the earlier the crime was committed during the last two decades, the more likely would execution be the outcome for the offender with mental retardation. This is true.

The crimes of the executed were committed significantly earlier than those of the spared.[30] All crimes of the executed were committed between 1976 and 1981. No crimes committed after 1981 have been punished by execution, and the years the crimes were committed of those spared have extended into 1989.

Similarly, there is a significant difference in the year of the final decision between the executed and the spared. The determination of the outcome is significantly earlier for those who were executed compared to those who have been spared.[31] All eleven executions took place between 1984 and 1990. The last occurred on May 16, 1990. The decisions to spare the lives of murderers with mental retardation took place between 1985 and 1991, with more than eight in ten made between 1988 and 1991.

Clearly, a change is occurring. More people with mental retardation have been spared from execution in the last part of the eighties and the early nineties than in the early part of the eighties. Some slowing of executions is occurring. The general opposition of the public to such executions, the passage of the federal ban on them, and the increasing numbers of states providing legislative prohibitions[32] are apparently having an effect.

However, the executions continue despite the outrage in Georgia over the execution of Jerome Bowden in 1986 and the *Penry* decision in 1989, and because of the substance of *Penry*. Two men with mental retardation (Prejean and Anderson) were executed in 1990. The *Penry* dictum with case-by-case decision making has not worked to prevent all executions of persons with mental retardation.

VIOLENCE AND EXECUTION

> . . . the offense of murder was outrageously and wantonly vile, horrible and inhuman in that it involved torture to the victim and depravity of mind on the part of the defendant.
>
> *Death Penalty Statutes*[33]

It goes without saying that all murders are violent. Yet there are degrees of violence. A sadistic, premeditated murder of multiple victims involving rape, torture, cruelty and excessive brutality is more violent than one that was unpremeditated but resulted when the perpetrator responded to a single victim's defense attempts in the course of a robbery or rape, when the victim(s) had tormented the killer because of his mental retardation, when the subject was an accomplice and played a minor role in the murder, or when the victim was shot and died without prolonged torment. Thus the crimes of the sample group of murderers with mental retardation can be classified as excessively and severely violent or not excessively violent. A severely violent crime involves brutality, rape, and/or infliction of extended mental anguish and/or physical pain. A crime of low violence is one which involves no rape, torture, prolonged victim suffering and no premeditation. It may have resulted from victim provocation.

Twelve (55 %) of the people with mental retardation perpetrated the most severely violent crimes. Of these, eight (67 %) were executed, and four (33 %) were spared.

The executed are Arthur Goode, self-declared pedophile, who tortured and murdered little boys; Ivon Stanley, who with another man, kidnapped a businessman, beat him multiple times with a hammer and shovel, forced him to lie in a shallow grave where he was buried alive; Morris Mason who tied his seventy-one year old victim to a chair, nailed one of her hands to it, hit her with an axe and set her house on fire causing her to burn to death; Terry Roach who, along with two other young men, selected a teenage couple at random on Lover's Lane, shot the boy, gang raped the girl and shot her multiple times in the back of the head; Willie Celestine who broke into an old woman's home in the middle of the night, raped her, beat her face to a pulp, and strangled her to death; John Brogdon who together with another teenager, raped, tortured and murdered an eleven-year-old girl; Horace Dunkins, Jr. who, on the afternoon of the crime declared he was out to "get some pussy from a White lady"[34] and randomly selected a white mother of four to rape and mutilate with sixty-six knife lacerations all over her body, including wounds to the pelvic cavity; and Alton Waye who raped a woman who came to the door when he knocked in the middle of the night, used a butcher knife from her kitchen to stab her forty-two times, and beat her face until it was beyond recognition.

Persons with mental retardation who were eventually pardoned and whose crimes were extraordinarily violent include Johnny Westbrook who, with an accomplice, raped a woman, kidnapped her and forced her to drive to a bank to withdraw money for him, took another woman who came to her aid along with them, and beat them both to death with a board; George Dungee who participated in the rape, mutilation and shooting death of Mary Alday; Limmie Arthur who murdered his drinking partner with multiple blows of an axe; and Eddie Lee Spraggins who raped and stabbed his female victim multiple times, partially disemboweling her.

The crimes of eleven persons with mental retardation are less severe and without excessive violence. Three (33 %) among these were executed. These include Jerome Bowden, who did not rape or torture his fifty-five year old female victim, but hit her twice with a gun butt, crushing her skull; Larry Anderson who was duped into being the trigger man by his relatives in the shooting death of his brother-in-law in a plot they hatched to collect insurance; and Dalton Prejean who shot a policeman who had stopped his car because the officer roughed up his brother.

Eight persons whose crimes were not excessively violent (73 %) were pardoned. These include Herbert Welcome who shot his aunt and her boyfriend in a fight after years of being ridiculed and tormented by them for having mental retardation; William Smith who only intended to rob and not murder "Old Dan," the storekeeper, but killed him in an impulsive reaction when he came after Smith with a hammer; Son Fleming, who together with two other men shot and killed a local sheriff in a swamp; Ronald Monroe, who allegedly climbed in the window of his next door neighbor in the middle of the night and stabbed her seven times, causing her to bleed to death, because he had been evicted from his home; Larry Jones who hit a robbery victim over the head with a wrench: Leonard Jenkins who shot and killed a police officer during the coarse of a bank robbery; Jerome Holloway who beat his elderly victim to death with a stick and a kerosene lamp: and, Gary Edgington who held the female teenage victim while his accomplice stabbed her but did not physically harm her himself.

FIGURE 5.13 compares the relative violence quotients of the murders committed by the twenty-three persons with mental retardation and their final life or death fate.

The numbers displayed in the graph show the beginnings of a relationship between the violence severity of the crime and the execution/spared ratio. As the crime's brutality increases, the chances of being executed seem to become greater. This apparent difference in the average violence quotient of the executed and spared is almost statistically

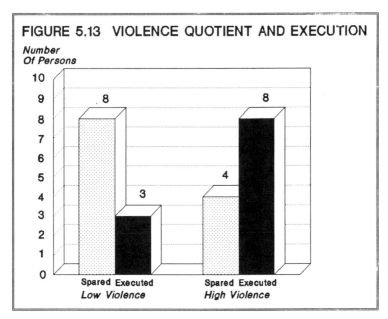

FIGURE 5.13   VIOLENCE QUOTIENT AND EXECUTION

significant.[35]

If rational outcomes prevail, then the persons who committed the most violent crimes should be executed, and those who did not commit excessively violent crimes should be spared. This is close to being the case.

LEADERS AND FOLLOWERS: PERPETRATORS AND ACCESSORIES

> *The hand of one is the hand of all.*
> *--Principle of the Common Law*[36]

Eight (36 %) of the offenders in the sample were the sole perpetrators of their crimes. An equal number (36 %) acted in concert with one other person. Four persons with mental retardation (17 %) had two accomplices. Three in the sample (13 %) had three accomplices in their crimes. FIGURE 5.14 illustrates this.

Of the eight persons who acted alone in their crimes, three (37 %) have been executed. Five (63 %) have had their death sentences reduced. Thus mentally retarded persons acting alone have a greater chance of being spared than executed.

The eight offenders who acted in concert with one other person when

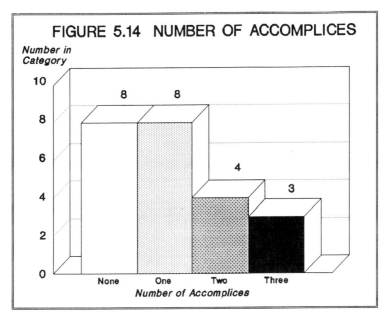

FIGURE 5.14   NUMBER OF ACCOMPLICES

they committed the crime have exactly the opposite ratio in outcome. Five (63 %) were executed and three (37 %) were spared.

Half (50 %) of the four persons who had two accomplices, and two-thirds (67 %) of those with three accomplices, respectively, were executed. One of each classification (33 %) was spared. FIGURE 5.15 shows these percents.

Theoretically, what happens to mentally retarded persons with co-defendants should be reasonably related to whether they were the leader and principal offender or a mere accessory who followed another person of more wit and cunning. Nevertheless, in most states the law holds all participants in a murder equally responsible, even though principal perpetrators are logically more responsible and accountable than accessories who are led into a crime by another person who is the instigator.

Similarly, as more persons participate in a crime, responsibility becomes diluted, and the mentally retarded person may not be as ultimately accountable as if he acted alone.

FIGURE 5.15 shows the exact opposite of theory. Relatively more of the sole perpetrators were spared (five men) than executed (three men). The majority of those who acted with one or more other persons (eight of fifteen) were executed. This apparent anomaly has no statistical import.[37]

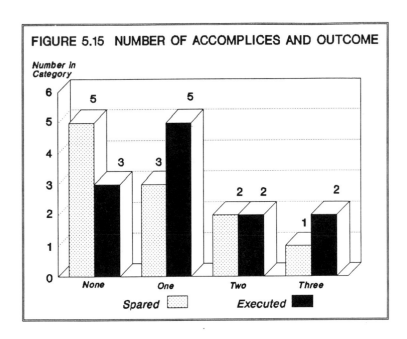

FIGURE 5.15 NUMBER OF ACCOMPLICES AND OUTCOME

Just as the common law and many state statutes hold that it should, whether a mentally retarded person was the leader, instigator and principal offender or an accessory who was led or coerced by others to participate in the crime makes no difference in outcome.[38]

WEAPONS USED

Guns and knives are the weapons of choice of mentally retarded murderers. Seven people used guns, while six used knives. Four of the offenders using knives also employed secondary methods (a hammer, gun butt, fists and fire) to beat or burn, as well as stab, their victims to death. The remaining nine used a variety of weapons to bludgeon or chop their victims to death, including an axe, a two-by-four board, an unidentified blunt object, a kerosene lamp and stick, a wrench, a brick and broken glass, and strangulation.

The choice of weapon makes no difference whatsoever in the outcome of the sentence. The weapon used is not a factor in the final sentence determination.[39]

VICTIM CHARACTERISTICS

The most difficult cases to talk about are the heinous murders of young children, [and] helpless victims of some kind . . . .
James W. L. Park, *Amazing Grace*

Several characteristics of victims may be related to the outcome of perpetrators who commit capital crimes. These include the number of victims, their race, gender, age, and whether they are handicapped or not. This section looks at each of these characteristics in sequence.

NUMBERS OF VICTIMS

Generally speaking, the murder of more than one victim is considered to be an aggravating circumstance. The more victims, the worse the crime. Thus mentally retarded murderers who killed multiple victims during the crime or in a crime spree over several days should theoretically have a greater chance of being executed than those who killed just one person.

As FIGURE 5.16 shows, seventeen people in the sample (74 %) were subjected to the death penalty for killing one victim, and six persons (26 %) killed multiple victims.

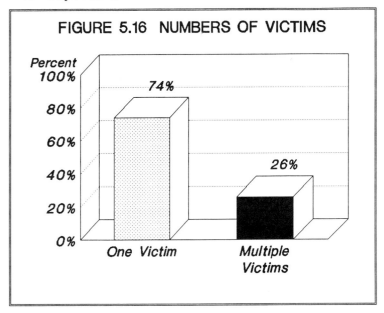

FIGURE 5.16 NUMBERS OF VICTIMS

Of the seventeen persons with mental retardation with a single victim, eight (47 %) were executed and nine (53 %) were spared. Of the six with multiple victims, half were executed, and half were spared. These figures show that there is only a marginal difference in the final outcomes of offenders with one and multiple victims. FIGURE 5.17 shows this virtual lack of differences in the rates of execution and reprieve of persons with one and multiple victims.

The chart illustrates that the number of victims has absolutely no relationship to whether a mentally retarded murderer lives or dies.[40] The decision to spare or execute is clearly related to other factors than the number of victims.

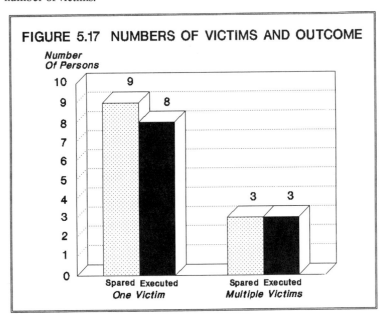

FIGURE 5.17 NUMBERS OF VICTIMS AND OUTCOME

THE "RACE-OF-THE-VICTIM" EFFECT[41]

> *Until we accept that a black life is just as vital to our well-being as a white life, we will remain the most violent people on earth.*
> --David Gergen, *Death on Our Doorsteps*[42]

In virtually every study that has been conducted on the subject, the results have shown that the race of the victim in any murder is related to the imposition of capital punishment. When the victim is white, the perpetrator is far more likely to receive the death penalty than when the victim is black.[43] This analysis of the victims of mentally retarded killers affirms that conclusion. It also shows that once the sentence is imposed, it is far more likely to be carried out if the victim was white than if the victim was African American.[44]

As FIGURE 5.18 shows, seventeen (74 %) of the victims of the killers in the sample were white. Five (22 %) were African American. One person (Welcome - 4 %) had both a black and white victim.

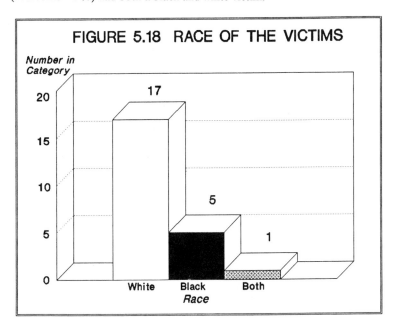

FIGURE 5.18 RACE OF THE VICTIMS

Thus a person with mental retardation who kills a White is 2.5 times as likely to get the death penalty as one who kills an African American.

Of the seventeen murderers who killed white victims, eleven (65 %) were executed, and six (35 %) were spared. However, of the six persons who killed African Americans (including Welcome), none was executed. If a person with mental retardation kills a white person, then the execution chances are almost two in three. If he or she kills an African American, there is virtually no chance that execution will follow upon the death sentence.

In sum, with discretionary sentencing, racial discrimination is blatant. Black on White gives a substantial chance of being executed, but Black on Black is not worth dying for. FIGURE 5.19 compares outcomes based on the victims' race.

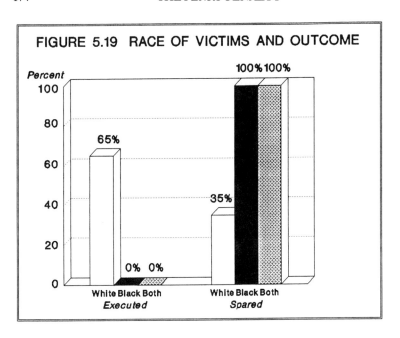

FIGURE 5.19   RACE OF VICTIMS AND OUTCOME

GENDER AND SEXUAL ASSAULT

Female victims are considered more vulnerable than male victims because of their generally lesser physical strength and ability to defend themselves from a stronger male aggressor. Where the female victim was raped, the crime is doubly aggravated by both vulnerability and the grave psychological and physical harm of rape.

Thirteen (52 %) of the primary victims in the sample were females.[45] The killers of six of these (46 %) were executed, but seven (54 %) were spared. Ten of the victims (48 %) were males. Half of the ten men who killed male victims were executed, and half were spared. The one person who killed both his aunt and her boyfriend was also spared. As FIGURE 5.20 depicts, the outcome of the mentally retarded death penalty is completely insensitive to victim gender.[46]

When the targets of the crimes are also raped or sodomized, as with nine of the victims, the likelihood of execution should increase. However, this is not the case. As FIGURE 5.20 also shows, the chances of the mentally retarded perpetrator being executed do increase slightly when a murder victim is also sexually assaulted, but this increase is not statistically significant.[47]

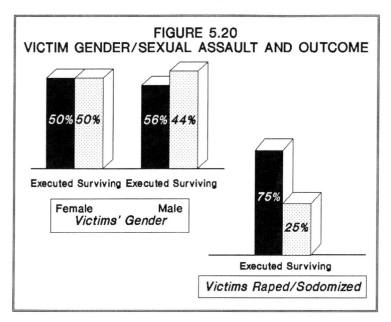

FIGURE 5.20
VICTIM GENDER/SEXUAL ASSAULT AND OUTCOME

Thus the outcome for mentally retarded murderers is not dependant in any fashion on the victim's gender and whether a sexual assault occurred or not. Other factors account for which mentally retarded killers are executed and which are spared.

AGE VULNERABILITY

Age, like the sex of the victim, is theoretically related to crime severity and sentence outcome. Children and elderly victims are more vulnerable to crime because of their years. In rational sentencing schemes,[48] crime severity is aggravated when the victim is either young or old.

The victims of mentally retarded killers are frequently children or the elderly. Three victims in this sample were under eighteen. Eight were over sixty. This high rate of age-handicapped victims (49 %) occurs because the mentally retarded tend to associate with children who are more similar to them emotionally and intellectually than their age-specific peers. Alternatively, the mentally retarded may validate their own self-worth by associating with and helping older people who are not fully mentally or physically functional because of their extensive years. Many elderly may need the assistance that a mentally retarded person is willing to give them in return for the elderly person's friendship, that which they cannot get from people their own age who are so far superior in intellectual capabilities than they.[49] Thus the victims may become those very people who have befriended them and who are excessively vulnerable because of their age.

Of the eleven persons who killed victims who were age vulnerable, six (55 %) were executed, and five (45 %) were spared. Of the twelve who killed adults, five (42 %) were executed and seven (58 %) were spared. These differences in the rates of execution based on the age vulnerability of the victim are not statistically significant.[50] Thus despite the legal principle which holds that a child or elderly murder victim creates an aggravating circumstance, age handicapped victims did not work consistently to determine the outcome among this sample of mentally retarded offenders. FIGURE 5.21 displays the distribution of the executed and the spared based on victim vulnerability.

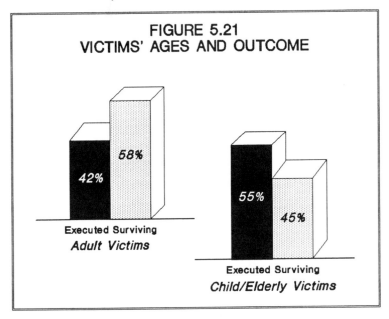

PHYSICAL HANDICAP

One last victim trait - vulnerability because of physical handicap - requires analysis. Three men, Arthur, Bowden, and Welcome, attacked or murdered handicapped victims. Of these three, one was executed (Bowden), and two (Welcome and Arthur) have been spared. Thus although there were very few handicapped victims, when the victim is physically impaired, it apparently doesn't increase the probability of execution as theory suggests it should.

SUMMARY

RANDOMNESS OF OUTCOME

Based on the total sample of murderers with mental retardation who have had a final determination made, the chances of being executed or spared are exactly even. Half of those whose sentence outcomes are final have been killed. Half have been spared.

However, this apparent randomness disappears, and the picture of why persons with mental retardation are executed becomes clearer, when the characteristics of the perpetrators, the circumstances of the crime, and the characteristics of the victims are considered. Some characteristics have been shown to be significant and powerful predictors of execution. The next section summarizes these.

IMPORTANT CHARACTERISTICS IN OUTCOME

The younger a murderer is at the time of the crime, the more likely he or she is to be executed. The average age of the executed when they committed their crimes was twenty-one; of the spared, thirty-one.

The race of the victim is determinative in whether a person with mental retardation lives or dies. When the victim is white, the perpetrator is far more likely to be executed than when the victim is African American.

A general slowing of the rate of executions of persons with mental retardation occurred in the last part of the nineteen eighties and early nineteen nineties. As time has progressed beyond 1976 when the death penalty was reinstated, the chances of being executed have decreased. The majority of reprieves from the death penalty for persons with mental retardation occurred between 1988 and 1991, largely due to the passage of Georgia's statute banning the death penalty for offenders with mental retardation. No reprieve occurred prior to 1985.

Married or previously married offenders have a better chance of having their sentences vacated than those who have never been married.

Persons with I.Q.s in the borderline or upper level of mild retardation have somewhat greater chances of being executed than those in the lower level of the mild category or in the moderate or severe classifications.

Persons with more education have a greater chance of being executed than those with minimal or no formal education.

Murderers with mental retardation who committed their crimes in the South have far greater chances of being executed than those whose crimes were committed elsewhere in the United States. No persons with mental retardation have been executed outside the South. Chances of being saved

from execution are greatest in the Midwest.   Two people with mental
retardation have been spared there.

CHARACTERISTICS INSIGNIFICANT IN OUTCOME

Although theory suggests that some characteristics ought to be related
to whether a defendant is executed or spared, they could not be shown to
have such a relationship. These are summarized in this section.

Race is an important characteristic in whether a murderer with
mental retardation receives the death penalty. More than three out of four
murderers with mental retardation who have been given death sentences are
African Americans. However, there is no consistent difference in the race of
the executed and spared.

There is no significant difference in the time spent on Death Row of
the executed and spared. Both groups spent about eight years awaiting their
fates.

Although criminal history is an important factor in rational sentencing
schemes, it is not related to whether a person with mental retardation
receives the death sentence or is eventually executed or not. First offenders
were executed, and murderers with prior homicides were spared.

An offender who is dually diagnosed as both mentally ill and having
mental retardation is just as likely to be executed as one who is not mentally
ill. One who suffers from brain damage is equally likely to be executed as
one who is not brain damaged.

Murderers with mental retardation who were brutalized and abused
as children have just as great a chance of being executed as those who were
not.

Whether a crime was excessively violent or not makes no difference in
the outcome of murderers with mental retardation.

Whether the person with mental retardation was the sole perpetrator
or principal offender, whether he had one or more accomplices and was a
follower rather than instigator is unrelated to the final outcome.

Whether the victim was male or female has no relationship to
execution or reprieve. Equally unimportant is whether the victim was
sexually assaulted.

Whether the victim was age vulnerable, that is, a minor or an elderly
person, has no bearing on the final outcome. Similarly, whether the victim
was physically handicapped or not is unrelated to final outcome.

FIGURE 5.22 lists these characteristics in summary fashion.

FIGURE 5.22
SUMMARY OF CHARACTERISTICS AND OUTCOME

Significant	*Insignificant*
Perpetrator's Age	Perpetrator's Race
	Years on Death Row
Victim's Race	Criminal History
	Mental Illness
Year of the Crime	Child Abuse
	Brain Damage
Marital Status	Violence Quotient
IQ	Principal Offender/Accessory
	Number of Accomplices
Education	Victim's Gender
	Sexual Assault on the Victim
Crime's Location	Victim Age Vulnerability

A PREDICTION OF EXECUTION

The simple relationships between execution and the factors listed above (age at the time of the crime, race of the victim, year of the crime, marital status, offender's race, state in which the crime occurred, educational level, and I.Q.) were further investigated by additional statistical procedures.

Interestingly, the age of an offender with mental retardation when the instant crime was committed, and the person's I.Q., educational level, and marital status are highly interrelated.[51] The older the person was at the time of the crime, the lower was his I.Q., the fewer years of schooling did he have, and the more likely was he to be married. Older men had greater probabilities of being in the bottom rungs of intelligence with correspondingly lower educational levels. Younger murderers were unlikely to be married, were somewhat brighter (although still mentally retarded) and had correspondingly higher educational levels.

However, when all of the factors that are individually correlated to execution are considered together, the explanatory power of education, I.Q. and marital status disappear. Of these four, only age remains significantly important. This means, that where the mentally retarded are concerned, education, I.Q. and marital status are simply the accompaniments of age. Age is the really powerful predictor of whether a mentally retarded person is executed or not.

Second in importance in the prediction of execution is the race of the victim. The year of the crime also remains an important characteristic.[52] FIGURE 5.23 summarizes this statistical explanation of execution.

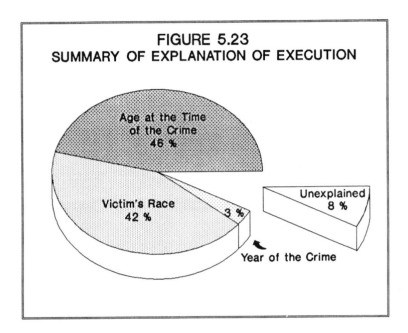

FIGURE 5.23
SUMMARY OF EXPLANATION OF EXECUTION

Age at the Time of the Crime 46 %

Victim's Race 42 %

3 %

Unexplained 8 %

Year of the Crime

CONCLUSIONS

The death sentence outcomes of mentally retarded murderers are exactly even and entirely random when no explanatory elements are taken into account. An offender with mental retardation is just as likely to be executed as not. When the circumstances of the crime, offender traits, and victim characteristics are studied, however, illuminating details of disquieting sentencing patterns emerge.

Many actors and factors shape the final decision to execute or not. These decision components should be rationally related to the outcome, that is, they should influence the life or death decision as reason, theory, sentencing standards and justice suggest they should. However, this is not always the case.

Some situational aspects make no sense at all. They do not influence the outcome when theory suggests they should. Factors without significant influence include the offender's criminal history, his mental illness, brain damage or childhood abuse, the victim's age or sex, and whether the victim was sexually assaulted or physically handicapped. None of these have any meaningful bearing on the life or death situations of offenders with mental retardation as rationality suggests they should.

Some independent decision components, in equity, should not be related to the executions of persons with mental retardation, but are. Or, they are inversely related to the outcome, that is, they have the opposite effect from what rational decision making dictates.

What this means *in toto* is that the discretion of the sentencing process does not lead to totally random outcomes. Nevertheless, whether a murderer with mental retardation ultimately lives or dies falls far short of rationality and equity. Disparity and discrimination exist in the outcome, especially when:

> younger offenders have far greater chances of being executed than older ones;

> the perpetrator is virtually certain to live if the victim is an African American, but when the victim is white, there is a high probability of being executed;

> execution chances were greater between 1976 and 1985 than after 1985;

> the married have a better chance of being spared from execution than the unmarried;

> offenders in the lower levels of mental retardation are spared more frequently than those in the higher levels;

> offenders with lower educational levels are spared more frequently than those with higher levels;

> the chances of dying are greater in certain areas of the South than in any other part of the country;

> nine out of ten men with mental retardation who receive the death sentence are African Americans.

Such discretionary discrimination and disparity dictate the demise of the death penalty for offenders with mental retardation. The 3-D's of sentencing offenders with mental retardation to death argue for its abolition. When crimes taking place in the seventies or early eighties continue to be punished by execution into the nineties even though the dehabilitating effects of mental retardation are more widely known, and public opinion is against it, then it ought to be stopped.

Discretion should be removed. Common decency cries out for a consistent determinative formula. The imposition of the death penalty on all people with mental retardation should be abolished. The empirical evidence from these death penalty cases of offenders with mental retardation dictates this response. In fairness, justice and equity, it allows no other.

¹*See* Chapter 3. A DEATH ROW DOZEN, and Chapter 4. THE SURVIVORS, *supra.*

²Ian Gray and Moira Stanley, eds., "Introduction," 16. This and the following quotes in this chapter, Watt Espy, "American Gothic," Reverend Joseph Ingle, "Strange Fruit," Darryl Bell, "Checkmate," Bryon Eshelman, "Death Row Chaplain," Clive Stafford Smith, "An Englishman Abroad," and James W.L.Park, "Amazing Grace," are taken from *A Punishment in Search of a Crime* (New York: Avon Books, 1989), pages 51, 144, 140, 155, 130, respectively.

³Nathanial Lipscomb, who committed his crime in 1959 and who was executed in 1961 is excluded from this analysis because his case is atypical, having occurred prior to the reauthorization of the death penalty by the Supreme Court in 1976.

⁴Lawrence A. Greenfield, "Capital Punishment 1990," Department of Justice, Bureau of Justice Statistics, 1991, 1.

⁵"40 % on Death Row Are Black People, New Figures Show," *New York Times*, 30 September 1991, sec. A.

⁶Pearson's R = -.293, probability = .241. T = 1.05 with 21 degrees of freedom and a two-tailed probability of .304, based on the pooled variance estimate.

⁷Reed, "Legal Rights," 412.

⁸The difference in the average I.Q.s of the two groups is close to being statistically significant. Pearson's R = .348, probability = .086. T = -1.87 with 20 degrees of freedom and a two-tailed probability of .076, based on the pooled variance estimate.

⁹For education and executed/spared, Pearson's R = .530, probability = .014. T = -2.42 with 15 degrees of freedom and a two-tailed probability of .029, based on the pooled variance estimate. The educational levels of five of the persons in the sample are unknown.

¹⁰Pearson's R = -.485, probability = .024. T = .93 with 20 degrees of freedom and a two-tailed probability of .292, based on the pooled variance estimate.

¹¹The marital status of one person (Spraggins) is unknown.

¹²Pearson's R = -.679, probability = .001. T = 3.21 with 21 degrees of freedom and a two-tailed probability of .001, based on the pooled variance estimate.

¹³Limmie Arthur stated that, "'I don't understand a whole lot of what was going on. . . . I had to listen real close . . . and I get lost very quick. . . . It's bad. It's bad to be retarded." *See* Marcus, "Retarded Killer's," sec. A.

¹⁴John Curtain, President, American Bar Association, quoted in Linda P. Campbell, "Death Row Appeal Process Mangles Notions of Fairness, Justice," *Chicago Tribune*, 19 May 1991, 12.

¹⁵Pearson's R = .088, probability = .344. T = -.41 with 21 degrees of freedom and a two-tailed probability of .688, based on the pooled variance estimate.

¹⁶T = 2.80 with 21 degrees of freedom and a two-tailed probability of .011, based on the pooled variance estimate.

¹⁷Pearson's R = .915, probability = .000.

[18]"Rehnquist Urges Reform of Death Penalty Appeals," *Crime Prevention Press* (Spring 1989) 3.

[19]For example, the U.S. Sentencing Commission, Arkansas, Delaware, Kansas, Minnesota, Ohio, Oregon, North Carolina, Texas, Washington and several other states. *See* Donna Hunzeker, "Can States Make Sentencing a Science?" *State Legislatures* (October 1992):19-20.

[20]*See for example* ILL. ANN. STAT. ch. 38, s. 9-1 (b)(1)(1991); MO. REV STAT. S. 565.032(3)(1)(1991).

[21]Pearson's R = -.069, probability = .430. T = -1.07 with 18 degrees of freedom (the criminal history of two persons is unknown) and a two-tailed probability of .299, based on the pooled variance estimate.

[22]477 U.S. 399 (1986).

[23]No statistically significant difference exists between the rates of execution of the mentally ill and the non-mentally ill. Pearson's R = -.000, probability = .500. T = -.15 with 21 degrees of freedom and a two-tailed probability of .666, based on the pooled variance estimate.

[24]Deann Dorman Logan, "From Abused Child to Killer: Positing Links in the Chain," (Draft) California Appellate Project, 23 August 1991.

[25]Fleming v. State, 250 Ga. 687, S.E.2d 339 (1989).

[26]Russell Snyder, "Lawyer Activists 'Horrified' over Death Penalty Process," United Press International, Dateline: Washington, D.C., 8 November 1990.

[27]GA.CODE ANN. s 17-7-131(j)(Supp. 1988).

[28]Arkansas, Kentucky, North Carolina, and Tennessee. *See* George Cole, *American System of Criminal Justice*, (Pacific Grove, CA: Brooks/Cole Publishing Company, 1989), 486.

[29]Arizona, California, Colorado, Connecticut, Delaware, Idaho, Indiana, Maryland, Missouri, Montana, Nebraska, Nevada, New Hampshire, New Jersey, New Mexico, Oklahoma, Oregon, Pennsylvania, South Dakota, Utah, Washington, and Wyoming. *Id.*

[30]Pearson's R = -.543, probability = .012. T = 1.84 with 20 degrees of freedom and a two-tailed probability of .080, based on the pooled variance estimate. F = 5.38 and a probability of .014.

[31]Pearson's R = -.395, probability = .058. T = 1.83 with 21 degrees of freedom and a two-tailed probability of .082, based on the pooled variance estimate.

[32]As of July, 1992, Georgia, Kentucky, Tennessee, Maryland and New Mexico had passed laws forbidding the mentally retarded death penalty.

[33]Aggravating circumstance for the crime of first degree murder that makes a defendant death eligible, as stated in GA.CODE ANN. s 17-10-30(b)(7) and many other states' death penalty statutes.

[34]Dunkins v. State, 437 S.E.2d 1349 (1983).

[35]Pearson's R = .383, probability = .065. T = -1.96 with 20 degrees of freedom and a two-tailed probability of .063, based on the pooled variance estimate.

[36]Principle of the Common Law, as stated by David G. Stout, "The Lawyers of Death Row," *New York Times*, 14 February 1988, sec. 6.

[37]Pearson's R = .189, probability = .200. T = -.70 with 21 degrees of freedom and a two-tailed probability of .492, based on the pooled variance estimate.

[38]Pearson's R = .203, probability = .217. T = -.80 with 15 degrees of freedom (no determination of the leadership role or lack thereof could be made for six of the people in the sample) and a two-tailed probability of .434, based on the pooled variance estimate.

[39]T = .44 with 21 degrees of freedom and a two-tailed probability of .662, based on the pooled variance estimate.

[40]Pearson's R = -.100, probability = .325. T = .46 with 21 degrees of freedom and a two-tailed probability of .650, based on the pooled variance estimate.

[41]Benjamin R. Civiletti, "Racial Bias Permeates States' Use of the Death Penalty," *The (Wilmington, DE) News Journal*, 11 July 1990, sec. A.

[42]David Gergen, "Death on Our Doorsteps," *U.S. News and World Report*, 7 October 1991, 98.

[43]In 1990, the congressional General Accounting Office evaluated twenty-eight studies of the way capital punishment has been implemented in the United States. It found that "in otherwise similar circumstances, the killer of a white is far more likely to receive the death penalty than is the killer of a black." *Id. See also* McCleskey v. Kemp, 481 U.S. 279, 107 S.Ct. 1756 (1987).

[44]Where the victim's race is coded 0 for white and 1 for black, and spared is coded 0 and executed is 1, Pearson's R = -.461 with a probability = .031. T = 2.21 with 19 degrees of freedom (Spraggins' victim's race is unknown) and a two-tailed probability of .040, based on the pooled variance estimate.

[45]The figure includes Herbert Welcome who killed both a man and a woman.

[46]T = .00 with 20 degrees of freedom (excluding Welcome) and a two-tailed probability of 1.000, based on the pooled variance estimate.

[47]T = -1.45 with 21 degrees of freedom and a two-tailed probability of .161, based on the pooled variance estimate.

[48]*See for example*, Sentencing Accountability Commission, Delaware Sentencing Standards (1986).

[49]Robert Perske, *Unequal Justice*, (Nashville, TN: Abingdon Press, 1991), 18.

[50]Pearson's R = .129, probability = .279. T = -.60 with 21 degrees of freedom and a two-tailed probability of .558, based on the pooled variance estimate.

[51]The following is the correlation matrix of these four variables:

Correlation
1-tailed Significance

	Education	I.Q.	Marital Status
Age At Crime	-.758	-.571	.331
	.000	.008	.097
Education	-	.436	-
	-	.040	Not significant

[52]The following is the stepwise regression equation for age at the time of the crime, race of the victim, year of the crime, marital status, educational level, and I.Q., with whether the subject was executed or pardoned as the dependent variable:

Order of Entry	Variable	Multiple R	Multiple R²	T	Sig of T
1.	Age at Crime	.67867	.46060	-3.579	.0000
2.	Victim's Race	.94261	.88851	-5.491	.0000
3.	Year of Crime	.96065	.92285	-2.405	.0318
	Constant			15.095	.0000

Not Entered in the Equation

Variable	Partial Correlation	T	Sig of T
I.Q.	-.05474	-.190	.8525
Marital Status	-.29352	-1.064	.3084
Education	.11179	.390	.7036

6

Legislative Initiatives To Abolish The Death Penalty for Offenders with Mental Retardation

INTRODUCTION

The clearest and most reliable objective evidence of contemporary values is the legislation enacted by the country's legislatures.
--Majority Opinion, *Penry v. Lynaugh*

The State of Georgia's execution of Jerome Bowden in 1986 began the nationwide thrust to use legislation to ban executions of persons with mental retardation. In 1988, in reaction to Bowden's death and his curiously prophetic statement as he was about to die in the electric chair that he hoped that his dying would "bring some light to this thing that is wrong,"[1] the State of Georgia and the federal Congress became the first legislative bodies to prohibit executions of people with mental retardation.

The following year,[2] the U. S. Supreme Court made its *Penry* decision[3] in which it stated that defendants with mental retardation can be executed on a case-by-case-basis as long as the sentencing authority considers the fact of their mental retardation in determining the sentence. This *Penry* penalty accelerated the legislative push around the country to prevent executions of people with mental retardation. As a result of *Penry*, experts in the field of handicapped law issued a call for other legislatures in states with the death penalty to follow the lead of Georgia and the U.S. Congress.

Advocates of human and civil rights around the nation have risen to that call, some successfully, and some with lesser results. This chapter summarizes the statutory attempts to ban the execution of persons with mental retardation since 1986. It delineates the various approaches that have been taken to the issue and summarizes the legislative history of the movement to ban executions of persons with mental retardation.

PROGRESS TO DATE

To summarize the progress to date, the federal government in 1988 adopted a ban on the death penalty for people with mental retardation in its generally "get tough" crime legislation. The U.S. Senate proposed a similar ban in the death penalty provisions of the Crime Control Act of 1990 but all death penalty provisions were deleted from the bill prior to passage.[4]

Among the states, four others besides Georgia - Maryland, Kentucky, Tennessee and New Mexico - have statutorily prohibited executions of individuals with mental retardation. Four - Delaware, South Carolina, Texas and Virginia - have adopted mental retardation as a mitigating factor in the criminal sentencing process. The legislatures of Delaware, South Carolina and Virginia have also considered a complete ban on executions of persons with mental retardation, as have twenty other states with the death penalty. These are Arizona, Arkansas, Colorado, Connecticut, Florida, Idaho, Illinois, Indiana, Louisiana, Mississippi, Missouri, Nebraska, New Jersey, North Carolina, Ohio, Oklahoma, Oregon, Pennsylvania, Utah and Washington.

Fourteen states have no death penalty at all and so do not need to act in this area. These are located mostly in a northern tier which includes Alaska, Iowa, Maine, Massachusetts, Michigan, Minnesota, New York, North Dakota, Rhode Island, Vermont and Wisconsin. Outside this tier are Hawaii, Kansas and West Virginia.

The remaining seven states with the death penalty have taken no legislative action. Their locus is mostly in a western and southwestern tier of states which includes Alabama, California, Montana, Nevada, New Hampshire, South Dakota, and Wyoming. FIGURE 6.1 shows the geographic distribution of state legislative actions which ban capital punishment for individuals with mental retardation.

THE GEORGIA STORY

Where there is no vision, the people perish.
Proverbs 28:18

INTRODUCTION

Georgia is a most unlikely spot for the birthing of death penalty reform. Dating back to Sherman's march on Atlanta during the Civil War, Georgia has a long history of solving problems by death and destruction. Buried in the Death Belt of the deep South, it maintains strong vestiges of the deep-seated prejudices and racial cleavages remaining from the era of slavery. The harsh use of the death penalty, particularly against African Americans and persons with mental retardation, is a reflection of this broader social fabric and regional heritage. Indicators of Georgia's lethal legacy include its high rank in numbers of executions among the executing states and its premier status as the source of landmark death penalty case law. These issues are examined next.

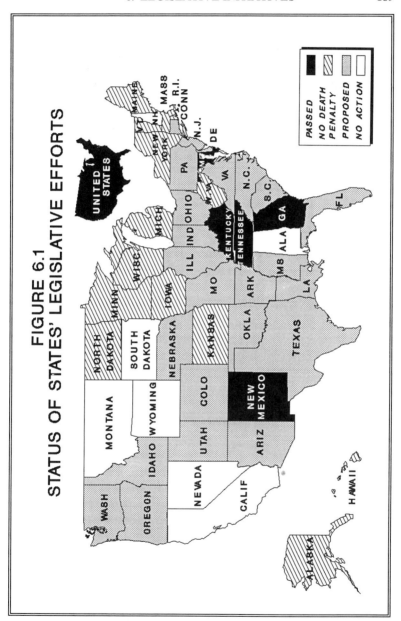

FIGURE 6.1
STATUS OF STATES' LEGISLATIVE EFFORTS

GEORGIA'S EXECUTION LEGACY

Georgia's contemporary execution history evidences its lethal legacy. Among the American states, Georgia ranks fourth in the number of executions carried out since 1976. As the next table shows, as of March 31, 1992, fifteen people had died there by execution. Of the eighteen executing states,[5] only Texas, Florida and Louisiana had executed more persons.

FIGURE 6.2 RANK OF EXECUTING STATES
BY NUMBER OF EXECUTIONS AS OF MARCH 31, 1992

Rank	State	Number	Percent of Total
1.	Texas	46	27.5
2.	Florida	27	16.2
3.	Louisiana	20	12.0
4.	**Georgia**	**15**	**8.9**
5.	Virginia	13	7.8
6.	Alabama	9	5.4
7.	Missouri	6	4.0
8.	Nevada	5	3.0
9.	Mississippi	4	2.4
10.	North Carolina	4	2.4
11.	South Carolina	4	2.4
12.	Arkansas	3	1.8
13.	Oklahoma	3	1.8
14.	Utah	3	1.8
15.	Indiana	2	1.2
16.	Illinois	1	.6
17.	Delaware	1	.6
18.	Wyoming	1	.6

Using a slightly different measure, per thousand persons of population, Georgia is also fourth in the number of executions. Only Louisiana, Nevada and Texas rank higher. FIGURE 6.3 shows the distribution of the executing states by numbers of executions per thousand persons of population.

FIGURE 6.3 RANK OF EXECUTING STATES BY POPULATION AS OF MARCH 31, 1992

Rank	State	1990 Population	Executions per Thousand Persons
1.	Louisiana	4,219,973	.00474
2.	Nevada	1,201,833	.00416
3.	Texas	16,986,510	.00271
4.	**Georgia**	**6,478,216**	**.00232**
5.	Alabama	4,040,581	.00223
6.	Wyoming	453,588	.00220
7.	Virginia	6,187,358	.00210
8.	Florida	12,937,926	.00209
9.	Utah	1,722,850	.00174
10.	Mississippi	2,573,216	.00155
11.	Delaware	666,168	.00150
12.	Arkansas	2,350,725	.00128
13.	South Carolina	3,486,703	.00115
14.	Missouri	5,117,073	.00098
15.	Oklahoma	3,145,585	.00095
16.	North Carolina	6,628,637	.00060
17.	Indiana	5,544,159	.00036
18.	Illinois	11,430,602	.00009

GEORGIA'S INFLUENCE ON THE LAW

Besides its high rank as an executing state, Georgia also holds the premier place in the legal history of the death penalty. Some of the most significant case law influencing the perpetuation of the death penalty and its disproportionate use against minorities in the United States has derived from Georgia. In 1972, in the case of *Furman v. Georgia*,[6] the U.S. Supreme Court declared Georgia's death penalty to be unconstitutional. Almost immediately, courts all over the country voided existing death statutes on the same grounds.

Subsequently, almost three quarters of the American states, including Georgia, moved to redraft their death penalty statutes to conform to the mandates of *Furman*.[7] In 1976, the U.S. Supreme Court once again addressed the issue in a Georgia case, *Gregg v. Georgia*.[8] This time the Court upheld the newly crafted and enacted death penalty statutes, and the executions began again shortly thereafter. These two bench mark opinions are examined here as a part of Georgia's legal capital punishment legacy. An examination of this legal background is a necessary prelude to an understanding of how Georgia could become the first state to legislatively ban executions of individuals with mental retardation.

FURMAN V. GEORGIA

> *Death is today a cruel and unusual punishment.*
> --Justice William Brennan, *Furman v. Georgia*

In 1972, the U.S. Supreme Court heard the appeals of three capital defendants together, two from Georgia and one from Texas. Portentously, two of the three had diagnoses indicative of mental retardation. All three defendants were African Americans. Two of the defendants had been convicted under Georgia law, one for rape and one for murder. Georgia permitted execution for both these crimes.[9] The third was convicted of rape under Texas' death penalty law which also allowed execution for this crime.[10]

The first defendant, Furman was a twenty-six year old Georgian with a sixth grade education. He was diagnosed with "Mental Deficiency, Mild to Moderate, with Psychotic Episodes associated with Convulsive Disorder." He had entered the home of a white man, the father of six, at night and shot and killed him "through a closed door."[11]

Branch, the second defendant, was a Texan with a fifth grade education who ranked in the bottom "fourth percentile" of his class. He was found to be "a borderline mental deficient" with a "dull intelligence." His I.Q. was "well below the average I.Q. of Texas prison inmates." He had raped a sixty-five year old white widow.[12]

Jackson, the third defendant, was a twenty-one year old Georgian of average intelligence who had also been convicted of rape.[13]

In keeping with the enormity of the issue, Justices Douglas, Brennan, Stewart, White, and Marshall each wrote separate concurring opinions in support of the ruling. Justices Blackmun, Powell and Rehnquist dissented.

In the first concurring opinion, Justice Douglas reviewed the historical context of the Eighth Amendment and found the statutes in question to be unconstitutional under it. He held that the imposition of death in all three cases was cruel and unusual punishment.[14]

He based his reasoning on two arguments. First, the statutes in question allowed for juries and judges to have almost "uncontrolled discretion" in determining who lives and who dies. They contained "no standards" by which this determination should be made so that the decision relied on "the whim of one man or 12."[15]

Second, in reasoning directly foreshadowing the defense arguments in *McCleskey v. Kemp*[16] twenty years later, Justice Douglas squarely addressed the racially discriminatory application of the death penalty. Because of the lack of reasonable standards for application, the death penalty had been systematically and discriminatorily applied "selectively to minorities whose numbers are few, who are outcasts of society, and who are unpopular, but whom society is willing to see suffer though it would not countenance general application of the same penalty across the board."[17] In practice, he stated, "the death sentence is disproportionately imposed and carried out on the poor, the Negro, and the members of unpopular groups."[18]

In short, Justice Douglas reasoned that discrimination against minorities resulted because the statutes contained nothing to prevent it.

In the second concurring opinion, Justice Brennan stated four reason why "death is today a cruel and unusual punishment."[19] First, the deliberate killing by the state of a human being is a denial of basic human dignity.[20] Second, execution is arbitrarily inflicted on some few and not others, and so "smacks of little more than a lottery system."[21] Third, as evidenced by several factors, contemporary society at the time rejected execution. These included the controversy that has always surrounded it, the continuous attempts to make the method more humane, the narrowing of the crimes for which it was inflicted, the refusal of juries to convict when they found execution to be inappropriate, and the rarity with which it was used.[22] Fourth, it was patently unnecessary because a lesser punishment, life in prison, served just as well.[23]

In sum, Justice Brennan stated:

Death is an unusually severe and degrading punishment; there is a strong probability that it is inflicted arbitrarily; its rejection by contemporary society is virtually total; and there is no reason to believe that it serves any penal purpose more effectively than the less severe punishment of imprisonment. . . . [24] [T]he states may no longer inflict it.[25]

In the third concurring opinion, Justice Stewart wrote that execution is cruel and unusual because it was as random as "being struck by lightning,"[26] and was "wantonly and freakishly imposed."[27] If it had any rational basis at all, it was the "constitutionally impermissible basis of race."[28]

Justice White, writing the fourth concurring opinion, reasoned that execution itself was not unconstitutional, but that under the current statutes "there is no meaningful basis for distinguishing the few cases in which it is imposed from the many in which it us not."[29]

Justice Marshall wrote the last concurring opinion. He reviewed case law interpretation of the Eighth Amendment going back to 1879. This analysis showed the historical evolution of the interpretation of what cruel and unusual punishment was in the United States.[30] The most important principle derived from this review was that what is cruel and unusual "must draw its meaning from the evolving standards of decency that mark the progress of a maturing society."[31] This meant, of course, that the Court was not bound by the precedent of having formerly determined capital punishment to be constitutional. Thus, considering the evolution of case law, punishment might be considered cruel and unusual under four principles. First, it causes so much pain and suffering that civilized people don't tolerate it.[32] Second, it is unusual in that it "was previously unknown" as a punishment "for a given offense."[33] Third, it is "excessive and serves no valid legislative purpose."[34] Fourth, "it may be invalid if popular sentiment abhors it."[35]

Justice Marshall then examined the history of capital punishment to see if this was now the case.[36] Because grass roots abolition movements had been only partially successful, he went on to examine whether abolition was "demanded by the Eighth Amendment itself," based on whether "less severe penalties would satisfy the legitimate legislative wants as well as capital punishment."[37]

After reviewing the six possible purposes of capital punishment,[38] he concluded from his review that:

1. Retribution for its own sake is improper.[39]

2. Capital punishment deters no better than life imprisonment and "is not necessary"[40] nor "justified on the basis of its deterrent effect."[41]

3. Since most murderers never commit additional murders, it is excessive as a means to prevent recidivism.[42]

4. If it "is used to encourage guilty pleas and thus deter suspects from exercising their rights to jury trials under the Sixth Amendment, it is unconstitutional."[43]

5. The United States "has never formally professed eugenic goals," and if it did, we would need tests to determine which murderers are incurable and which can benefit from treatment. No tests then existed.[44]

6. Last, it is less costly to imprison for life than to execute.[45]

Based on this reasoning, Justice Marshall concluded that "the death penalty is an excessive and unnecessary punishment that violates the Eighth Amendment"[46] and "is morally unacceptable to the people of the United States at this time in their history."[47]

Thus the death penalty statutes of Georgia and Texas, and, by implication, those of the thirty-nine other states that had similar ones at the time, were unconstitutional.

Subsequent to *Furman*, the state legislatures hastened to meet the objections of the Supreme Court majority to their death penalty statutes. In the next four years, thirty-five states and the federal Congress enacted new death penalty provisions with more definitive and structured procedures[48] to remove the "untrammeled discretion"[49] that juries formerly had.

Based on the recommendations of the Model Penal Code,[50] the new statutes took the form of providing for several procedural safeguards to restrict jury discretion. First, these new laws adopted a bifurcated capital trial system in which guilt was initially determined in a trial of fact, and the punishment was assessed in a later sentencing hearing. In this penalty phase of the trial, additional aggravating and mitigating evidence was admissible.[51]

Second, the laws spelled out aggravating factors and generally enacted a requirement that at least one such factor be present beyond a reasonable doubt for the defendant to be sentenced to death. In addition, any mitigating circumstances that might ameliorate the penalty could also be introduced. The jury was required to weigh aggravating against mitigating factors to determine the appropriate sentence.[52]

Third, the laws provided for automatic review of the death sentence by the state's Supreme Court.[53]

Last, the appellate court was usually required to consider whether passion, prejudice or some other arbitrary factor played a part in the imposition of the sentence, and to make a proportionality review to determine if the punishment was in keeping with that assessed in other similar cases.[54]

In 1976, the U.S. Supreme Court examined the constitutional validity of these concepts in a case which again originated in the State of Georgia and was a challenge to that state's revised death penalty statute. The case is Gregg v. Georgia.[55]

GREGG V. GEORGIA

> *We now hold that the punishment of death does not invariably violate the Constitution.*
>
>   -- Majority Opinion, *Gregg v. Georgia*

With these words, the U.S. Supreme Court once again authorized the use of the death penalty.[56]

On November 12, 1973, Tony Gregg and a sixteen-year-old juvenile, Floyd Allen, were hitchhiking in Florida to go to Asheville, North Carolina. Two men, Fred Simmons and Bob Moore, picked them up. Both men were intoxicated.

At one point in the trip, the four stopped to relieve themselves by the side of the road. As Simmons and Moore came back up an embankment to the parked car, Gregg announced to Allen his intention to rob them. Simmons had earlier flashed a roll of bills when he purchased a different car after the original one broke down.

Gregg steadied his elbows against the hood of the car and pointed a pistol towards the embankment. He shot each man as he appeared over the rise.[57] Gregg then went up to each and shot them again in the head execution style. Both died from their wounds. For these crimes, Gregg was given the death penalty under the State of Georgia's new death penalty statute.[58]

In reviewing the case, the U.S. Supreme Court reasoned in three stages. First, it examined the preliminary issue of whether the *Furman* court had held the death penalty to be unconstitutional *per se*. It found that the *Furman* court had not. Only two justices in *Furman* (Brennan and Marshall) had arrived at the conclusion that the death penalty was cruel and unusual punishment in and of itself.[59] Four justices (Burger, Blackmun, Powell and Rehnquist) had held that it was not unconstitutional *per se*.[60] Three (Douglas, Stewart, and White) had held that the statutes were unconstitutional as applied, but had left open the question of the constitutionality of the death penalty itself.[61] Thus there was no unanimity on the issue, and the death penalty was not necessarily cruel and unusual punishment. Consequently, it could not be held to be universally void.

Second, the Court examined the provisions of the Georgia death penalty statute to see if they were sufficient to provide the necessary safeguards and structure to prevent the arbitrary, capricious and freakish application of the death penalty that had voided the law in *Furman*. It found that the Georgia "statutory scheme" was adequate for this purpose.[62] It provided for a bifurcated trial with a sentencing hearing which allowed for the introduction of any mitigating evidence, and required that the jury find by a unanimous vote that at least one of ten statutory aggravating factors[63] existed beyond a reasonable doubt. The jury thus was required to consider the nature of the offense and the character of the offender in making its sentencing determination.[64]

The statute also provided for automatic appeal to the Georgia Supreme Court. That court was required to rule out passion, prejudice or other arbitrary factors as determinants of the sentence. It was also required to determine whether the evidence supported the jury's finding of at least one aggravating factor, and to make a proportionality review of other cases in which the death penalty was imposed in the State to see if it was excessive or freakishly applied in this instance.[65] In short, the statute was sufficient to remove arbitrary discretion.

Last, the Court held that the statute in this case was rightly and conscientiously applied in all stages (prosecutor, jury and appellate review).[66] Thus Gregg's death sentence, the Georgia statutory scheme, and the death penalty itself were constitutionally valid.

In the dozen or so years after the death penalty was authorized again in the *Gregg* case, little changed in the pattern of its application in Georgia, or elsewhere in the nation. Execution continued to be applied disproportionately to minorities, especially African Americans and people with mental retardation.

Eleven years later, substantial evidence of racial bias in the application of capital punishment was again presented to the U.S. Supreme Court from a Georgia case. However, contrary to the reasoning in *Furman* and in keeping with the philosophy of *Gregg*, the Court found such racial bias to be no constitutional bar to execution. The next section examines the reasoning of the Supreme Court which brought it to this conclusion.

McCLESKEY v. KEMP: RACE AND EXECUTION IN GEORGIA

> *[Statistical evidence of racial discrimination] does not demonstrate a constitutionally significant risk of racial bias affecting the Georgia capital sentencing process.*
> --Majority Opinion, *McCleskey v. Kemp*

In 1987, Georgia litigation once again became the focal point of a constitutional decision which influenced the relationship between the death penalty and minorities, in this instance African Americans. The seminal case in this area is *McCleskey v. Kemp*.[67]

The U.S. Supreme Court held in *McCleskey* that racial disparity in the application of death sentences is not "a major systemic defect"[68] and presents no obstacle to execution. The defendant, Warren McCleskey, was a African American who had been sentenced to death for his part in a robbery of a furniture store in Fulton County, Georgia. A white policeman was shot and killed during the crime. Conflicting evidence existed concerning who fired the shots that killed the officer, but McCleskey was nonetheless convicted of murder and sentenced to death.[69]

In the appeal of McCleskey's case, the defense had argued that statistics concerning two thousand Georgia murders in the 1970s[79] showed that racial bias in the imposition of the death penalty existed in at least two situations. First, a defendant is far more likely to receive the death sentence when the victim is white rather than African American, and secondarily, when the defendant himself is African American rather than white.[71] These data were derived from the so called "Baldus Study" of capital sentencing in Georgia.[72] McCleskey exactly fitted both circumstances.

The Court refused to accept these arguments as proof of discrimination against McCleskey. It stated that discrepancies in sentencing such as these are "an inevitable part of our criminal justice system."[73] Such racial disparities in the impact of death sentencing present no constitutional bar to execution as long as adequate procedural safeguards are legislatively established to make the sentencing process "as fair as possible."[74] Echoing *Gregg*, once again the Court held that the Georgia death penalty statute provided for multiple and sufficient safeguards. These included a "bifurcated guilt and sentencing proceeding," the existence of at least one statutory aggravating factor, the admission into evidence of any "mitigating evidence" whatsoever, "particularized inquiry" into the nature of the offense and the character of the offender, and finally, "automatic appeal."[75] These procedures were more than adequate to ensure a fair process.

To show a constitutional violation in a specific case, the defense must establish that a "racially discriminatory purpose"[76] existed in this individual's case, or in the intent of drafters of the statute.[77] No such proof was made for McCleskey. Thus there was no constitutional necessity to prevent all racial disparity in the application of the death penalty.[78]

McCleskey's appeal had been based on plentiful data concerning racial disparity in the application of the death penalty during the 1970s both before and after *Gregg*. Besides the Baldus Study, another well-known analysis of racial disparity in the death penalty in seven executing states showed that a killer of a white victim in Georgia was ten times as likely to receive the death penalty as someone who kills an African American victim.[79] This ratio was greater than that in any other state, including Florida (eight to one), Illinois (six to one), Mississippi (six to one) and North Carolina (four to one).[80]

Subsequent to these studies, nothing in the pattern of racial disparity in the imposition of the death penalty in Georgia (and more specifically, the carrying out of executions) has changed. As FIGURE 6.4 shows, fifteen defendants have been executed since *Gregg*. Warren McCleskey is the last. Two of the fifteen executed (13 %) were mentally retarded. Eleven (73 %) were African Americans. Four were Whites (27 %). All of the victims except two (87 %)[81] were Whites.[82] The fact of mental retardation, the race of the victim and the race of the perpetrator continued to be disproportionately correlated with who was executed in Georgia.

FIGURE 6.4 CHARACTERISTICS OF GEORGIA'S EXECUTED

Name	Date Executed	Race	Race of Victim
1. John Eldon Smith	12/15/83	Black	White
2. Ivon Stanley (m.r.)	7/12/84	White	White
3. Alpha Otis Stephens	12/12/84	Black	White
4. Roosevelt Green	1/09/85	Black	White
5. Van Roosevelt Solomon	2/20/85	Black	White
6. John Young	3/20/85	Black	Asian
7. Jerome Bowden (m.r.)	6/24/86	Black	White
8. Joseph Mulligan	5/15/87	Black	Black
9. Richard Tucker	5/19/87	Black	White
10. William Boyd Tucker	5/28/87	White	White
11. Billy Mitchell	9/01/87	Black	White
12. Timothy McCorquedale	9/21/87	White	White
13. James Messer	7/28/88	Black	White
14. Henry Willis	5/18/89	White	White
15. Warren McCleskey	9/25/91	Black	White

Mental Retardation

Non-Mentally Retarded	13	87 %
Mentally Retarded	2 -	13 %
Total	15	100 %

Race of Perpetrator		Race of Victim	
Black	11 - 67 %	Black/Asian	2 - 13 %
White	4 - 33 %	White	13 - 87 %
Total	15 100 %	Total	15 100 %

A "NEW SOUTH" DIALECTIC

In Georgia, the issues of the disproportionate execution of African Americans and people with mental retardation are inescapably intertwined in a double thread of discrimination. Nevertheless, outside the entrenchment of this double disparity in capital punishment, and perhaps because of it, another process, a "New South" dialectic, is also at work in modern Georgia.

In the thesis of the dialectic, Georgia litigation was the most significant determinant of the perpetuation of the death penalty and its inequitable application to African Americans and persons with mental retardation. However, the *Furman* decision laid the cornerstone for the dialectical antithesis to the constitutional validation of this disparity which occurred in *Gregg* and *McCleskey*.

The electrocution of Jerome Bowden in 1986 provided addition materials for the building of the antithesis. Bowden's execution received considerable local media attention. The fact of his mental retardation had not been well known in Georgia prior to his execution. Public reaction to this event began the legislative reform movement.[83] It propelled a new legislative synthesis which righted one prong of the dual disparity - the disproportionate application of capital punishment as applied to people with mental retardation.

The time was ripe for this reform. Deep within the Death Belt caricature of the Old South, another Georgia had been developing. Atlanta had become a cosmopolitan city, a melting pot with international links and strong economical and cultural ties outside its own region. The *Atlanta Journal and Constitution*, the local newspaper, maintained a national readership and a reputation for excellence. The Georgia prison system had been highly reformed with one of the best programs in the country for offenders with mental retardation. A solid core of correctional officials understood and responded to the disabilities of offenders with mental retardation.[84]

These factors all contributed to the development of an enlarging group of knowledgeable and enlightened public policy makers who took the Bowden message to heart. They would no longer remain silent in the tug of war of values that underlay the moral issues surrounding the application of the death penalty in Georgia. Bowden's execution became the rallying point for this group to adopt an egalitarian policy that persons with mental retardation would no longer be executed in their state.

To that end Georgia policy makers, first its legislature and then the state courts, brought the new synthesis to fruition with the passage of the first law in the nation to ban executions of persons with mental retardation. The next section analyzes this landmark in the legal history of Georgia, and of capital punishment and offenders with mental retardation.

The equitable synthesis was complete when the Georgia Supreme

Court in *Fleming v. Zant* applied the principle that execution of persons with mental retardation is cruel and unusual punishment under the Georgia Constitution retroactively to those who had been convicted prior to the statute's enactment.[85] The subsequent section examines the reasoning of this case.

ANALYSIS OF THE GEORGIA STATUTE: THE "GUILTY BUT MENTALLY RETARDED ACT"

Introduction. In early 1988, Georgia law already accounted for the legal treatment of criminals who suffered from insanity and mental illness and used their illness as a defense in criminal prosecutions.[86] The law established verdicts of "not guilty by reason of insanity,"[87] and "guilty but mentally ill" for felonies, including murder.[88] It also made provisions for assessment of the defendant's mental condition,[89] holding of a hearing on the factual basis of the claim of insanity or mental illness when a plea was entered,[90] charges to the jury concerning what would happen to the defendant if they found either verdict at trial,[91] and procedures to follow should the defendant be found not guilty by reason of insanity or guilty but mentally ill.[92] The law also arranged for placement either with the Department of Corrections or the Department of Human Resources, as appropriate, based on the verdict, evaluation and results of the hearing.[93] Thus Georgia law provided for the humane and sensible treatment of insane and mentally ill persons who committed crimes.

Since this procedural structure was already in place and operational, it was logical and convenient that the verdict of guilty but mentally retarded, the prohibition of the execution of persons with mental retardation convicted of capital crimes, and the procedures for the care and habilitation of these offenders be combined with, and added to, this statute. How defendants found guilty but mentally retarded would be treated, both those convicted of capital and lesser felonies, logically followed the same procedures. Thus in 1988, when the issue of capital punishment as applied to offenders with mental retardation was ripe for legislative action, this insanity statute was amended to include the "guilty but mentally retarded" verdict[94] and to apply the same procedures to offenders with mental retardation.

Provisions Applying to Guilty but Mentally Retarded Offenders. In the first provision applying to offenders with mental retardation, a standard definition of mental retardation was added to the definitions section of the statute. Mentally retarded was defined as "having significantly subaverage general intellectual functioning resulting in or associated with impairments in adaptive behavior which manifested during the developmental period."[95]

To the possible verdicts of "guilty," "not guilty," "not guilty by reason of insanity," and "guilty but mentally ill" for felonies, a verdict of "guilty but mentally retarded" was also authorized for all felonies.[96]

The plea of guilty but mentally retarded was coupled with the plea of guilty but mentally ill in all sections of the statute, and the procedures for dealing with each plea became exactly the same. Neither plea can be accepted until a hearing is held as to the "factual basis" of the defendant's mental retardation based on an evaluation which must be conducted by "a licensed psychologist or psychiatrist." The court is required to be satisfied that the defendant was in fact mentally retarded at the time the crime was committed before such a plea can be accepted.[97]

When a defendant goes to trial and enters a "defense of insanity"[98] or contends that he or she "was otherwise mentally incompetent under the law"[99] at the time the crime was committed, the court is required to instruct the jury that they can find verdicts not only of guilty, not guilty, not guilty by reason of insanity, and guilty but mentally ill. They can also find a verdict of guilty but mentally retarded.[100] The strictest "reasonable doubt" standard of proof is required for the jury to find a verdict of guilty but mentally retarded, that is, it must find that the defendant is both guilty and mentally retarded "beyond a reasonable doubt,"[101] rather than more loosely by the preponderance of the evidence.[102]

The court must charge the jury concerning a verdict of guilty but mentally retarded that, based on this verdict, the defendant "will be given over to the Department of Correction or the Department of Human Resources, as the mental condition of the defendant may warrant."[103] Thus the jury is generally made aware of the procedures that will be followed if it finds this verdict. This charge is intended to show the jury that the defendant would not be set free should they find him or her guilty but mentally retarded.[104]

Once either a verdict or plea of guilty but mentally retarded has been determined, the defendant must be sentenced in the same way as one who is found guilty, with one exception.[105] This exception is that "in any case in which the death penalty is sought . . . the death penalty shall not be imposed and the defendant shall be sentenced to imprisonment for life." The provision took effect in trials beginning "on or after July 1, 1988."[106] In this way the statute prospectively, but not retrospectively, prohibited capital punishment for offenders with mental retardation.

Given that a capital defendant with mental retardation is to receive a sentence of life in prison according to this provision, the law also contains procedures for the person's appropriate care and treatment. A "psychiatrist or licensed psychologist from the Department of Human Resources" must make an evaluation of the defendant after sentencing but prior to admission to the jurisdiction of the Department of Corrections.[107] The law requires the Board of Human Resources to develop rules and regulations for the carrying out of this evaluation.[108]

If the evaluation and hearing indicate that the defendant is not in need of immediate hospitalization, then he or she will be given over to the Department of Corrections. Corrections will commit the offender to "an appropriate penal facility" where he or she shall receive the treatment that is psychiatrically indicated for his or her mental retardation, within the fiscal constraints of the Department of Corrections.[109] Practically, this means that these offenders will be assigned to the mental health and mental retardation unit for men located at the Georgia State Prison in Reidsville, or any of a dozen or so other such units located in penitentiaries around the state.[110]

If the offender goes to a penal facility and a later psychiatric assessment indicates that his or her mental retardation requires more intensive treatment than the Department of Corrections can give, then he or she must be transferred to the Department of Human Resources for such treatment. The law requires these two agencies jointly to develop rules and regulations for the inter-transfer between them of persons convicted with these verdicts.[111]

If the evaluation and hearing show that the offender requires immediate hospitalization, then the Department of Corrections must transfer the person to a mental health facility under the jurisdiction of the Department of Human Resources for such treatment as is indicated according to the rules and regulations that have been developed.[112]

Conclusion. In conclusion, the Georgia statute is comprehensive and all inclusive. It provides for a finding of mental retardation which statutorily must mitigate the punishment in capital crimes and can do so in lesser felony cases. It forbids the execution of persons convicted of capital crimes who have mental retardation and provides for appropriate care and habilitation of these offenders as professionally determined, either by corrections or mental retardation services, throughout their life imprisonment. The statute thus becomes a model for other states to follow in implementing a ban on capital punishment for persons with mental retardation.

The Georgia statute anticipates the problems of the *Penry v. Lynaugh* decision. It provides a definitive answer to the U.S. Supreme Court which went unheeded in *Penry.* If John Paul Penry or any other offender with mental retardation would have had the good fortune to be brought to trial in Georgia, he would have been punished for his crime, but he would also have been justly treated by the law, the courts, and correctional and treatment personnel according to his diminished mental capacity and criminal responsibility. He would not have been brought to the brink of execution. The accident of geography should not result in the unequal treatment of offenders with mental retardation which now exists from state to state in such a grave matter as the carrying out of deliberate death.

FLEMING V. ZANT

> *The execution of mentally retarded offenders violates the Georgia constitutional guarantee against cruel and unusual punishment.*
> -- Majority Opinion, *Fleming v. Zant*

Since the Georgia statute banning capital punishment for offenders with mental retardation was prospective and not retrospective, that is, it applied only to persons who went on trial after July 1, 1988, offenders with mental retardation already on Death Row in Georgia were still facing execution. One such offender was Son Fleming. He was convicted and sentenced to death for a crime committed in 1977 more than a decade before the passage of the law.[113]

Shortly after the enactment of the statute, Fleming's attorneys appealed his death sentence to the Georgia Supreme Court. They sought to have it overturned on the basis that the law should apply to all offenders with mental retardation sentenced to death, not just those convicted after the passage of the death penalty prohibition.[114] The court granted a stay of execution on July 12, 1989, just a few hours before Fleming was scheduled to be executed, in order to hear these arguments.[115]

The defense presented three arguments based on the effective date of the statutory ban on executions of persons with mental retardation. First, they argued that the distinction between those offenders with mental retardation tried before and after the effective date was arbitrary and capricious and discriminated among offenders with mental retardation without a rational basis. Due process and equal protection required that the provision be applied retroactively. The court rejected this argument, saying that the distinction between the two is based on "a reasonable relationship to a legitimate legislative concern for the finality of criminal convictions," and that "the classification is neither arbitrary nor discriminatory."[116]

Second, the defense argued that Fleming's sentence was "disproportionate to that imposed against similar defendants in similar cases in Georgia,"[117] since "no case will again come before this Court for direct review of a death sentence imposed on a mentally retarded person."[118] The Georgia court also dismissed this reasoning. Since "no judicial determination" had ever been made that Fleming had mental retardation, it would be improper at this time to undertake another proportionality review.[119]

The last argument of the defense was that execution of persons with mental retardation is cruel and unusual punishment forbidden by the Eighth Amendment of the U.S. Constitution and the Constitution of the State of Georgia.[120]

The Georgia Court first noted that what constitutes cruel and unusual punishment changes as societal values change.[121] Then, relying on *Penry v. Lynaugh* as precedent, it held that execution of persons with mental retardation is not cruel and unusual punishment based on the Eighth Amendment because there was no "national consensus" at the time to that effect.[122]

The Court then noted that it uses several types of "objective evidence" to measures societal consensus. Primary among these are legislative actions. Other measures can include public opinion polls, studies, and the actions of "sentencing juries."[123] The Court then cited three such measures. First and foremost, the Georgia state legislature passed the prohibition of execution of mentally retarded offenders.[124] Second, the Senate passed Senate Resolution 388 which encourages "the Board of Pardons and Paroles to give special consideration to commuting the [death] sentences of mentally retarded offenders." The Resolution further stated that such executions destroy "public confidence in the criminal justice system."[125] Last, although the Georgia court stated that it would not "rely on" such public opinion polls to demonstrate a public consensus, it cited a Georgia state poll which showed that two-thirds of Georgians oppose executions of offenders with mental retardation, while three-quarters support capital punishment generally.[126] It noted that the *Penry* case and the Senate Resolution also referenced this poll.[127]

Based on this evidence, the Court concluded that:

> The legislative enactment reflects a decision by the people of Georgia that the execution of mentally retarded offenders makes no measurable contribution to acceptable goals of punishment. . . . federal constitutional standards represent the minimum, not the maximum, protection that this state must afford its citizens. . . . this state's consensus is clear. . . . although the rest of the nation might not agree, under the Georgia Constitution, the execution of the mentally retarded constitutes cruel and unusual punishment.[128]

The Court also was careful to say that it was not holding capital punishment for offenders with mental retardation to be unconstitutional *per se* or forever. It noted that the consensus then extant among the citizens of Georgia might change at some time in the future.[129]

Finally, the Court addressed Fleming's appeal and set out a two stage procedure by which determinations of mental retardation should be made in cases in which the defendant was already under a death sentence. When the defendant petitions for *habeas corpus* and alleges mental retardation, the *habeas corpus* court must first make a determination as to whether there is "sufficient credible evidence . . . to create a genuine issue" concerning the alleged mental retardation of the Death Row inmate. This evidence must include at a minimum, "one expert diagnosis of mental retardation."[130] The court can hold a hearing on the issue or review the documentation that the defense presents, as it sees fit.[131] Should the *habeas* court find that there is a genuine issue of mental retardation, then it must remand the case back to the original trial court for a new jury trial on this single issue.[132]

In the new jury trial, the jury must weigh all the evidence presented concerning the defendant's mental retardation. It is not bound by the "testimony of expert witnesses" or any "test results."[133] In contrast to the statute which requires proof of mental retardation beyond a reasonable doubt, the defendant is required here to prove the existence of his mental retardation more simply by "the preponderance of the evidence."[134] If the jury finds that the defendant has mental retardation , then his or her death sentence will be automatically vacated.[135] However, the jury need not be told that this will happen.[136] Nor must potential jurors be "Witherspoon" qualified concerning their views and objections to the death penalty prior to being seated on the jury.[137]

In Fleming's case, there had never been a factual determination of mental retardation.[138] Thus his case was sent back to the *habeas corpus* court in Butts County for a determination as to whether there was sufficient evidence to hold a jury trial in Lanier County where Fleming was originally sentenced, on the issue of his mental retardation.[139]

CONCLUSION

Since the passage of the Georgia statute prohibiting execution of offenders with mental retardation and the *Fleming* decision making the law retroactive, several more offenders with mental retardation have been spared death sentences based on factual determinations of their mental retardation. These include the following.

> In July, 1988, the prosecutor in the case of George Elder Dungee decided not to seek the death penalty for him because of his mental retardation.[140]

> In August, 1988, the prosecution agreed not to seek the death penalty for Jerome Holloway, a man with mental retardation, in return for a guilty plea.[141]

> In August, 1988, the federal Eleventh Circuit Court of Appeals vacated the death sentence of William Alvin Smith on the basis that his mental retardation prevented him from voluntarily waiving his Miranda rights and from voluntarily confessing.[142]

> In December, 1988, after three previous trials and death sentences which were later overturned, the prosecution decided not to try Eddie Spraggins again in return for a guilty but mentally retarded plea.[143]

> In December, 1989, the Georgia Supreme Court held that the *habeas corpus* court's finding that a previously condemned killer, Eli Beck, was mentally retarded required a new jury trial on this issue.[144]

> In April, 1990, a jury found MacArthur Lawton, Jr. guilty but mentally retarded for the robbery and murder of two employees of a sporting goods store. Lawton was sentenced to five consecutive life sentences.[145]

> In 1991, the *habeas corpus* court granted a *de novo* jury trial to petitioner Timothy Foster, another previously convicted killer, on the issue of his mental retardation, and the Georgia Supreme Court filled

in the details of the procedures that must be followed in this trial.[146]

In June, 1992, the Georgia Supreme Court further elaborated on the procedures to be followed in another jury trial on a defendant's mental retardation. The defendant is Keith Patillo.[147]

Subsequent to *Zant* in 1990, Georgia has also withstood an attempt by a minority of State Senators to change the Georgia statute and to allow juries to determine whether offenders with mental retardation can be executed on a case-by-case basis.[148] In sum, the Georgia law is working[149] to prevent executions of offenders with mental retardation.

Since Georgia broke ground with the first statute in the country to prohibit application of the death penalty to persons with mental retardation and the U.S. Supreme Court established the *Penry* penalty, the national outrage at the constitutionally permissible execution of offenders with mental retardation has brought the issue to the legislative fore in other jurisdictions. Based on the Georgia precedent and as a result of *Penry*, shortly after the passage of the Georgia statute in 1988, the federal government followed Georgia's lead. The next section examines this federal statute.

THE FEDERAL ANTI-DRUG ABUSE ACT OF 1988[150]

The national election year of 1988 saw a confluence of major political events which shaped the evolution of death penalty legislation and its application to offenders with mental retardation at the national level.

Concerns of voters and policy makers alike over the national drug problem reached an apogee of fear and frustration. The drug addiction epidemic was virtually out of control, and law enforcement officials were seemingly unable to slow international drug trafficking or to stem the tide of illegal drugs into the country.[151]

Public opinion surveys showed major concern over the drug problem along with broad support for tough anti-drug measures.[152] Polls indicated equally strong general support for the death penalty.[153]

Along with these factors, not the least important consideration was that many elected officials were up for reelection in November. The congressional tapping of the public mood was such that many members of Congress feared that, without significant action on their part this year, they would not be around for another try in subsequent years. Few were willing to risk defeat by voting against the massive drug bill being proposed.[154]

As a result of these many factors, Congress compiled and passed one of the most significant "get tough"[155] crime statutes in recent history. This legislation, the Anti-Drug Abuse Act of 1988, launched Congress's all out "war on drugs."[156] The bill had originated in 1987 in the first session of the 100th Congress.

The bill included a new death penalty provision as part of the get tough philosophy. The capital punishment clause broadened then existent federal statutes which authorized capital punishment for only two very narrow types of crimes - air piracy resulting in death and espionage by military personnel.[157] Under the new law, the federal court has the option of applying the death penalty to drug "kingpins" convicted for any of three drug-related capital crimes.[158]

The first crime category targets major drug traffickers. It permits the death penalty to be applied to those who are involved in a "continuing criminal enterprise"[159] and who intentionally kill or cause "the intentional killing"[160] of another. A second category includes persons who intentionally kill or cause the killing of another during the commission of a major drug importation or distribution felony.[161] Last, anyone who kills or causes the death of a law enforcement officer during a drug crime can also be given death.[162]

Early in 1988 the Senate passed one version of the bill which included these death penalty provisions.[163] The bill then went through a series of major revisions in the House of Representatives throughout the spring.

As the summer wore on and the elections approached, the House continued to work the drug legislation.[164] While it was being prepared for vote by the House Rules Committee, Representative Sander M. Levin (D-Mich) introduced an amendment to exempt offenders with mental retardation from execution under the death penalty provisions. On August 8, 1988, Representative Levin stated to the Rules Committee that it was important to prevent further executions of persons with mental retardation because, to his knowledge, at least five had been executed nationally.[165] The House Rules Committee cleared the death penalty provisions with Levin's amendment attached for discussion by the full House.[166]

Representative Levin's amendment prohibiting executions of people with mental retardation was very simply stated. It says:

A sentence of death shall not be carried out upon a person who is mentally retarded.[167]

The death penalty provisions came up for debate on the floor of the House on September 8, 1988. The exclusion of persons with mental retardation was fully discussed and supported by the House.[168] Representative Donald Edwards (D-Calif) proposed additional language to clarify the Levin Amendment. Representative Edwards stated that his amendment intended to bring the mentally retarded exclusion provision into conformity with the definition of mental incompetency "recommended by the American Bar Association and the American Association on Mental Retardation."[169] He proposed the addition of the following words:

A sentence of death shall not be carried out upon a person who, as a result of mental disability--

(1) cannot understand the nature of the pending proceedings, what such person was tried for, the reason for the punishment; or

(2) lacks the capacity to recognize or understand facts which would make the punishment unjust or unlawful, or lacks the ability to convey such information to counsel or to the court.[170]

This amendment was accepted and included in the bill immediately after Levin's prohibition of mentally retarded executions.

Later in the day on September 8, the vote was finally called, and the House version of the bill passed by a wide 3 to 1 margin.[171] The bill then went back to joint committee of both houses for reconciliation with the Senate version.[172]

The reconciled version was reported out of committee to the floor just a little more than two weeks before the elections. In the wee hours of the morning of October 22, the final version of the Anti-Drug Abuse Act was approved by the House by an overwhelming margin of 346 to eleven. The Senate also approved, but only by voice vote.[173]

The Congress adjourned at 3:17 AM with a major drug crime law under its belt.[174] It had also taken a major step toward human rights by exempting offenders with mental retardation from its expanded death penalty provisions.

Conclusion. With two laws, one in Georgia and one at the federal level, effectively passed in the nation to prevent executions of offenders with mental retardation, it was only a short time before additional states were able to achieve similar results. Four more states to date have been successful in enacting this kind of legislation. The next section reviews the laws which ban capital punishment for offenders with mental retardation in the states of Maryland, Kentucky, Tennessee and New Mexico.

OTHER STATE STATUTES

MARYLAND

Introduction. On May 25, 1989, the State of Maryland became the second state in the nation to prohibit executions of offenders with mental retardation. On that date Governor William D. Schaefer signed "An Act

Concerning the Death Penalty - Mentally Retarded" into law.[175]

As the national debate on the issue intensified in 1988, the impetus in Maryland for outlawing the death penalty for persons with mental retardation came from two local factors. First, the last person to die in Maryland's gas chamber twenty-seven years earlier in 1961, Nathaniel Lipscomb, was said by his lawyers to have been mentally retarded.[176] The memory of that execution lingered and was well publicized[177] along side of the case of James Trimble who many thought might be the next to be executed in Maryland.[178]

James Trimble was a juvenile with an I.Q. of sixty-four, who was sentenced to death in 1982 at the age of seventeen for the kidnapping, rape and murder of a young woman in Baltimore County earlier that year.[179] He was on Death Row in Maryland in 1988 when Jerome Bowden was executed in Georgia, and the similarities of the two cases, as well as that of Lipscomb, were pointedly apparent to Marylanders.

The bill to ban executions of offenders with mental retardation was first introduced in the Maryland General Assembly in 1988. It passed in the Senate by a thirty-five to seven vote, but was stalled in the House of Delegates Judiciary Committee as the legislative session ended.[180]

In 1989, the bill was first worked again in the Senate Judicial Proceedings Committee. The Chair of that Committee opposed the bill.[181] Major support for the bill came from State Senator Margaret C. Schweinhaut (D-Montgomery).[182] Senator Schweinhaut was the second most senior legislator in the Maryland General Assembly, and was very well respected by her colleagues and the general public for more than thirty years of distinguished public service.[183]

On the day that the bill came to a vote in the Senate Judiciary Committee, the Chair called the question before Senator Schweinhaut and another supporter could get to the meeting. Both were on their way and rushing to make the vote. As a result, the vote was tied, four in favor of the bill, and four against. The bill thus died in committee for failure to receive a majority vote.[184]

However, in an unprecedented move, Senator Schweinhaut did not take this defeat as final. She asked the committee Chair for a rehearing, using all of her charm, prestige and personal power to persuade him to reconsider the bill at a time when all committee members were present.[185] The Chair at first denied her request but later agreed, saying he "wanted to be fair." In the new hearing held a week later, the bill was moved out of committee to the Senate floor by a six to five margin. The vote was exactly the same as it had been the previous year.[186]

On the day of the vote in the full Senate, Senator Schweinhaut delivered an eloquent speech in favor of the bill "that silenced the Senate chambers" and carried the vote by a wide margin.[187]

The battle then proceeded to the House of Delegates Judiciary Committee. After heated and extensive debate, a bill similar to the one that the Senate passed was reported out of this Committee on March 19 by a thirteen to nine vote.[188] Less than a week later the full House of Delegates passed the bill without debate by a wide margin.[189] Apparently all opposition had been vented. The Senate version was then reconciled to the House version,[190] and the Senate once again approved the bill.[191] Finally, the bill went to Governor Schaefer for signature.

The Debate. Throughout the debate, opponents of the bill made several arguments against it. First, they stated that the law was unnecessary. People with mental retardation don't get put to death anyway, because they lack the capability to form the criminal intent required to be condemned to death.[192] This argument was not persuasive, because the memory of Nathaniel Lipscomb's actual execution and knowledge of James Trimble's pending execution were real.

Second, many argued that the bill was a covert attack on the death penalty itself, a "Trojan horse" for capital punishment opponents.[193] They said that passage of this restriction on the death penalty was just an attempt to get the foot in the door to ban capital punishment completely. If people support the death penalty, then they could not support this end run around it.

Third, prosecutors opposed the bill by saying that it was not necessary and "doesn't do anything." It would be like "giving medicine to someone who wasn't sick" because the then existing law allowed "a person's mental capacity" to be considered as a mitigating factor.[194] Of course, they were correct in their statement that mental capacity could be used as a mitigating factor. But the actual and pending execution of offenders with mental retardation made this argument moot. It was all too apparent that using mental retardation as a mitigating factor does not prevent these executions.

Finally, others argued that the bill contained no "objective standard" to determine who has mental retardation. Consequently, the law could not be applied fairly.[195] Offenders with normal intelligence would attempt to escape execution under it.

This argument was countered successfully by bill proponents who stated that the bill included an objective standard of what mental retardation means which the courts and professionals had long accepted. Besides meeting this standard, defendants would have to show a history of deficient adaptive behaviors, such as inability to work or to get a license to drive a car. Even if a mistake was made in the determination of who has mental retardation, nothing would be lost. The offender would be imprisoned for life so that society would not be harmed.[196]

In sum, key to passage of the ban on executions of offenders with mental retardation in Maryland was the wide publicity of the facts that Maryland had actually executed a person with mental retardation and that another such execution was approaching. It is possible to conclude from this fact that the issue does not become real for the public and legislators until a person with mental retardation comes close to execution or is actually executed. This was the case in both Georgia and Maryland.

A second key factor in Maryland's success was backing by a well respected and senior legislator and her refusal to accept a temporary tactical defeat from opponents.[197] Staunch support from influential legislators is critical to successful passage. The federal debate and the support of Senators Joseph R. Biden, Jr. and Edward Kennedy also illustrate this point.

Third, supporters and lobbyists who could successfully counter the arguments of opponents also contributed to successful passage.

The Statute. Maryland's law prohibiting the execution of offenders with mental retardation takes a different approach than does Georgia's. It adds the prohibition to the state's capital punishment law concerning First Degree Murder, rather than to the law dealing with insanity and mental illness.[198] It contains no provisions for the care and treatment of mentally retarded offenders who are sentenced to life in prison as does Georgia's statute.

Turning to the law itself, a definition of mental retardation is first given.

> Mentally retarded means an individual has significantly subaverage intellectual functioning as evidenced by an intelligence quotient of 70 or below on an individually administered intelligence quotient test and impairment of adaptive behavior, and the mental retardation is manifested before the individual attains the age of 22.[199]

Thus the definition used is more explicit in two senses than that used in the Georgia statute. It defines subaverage intellectual functioning as a score of seventy or below on at least one individually administered I.Q. test. It also states when the mental retardation must have been manifested, that is, prior to age twenty-two, rather than the unspecified "developmental period," as Georgia law indicates.[200] This specificity of definition meets the objections made by Maryland opponents of the bill.

The law goes on to prohibit capital punishment for offenders with mental retardation by stating that:

> . . . if the person [found guilty of murder in the first degree] establishes by the preponderance of the evidence that the person was, at the time the murder was committed, mentally retarded, the person shall be sentenced to imprisonment for life or imprisonment for life without the possibility of parole and may not be sentenced to death.[201]

Thus the law uses a preponderance of evidence standard to establish mental retardation and does not require the more stringent "beyond a reasonable doubt" standard of proof statutorily required in Georgia.[202]

The law also addresses the issue of life imprisonment with or without parole by explicitly authorizing either of these sentences as possibilities. Georgia's law does not explicitly address this issue, but implicitly allows parole by not forbidding it.[203]

Thus Georgia and Maryland take substantially different approaches to achieve the same end.

Postscript. In December, 1989, six months after Maryland's law took effect, a mildly retarded man with an I.Q. of sixty-nine, Duane Richardson, was convicted of First Degree Murder and sentenced to life in prison. The sentencing jury agreed with the defense that the man should not be executed because of his mental retardation.[204]

The next year, James Trimble's death sentence was overturned.[205] However, it was not because of his mental retardation. This had never been factually proven in a court of law.

Instead, the Court of Appeals of Maryland vacated Trimble's sentence and remanded the case to the lower court to impose a life sentence. The Appeals Court reasoned that the trial judge had failed to instruct Trimble that should he elect to have his sentence determined by a jury and they failed to agree unanimously on the death sentence, he would automatically be sentenced to life.[206] Ordinarily, because of this technical error, the case would have been remanded to the trial court for a new sentencing hearing. However, because Trimble was less than eighteen years old at the time of the crime, and his new sentencing would occur after July 1, 1989, the time when the ban on juvenile executions took effect in Maryland, he could not be sentenced to death again. Thus his sentence was automatically commuted to life.[207]

Although the issue of removing Trimble from Death Row because of his mental retardation hovered in the background, a direct confrontation with it was avoided. In this way, the public opposition to his pending execution because of his mental retardation was assuaged without having to hold a new penalty hearing on the issue.

In sum, Maryland's new law, like that of Georgia, was beginning to have its intended effect.

TENNESSEE AND KENTUCKY

In 1990, with little national fanfare, the sister states of Tennessee and Kentucky became the third and fourth states, respectively, to ban executions of persons with mental retardation.

of persons with mental retardation.

Tennessee. In Tennessee, there was virtually no opposition to the legislation compared to what occurred in other states. Some members of the Tennessee Senate Judiciary Committee did say that they feared a "rash of appeals" from the seventy persons already sentenced to death in Tennessee.[208] Other senators argued that an adult with an I.Q. of a seven or eight-year-old "knows right from wrong" and therefore can be executed. They argued that a person who has "enough sense" to commit murder also has "enough sense to be executed."[209]

However, the basic premises that children and individuals with mental retardation who are "mentally children" aren't executed by "a civilized society" were far more persuasive.[210] During the first week of April, 1990, House Bill 2107, "An Act . . . To Prohibit the Imposition of a Sentence of Death for a Person with Mental Retardation,"[211] passed the house by an eighty-one to three margin.[212] A week later, the Senate version of the bill, S.B. 1851, passed by a vote of twenty-eight for it and three against.[213] Governor Ned McWherter signed the bill into law shortly thereafter.[214]

The law defines mental retardation in three parts:

Significantly subaverage general intellectual functioning; and

Deficits in adaptive behavior; and

The mental retardation must have been manifested during the developmental period, or by the age of eighteen (18).[215]

Next, it simply states that "no defendant with mental retardation at the time of committing first degree murder shall be sentenced to death."[216] The defendant has the "burden of production and persuasion" to establish mental retardation by "a preponderance of the evidence."[217] The "court" rather than the jury makes the determination of mental retardation,[218] and by implication, this must be made during the guilt/innocence phase of the trial.

If the "trier of fact," whether judge or jury, enters a verdict of "guilty of first degree murder" and a determination of mental retardation has been made at trial, then life imprisonment is automatic. No separate penalty hearing should be held.[219] By simply stating that the "defendant shall be sentenced to life imprisonment,"[220] the law does not address the issue of possibility of parole.

Tennessee's law also adds an interesting secondary feature. When the issue of mental retardation has been raised at trial and the court has found "that the defendant is not a person with mental retardation," the defense can still offer evidence of "diminished intellectual capacity as a mitigating circumstance" in the sentencing hearing.[221] This provision allows a second opportunity for the defendant to be spared the death penalty because of mental disability, even though a determination has been made that the disability does not meet all aspects of the definition of mental retardation. This clause was not in the original version of S.B. 1851, but was added in later in an amended bill as an additional safeguard for the rights of intellectually handicapped defendants.[222]

Thus Tennessee lawmakers took care not only to prohibit executions of defendants with mental retardation. They were also diligent to include case-by-case determination of mitigation due to diminished mental capacity as an alternative when mental retardation could not be proven at trial. This secondary opportunity to be spared from a death sentence is similar to the single standard established in the *Penry* case.

In sum, Tennessee was careful to ensure that the death penalty would not be automatically applied if mental retardation could not be proven by the preponderance of the evidence at trial.

The Tennessee statute contains no effective date so that the date of enactment by default became the effective date. The issue of retroactive application to any of Tennessee's Death Row inmates was not addressed.[223]

Kentucky. Also in April of 1990, Kentucky's Senate Bill 172, "An Act Relating to the Execution of the Mentally Retarded,"[224] became law with little commotion or national attention.

The bill defines the term offender to include both adults, and minors under eighteen who are tried as adults.[225] By implication, Kentucky did not preclude the execution of minors who do not have mental retardation.

A person who cannot be executed is "a seriously mentally retarded offender."[226] The word "seriously" is added to the phrase "mentally retarded" although the definition of the term is precisely the same as that which is universally accepted. Thus it has no real meaning other than to call attention to the fact that mental retardation is a serious, debilitating condition.

The definition states that a seriously mentally retarded offender is one "with significant subaverage intellectual functioning existing concurrently with substantial deficits in adaptive behavior and manifested during the developmental period."[227] Unlike Tennessee's law which does not contain the usual I.Q. delineation, significant subaverage intellectual functioning is here detailed as "an intelligence quotient (I.Q.) of seventy (70) or below."[228]

In contrast to Tennessee's procedures which call for a determination of mental retardation at trial, Kentucky's procedures for establishing that an offender is seriously mentally retarded require that this be done in a separate, pretrial proceeding. The defendant must file a motion with the court at least thirty days prior to the trial alleging that he or she is seriously mentally retarded. The defense may also provide evidence in support of this claim, and the State can offer evidence in rebuttal. The court must make a determination of the issue not more than ten days before the trial, that is, within twenty days of the filing of the motion.[229]

If a determination of serious mental retardation is made in these pretrial proceedings, then this determination governs.[230] The seriously mentally retarded defendant cannot "be subject to execution,"[231] but may be sentenced to any sentences other than death which are found in the other parts of Kentucky statutes that deal with capital crimes.[232]

Finally, Kentucky's statute specifically precludes retroactive application to offenders with mental retardation already sentenced to death. It states that it applies only to trials that begin after its effective date of July 13, 1990.[233]

In sum, the statutes of Tennessee and Kentucky take similar approaches to prohibiting executions of offenders with mental retardation, although they differ in some of the particulars of the definition of mental retardation and the procedures for making this determination. Both authorize the court to make a finding of mental retardation, and both provide for automatic life sentences if such a determination is made.

NEW MEXICO

New Mexico is the fifth state which bans executions of persons with mental retardation.[234] New Mexico's mental retardation death penalty statute was introduced, passed and signed into law within a two month period between January and March, 1991.[235]

The definition of mental retardation in the New Mexico statute is once again a variation of the standard definition. According to the statute, "'Mentally retarded' means significantly subaverage general intellectual functioning existing concurrently with deficits in adaptive behavior."[236] Onset during the developmental stage is not referenced.

The statute further elaborates on how the definition of mental retardation shall be detailed. "An intelligence quotient of seventy or below on a reliably administered intelligence quotient test shall be presumptive evidence of mental retardation."[237] Thus, for several reasons, mental retardation is more easily proven in New Mexico than in other states. Only one I.Q. test score in the standard range of mental retardation is needed. The permissible types and conditions of testing are broad, because the laws does not define the term "reliably administered." Finally, the court is directed to view this single measure as presumptive evidence that the defendant has mental retardation in absence of evidence to the contrary.

The statute also lays out procedures for the determination of mental retardation. Once a defendant has been found guilty of a capital offense, the defense may file a motion "requesting . . . that the penalty of death be precluded"[238] under the section that says that "the penalty of death shall not be imposed on any person who is mentally retarded."[239]

The court is required to hold a separate hearing to address this motion prior to the sentencing proceeding. In this hearing it must weigh the evidence that alleges that the defendant is mentally retarded against that which shows that he is not. The court must make a determination of the issue by the "preponderance of the evidence."[240]

If the court finds that the defendant is mentally retarded, then "it shall sentence him to life imprisonment"[241] because such a finding automatically precludes the death penalty. If the court finds that the death penalty is not automatically precluded, that is, that the defendant does not meet the definition of mental retardation by the preponderance of the evidence, then the defense may use the offender's "diminished intelligence" as mitigating evidence, both here and during the regular sentencing hearing.[242] Further, should a jury be seated for the penalty hearing, it "shall not be informed of any ruling [in the earlier special hearing] denying the defendant's motion" for an automatic life sentence.[243]

To summarize, according to the New Mexico statute, the defendant gets at least three chances to be spared the death penalty. The first is before the judge based on presumptive evidence of mental retardation and a preponderance of the evidence standard. Should the judge find that there is insufficient evidence to prove mental retardation, the defense may argue for mitigation by reason of diminished intelligence. Should this fail to persuade the judge, the defense may use the mitigation argument anew in the regular sentencing proceeding before a jury that is uninformed of the judge's ruling.

Thus if mental retardation doesn't automatically preclude death, the defense may use the weaker case-by-case approach established in *Penry*. It may argue that diminished mental capacity is mitigating evidence sufficient to prevent execution in this case. A jury may be persuaded where a judge was not, even though denying the death penalty via this path is more difficult.

To summarize, New Mexico's statute is broad in allowing evidence to prevent the execution of offenders with mental retardation. Only one I.Q. test is required for a determination of mental retardation, and the defense gets additional opportunities for the defendant's limited intelligence to be used to prevent execution should this fail.

LEGISLATION PENDING IN THE STATES

INTRODUCTION

This section summarizes the attempts of twenty-four states to ban executions of offenders with mental retardation legislatively. Included among these are those states (Delaware, South Carolina, Texas and Virginia) which have added mental retardation as a mitigating factor in capital cases, but which have stopped short of a complete ban.

ARIZONA

Early in 1992, the State of Arizona was approaching its first execution since 1963. Donald Eugene Harding was scheduled to die in April. In reaction to this disconcerting prospect, State Senator Manuel "Lito" Pena (D-Southwest Phoenix), a staunch opponent of the death penalty and chair of the Senate Judiciary Committee, led a legislative attach to ban the death penalty outright.[244] Introduced on February 20, 1992, his bill, Senate Bill 1472, would have repealed the state statute which authorizes the death penalty. A similar bill, House Bill 2237, was introduced in the Arizona House on February 5, 1992.[245]

S.B. 1472 was referred to the Senate Judiciary Committee. Despite Senator Pena's stature and support and the strong backing of churches and human rights activists, the Senator could not muster sufficient votes from his colleagues to move the bill out of committee to the full Senate.[246] Public opinion polls showed that "a large majority" of Arizona citizens supported executions.[247]

In order to salvage something from the situation, late in March, 1992, only days before Harding was about to die in the gas chamber, Senator Pena introduced a compromise bill. This amended version would have barred execution of persons with mental retardation and juveniles under the age of eighteen at the time they committed the capital crime. Senator Pena stated that he offered this compromise "as a step toward eventual repeal of capital punishment."[248] While Maryland opponents of the ban on executions of persons afflicted by mental retardation had used the foot-in-the-door argument to oppose the bill,[249] and supporters denied that this was their intent, in Arizona proponents openly, and, perhaps unwisely, stated this argument. Arizona Republicans in the Senate used the same argument to oppose the bill.[250]

Nevertheless, Senator Pena was able to get his modified bill out of committee by a narrow margin on April 7, 1992, the day after Donald Harding died a slow and "grisly" death in the Arizona gas chamber. The vote was split five to four "along party lines."[251] However, when the bill came to a vote on the Senate floor on April 20, 1992, it failed to receive the necessary votes to pass.[252]

As finally voted on, the bill would have required persons with mental retardation convicted of first degree murder to be sentenced to life in prison without the possibility of parole. However, the bill contained no definition of mental retardation nor procedures for determining if a defendant has mental retardation. This lack of a definition helped to defeat the bill. The missing definition, just like too vague a definition, was called a "loophole" that could be used as a defense[253] by virtually every capital defendant.

ARKANSAS

The State of Arkansas has made one attempt to prohibit executions of offenders with mental retardation. Senate Bill 739 was introduced in the Arkansas legislature on March 8, 1991. It went no further than that.

S.B. 739 would have prohibited capital punishment for persons with mental retardation, with adjudication of the issue of the defendant's mental retardation made before trial.

The bill contained a retroactive feature. It included provisions for the reduction of sentence if the determination of mental retardation was made after a death sentence had already been imposed.[254]

COLORADO

In 1992, Senator Regis F. Groff (D) and Representative Steve Ruddick (D) co-sponsored Colorado Senate Bill 55, a bill to prohibit the execution of offenders with mental retardation.[255] The bill followed the New Mexico statute's format. It consisted of a definition of mental retardation, provisions for a motion for a separate evidentiary hearing on the issue of the defendant's mental retardation in capital cases, presentation of evidence by the defense and prosecution, a standard of proof, automatic life imprisonment without parole if the offender is proven to have mental retardation, and an effective date for the bill's provisions.[256]

S.B. 55 contained a standard three part definition. A defendant with mental retardation is one who has "significantly subaverage intellectual functioning existing concurrently with substantial deficits in adaptive behavior and manifested during the developmental period."[257] The definition is not detailed in terms of I.Q. or developmental age.

The bill provided for a separate hearing on the issue of mental retardation for Class 1 Felonies (murders) should the defense file a motion seeking this hearing.[258] Prosecution and defense could both present evidence on the issue, and the defense carried the "burden of proof" by "clear and convincing evidence" to show that the defendant has mental retardation.[259] This standard of proof falls between the preponderance of the evidence and the beyond a reasonable doubt standards in the degree of difficulty of proof. Colorado is the only state to suggest this standard in its mental retardation legislation.

If the defendant is found to have mental retardation, then no penalty hearing is held. The defendant is automatically sentenced to life in prison without parole.[260] This mental retardation provision for life imprisonment is coupled with a similar one against executing juveniles who were under the age of eighteen at the time they committed the crime.[261]

The effective date of the bill was the date of passage. The bill applied to offenses committed after the date of passage rather than trials commencing after the effective date. Consequently, new trials for previously convicted Class 1 Felons would not fall under this law.[262]

An earlier version of the bill, House Bill 1020 b, was introduced in a special legislative session in September, 1991.[263] This bill contained the modifier "seriously" for mentally retarded and used the seventy or below I.Q. cutoff.[264] These were both deleted from the 1992 Senate bill. The mental retardation provisions were tied to amended proceedings for Class 1 Felony hearings[265] but were severed from them in the 1992 version. This may improve S.B. 55's chances of passage. Nonetheless, the bill failed to receive a favorable vote from the House in March, 1992, despite previously clearing the Senate in January.[266]

CONNECTICUT

In January, 1991, Representatives Joseph A. Adamo (D) and Stephen Dargan (D) proposed House Bill 5083, "An Act Concerning the Death Penalty," which contained a one line statement of limitation on the death penalty. It proposed that "the general statutes [of Connecticut] be amended to subject only persons over the age of eighteen *whose mental capacity is not significantly impaired* to the death penalty."[267] The bill contained no definition of what a significant impairment of mental capacity is. Assumably, mental retardation would be such a significant impairment so that offenders with mental retardation could not be executed should this legislation become law. However, the bill was introduced on January 9, 1992 and assigned to the Joint Committee on the Judiciary, where it died without movement in the 1992 legislative session.[268]

DELAWARE

The State of Delaware has twice attempted to pass legislation to ban the death penalty for persons with mental retardation. In 1990, the initial bill, Senate Bill 481, was sponsored by Senator Herman M. Holloway, Sr. (D-Wilmington). Representatives Jane P. Maroney (R-Talleyville) and Casimer S. Jonkiert (D) joined him as co-sponsors.[269]

Initial drafts of the bill were modeled on Georgia's "Guilty but Mentally Retarded" statute.[270] These drafts contained procedures for transfer of offenders with mental retardation convicted of capital crimes from the Department of Correction to the Division of Mental Retardation (DMR) based on the documented needs of the offenders.[271] The bill was initially worked by a non-legislative committee of the Sentencing Accountability Commission (SENTAC), the SENTAC Mentally Retarded Offender Committee.

Through a long process of negotiation with DMR in this committee throughout the spring of 1990, these procedures were eventually eliminated.

The bill was finally released from this committee by a three to two vote late in the second session of the 135th General Assembly. It was introduced on June 14, 1990, just two weeks prior to adjournment.[272] Thus it had little chance of passage in that session.

The bill as finally introduced in the Senate, S.B. 481, added a new section to the state's "Guilty but Mentally Ill" Statute.[273] The section contained a definition of mental retardation. "'[M]entally retarded' means:

> having 'significantly subaverage general intellectual functioning' which is interpreted to mean an intelligence quotient (I.Q.) score of 69 or less, and . . . resulting in or associated with 'deficits in adaptive behavior' which is interpreted to mean that the mentally retarded person does not have sufficient life skills to get along in the world without constant assistance from others, and . . . which 'manifested during the developmental period' which is interpreted to mean prior to age twenty-two (22).[274]

The bill described the "[a]ction to be taken upon plea of guilty, but mentally retarded in capital cases."[275] In trials that would begin

> after July 1, 1991, should the judge find in accepting a plea of guilty, but mentally retarded, or the jury or court find in its verdict that the defendant is guilty, but mentally retarded, the death penalty shall not be imposed and the court shall sentence the defendant to imprisonment for life without probation or parole.[276]

The bill provided for the determination of mental retardation to be made at trial based on the definition contained within the proposed statute. However, it provided for no standard of proof by which this decision would be determined. Earlier drafts of the bill had required that the trier of fact find that the defendant has mental retardation beyond a reasonable doubt in a separate hearing on the issue.[277] These procedures had been eliminated along with the inter-departmental transfer procedures.[278] By default, usual evidentiary and trial procedures would prevail.

The bill's effective date in initial drafts had been placed a year after anticipated passage. The intent was to allow for the transfer procedures between the Department of Correction and the Division of Mental Retardation to be developed and set in place. When these were removed prior to the bill's introduction, the year's lead time was left intact

Since it was apparent to the bill's drafter that delay in the introduction of the bill would cause it to have little chance of passage in the 1990 legislative session, another approach was also tried. The State's Sentencing Accountability Commission (SENTAC) had been legislatively charged with developing standards and guidelines for an equitable criminal sentencing system.[279] The standards it developed allowed judges to sentence outside adopted guidelines if mitigating or aggravating factors were present. Among the mitigating factors listed were "physical or mental impairment."[280] However, these standards gave the judges no explicit way to indicate that mental retardation was a mitigating factor that influenced their sentencing decision.

In the Spring of 1990, the author approached SENTAC to endorse the "Guilty but Mentally Retarded Act," or alternatively, to at least include mental retardation as an explicit mitigating factor to be used in sentencing. At its meeting in June, 1990, SENTAC refused to endorse the legislative ban on executions of persons with mental retardation. SENTAC's membership is largely comprised of members of the judiciary who are prohibited from making such endorsements.

Nonetheless, SENTAC agreed to make mental retardation an explicit factor listed among those that the Court can use to mitigate sentences outlined by the sentencing standards. SENTAC indicated that it did not find it necessary to adopt mental retardation as a mitigating factor legislatively, but that the phrase "mental retardation" could be added to the judges' sentencing sheets as an additional mitigating option for statistical purposes, that is, in order to keep track of the numbers of persons with mental retardation being sentenced outside the sentencing standards. Thus mental retardation was adopted as a mitigating factor in sentencing by SENTAC policy decision.[281]

When the 135th Legislative Session ended in June, 1990, S.B. 481 died with it. The author was determined to try again next year to get this legislation passed in the newly-elected 136th General Assembly. Over the winter, an attorney for the Community Legal Aid Society's Disabilities Law Program assisted in redrafting the proposed legislation in order to smooth out some of the rough spots and to give it a better chance for adoption. The result was House Bill 192/Senate Bill 101. Once again Senator Holloway and Representative Maroney were the primary sponsors.[282]

H.B. 192 and S.B. 101 were identical bills. The definition of mental retardation was modified to define significantly subaverage intellectual functioning as an I.Q. of seventy or below. "Deficits in adaptive behavior" was "defined as significant limitations in the defendant's effectiveness in meeting the standards of maturation, learning, personal independence, and/or social responsibility that are expected for his/or her age and cultural group." The developmental period was narrowed as the period "between conception and age 18."[283]

The procedures for making the determination of mental retardation were virtually the same as those contained in the 1990 version of the bill. In capital trials commencing after July 1, 1991, based on the definition of mental retardation contained in the bill, the judge could "accept a plea of guilty but mentally retarded, or the jury could find this verdict. Upon the court's acceptance of the plea or the jury's verdict, the defendant could not be sentenced to death but could be given any other sentence lawfully authorized for the offense.[284]

The plan in 1991 was to introduce the bill simultaneously in the House and Senate and work it through in each chamber. The bills were introduced on April 24 (S.B. 101) and April 25, 1991 (H.B. 192) respectively.[285] However, as the session progressed, the bill's backers developed a strategy to actively push H.B. 192 in the House. The bill was referred to the House Judiciary Committee and was placed on the Committee's agenda for review on May 8, 1991.

Although not a member of the Judiciary Committee, Representative Maroney attended the committee meeting. When it became apparent that the votes were not there to move the bill out of Committee to the House floor, Ms. Maroney asked that the bill be tabled until after a public hearing could be held on it.[286]

At that hearing which was held on May 14, 1991, the State's Attorney General and a representative of the professional mental retardation community spoke against the bill.[287] Thereafter, the Chair of the House Judiciary Committee refused to put the bill back on the Committee's agenda unless he could be assured that the votes were there to move the bill out of committee. Three votes of the six person committee were needed to do so. Two committee members were supportive, two were against, and two were undecided. Neither of the two fence sitters could be persuaded to be the swing vote, so the bill stayed in committee until summer adjournment on June 30, 1991.

The Second Session of the 136th General Assembly began in January, 1992. However, no further action was taken on either S.B. 101 or H.B. 192 in this session. Major elections were to be held this year in which all General Assembly members were facing re-election campaigns. The decision was made not to push such a controversial and politically sensitive item under these conditions. The bills died in committee at the Legislature's adjournment.

FLORIDA

Bills to ban the death penalty for offenders with mental retardation were introduced in the Florida legislature in three consecutive years - 1990, 1991, and 1992.

In the spring of 1990, Representative Dixie Sansom (R-Satellite Beach) sponsored House Bill 3029, and Senator Bob Johnson (R-Sarasota) introduced a similar bill, Senate Bill 1242.[288]

Although sponsored by two Republicans, the measures also had substantial support among Democrats. A Democratic Representative,

Eleanor Winstock of Palm Beach, stated that, although the public strongly supports the death penalty in general, its support is limited for the execution of persons with mental retardation.[289]

Additional backing came from the Association for Retarded Citizens of Florida, whose director stated, "'We're trying to do something about the issue before we can execute someone who is mentally retarded.'"[290] However, the coordinator of the Florida Department of Correction's impaired inmate services guardedly stated that, although she could not be certain, she believed that none of the three hundred and nine Death Row inmates in Florida have mental retardation.[291]

Florida law already provided for a separate penalty hearing for defendants who had been convicted of capital crimes but who were not yet sentenced.[292] The 1990 bills would have amended the procedures for this hearing to accommodate the mental retardation defense. The bills simply stated that a "defendant who establishes by a preponderance of the evidence that he meets the definition of retardation . . . . [which was stated elsewhere in Florida law] . . . shall not be punished by death."[293] That definition defines mental retardation as:

> significantly subaverage general intellectual functioning existing concurrently with deficits in adaptive behavior and manifested during the period from conception to age 18. 'Significantly subaverage general intellectual functioning, . . .' means performance which is two or more standard deviations from the mean score on a standardized intelligence test. . . . 'Adaptive behavior, . . .' means the effectiveness or degree with which an individual meets the standards of personal independence and social responsibility expected of his age, cultural group, and community.[294]

The bills also set out a procedure to be used to identify offenders with mental retardation among the more than three hundred Florida prisoners already condemned to death. This procedure would have been added to existing procedures for removing the insane from Death Row.[295]

The burden of initiating the process would fall to the Governor. Existing law required the Governor to appoint a three person panel of psychiatrists to examine a Death Row inmate when the Governor "is informed" that a person under sentence of death may be insane. The amended law would have required the Governor to appoint a panel of "three experts in the diagnosis and evaluation of mental retardation in the case of a convicted person who appears to be retarded." The governor would notify the panel that they were to examine the person "to determine whether he understands the nature and effect of the death penalty and why it is to be imposed upon him." All three panelists were required to be present during the examination, and the defense and state's attorneys could also be present.[296]

The panelists would issue a report to the Governor concerning their findings, and the Governor would make the final determination. If the Governor decided that the defendant "has the mental capacity to understand the nature of the death penalty and the reasons why it was imposed upon him," then he would issue the death warrant. If the Governor determined that the defendant does not have this capacity and has mental retardation, then he would have "the person . . . committed . . . to a Department of Correction . . . retardation facility. . . . "[297]

In sum, because Florida already had so many Death Row inmates, these bills were more concerned about the possibility of executing someone who was already condemned than about persons who had yet to be convicted. In placing the emphasis on existing Death Row inmates, the bills established a somewhat cumbersome process outside of the judicial system for identifying existing inmates with mental retardation and providing them with relief. These procedures undoubtedly doomed the bills to failure.

The House version of the bill was referred to several committees, including the Committee on Criminal Justice, the Appropriations Committee, and the Subcommittee on Prosecution and Punishment. It died on June 2, 1990 in the Committee on Criminal Justice without action. The Senate bill also failed to pass.[298]

In 1991, Representative Sansom reintroduced her bill into the House as H.B. 657. It fared no better than it did in the previous year.[299]

In 1992, the measure was tried once again. This time, Senate Bill 872 was introduced in January and referred to the Committees on Criminal Justice and Appropriations, where it died at the end of the legislative session.[300]

S.B. 872 substantially differed from the earlier versions. Rather than making the mental retardation determination a part of the regular sentencing hearing, the bill established procedures for a separate judicial hearing. When a person was convicted of a capital felony, and "upon motion of the defendant," the court would have been required to conduct a separate hearing, "without consideration of a sentence of death due to the defendant's allegation that he suffers from mental retardation. . . ." The purpose of the hearing would be to determine if the defendant meets the definition of mental retardation as defined elsewhere in the Florida statute.[301] The definition would be the same, generally accepted one.

The defendant would have been required to "establish by the preponderance of evidence that he meets the definition, . . . " and if he did so, then he would be sentenced to "life imprisonment without the possibility of parole for a minimum of twenty-five years."[302]

The bill required the court to issue a statement in writing outlining "its findings of fact and conclusions of law to justify the determination of mental retardation."[303] This requirement went beyond those of other states which proposed a separate mental retardation hearing and required merely a written statement of the findings without any legal opinion of fact and law.

To further clarify the intent of the procedures, the bill stated that a finding of mental retardation would not mean that the defendant was adjudicated incompetent nor that any "criminal charge or conviction" was thereby dismissed.[304]

The bill authorized the State to appeal from any finding that the defendant has mental retardation,[305] and made clear that, if the court found that the defendant "failed to prove that he" has mental retardation, then the case would proceed to an ordinary sentencing hearing to determine whether the sentence would be death or life imprisonment.[306]

Finally, the bill contained an effective date of October 1, 1992 for "offenses" rather than trials "committed on or after that date."[307] The issue of existing Death Row inmates and their retrials or other review on the issue of mental retardation was completely avoided.

Despite its more narrow focus - the elimination of the gubernatorial determination of mental retardation for existing inmates, the lack of any retroactive provisions, and the more detailed and precise determination of the retardation of defendants who are prospectively tried for capital crimes - the 1992 version of the bill also failed to pass.[308]

IDAHO

The State of Idaho attempted to pass legislation to ban executions of offenders with mental retardation in two successive years, 1991 and 1992. The first attempt was Senate Bill No. 1175.[309] Proposed in 1992, Senate Bill No. 140 was the second attempt.[310] With two relatively minor exceptions, it was virtually identical to the 1991 version.

The first section of each bill contained definitions of terms.

First, a defendant was defined as "an adult, or a minor under eighteen (18) years of age who is tried as an adult."[311]

Second, in the 1991 bill, a defendant with mental retardation was one "with significantly subaverage intellectual functioning existing concurrently with substantial deficits in adaptive behavior and manifested during the developmental period."[312] In the 1992 bill, the word "general" was added between the terms "subaverage" and "intellectual," so that the definition read "significantly subaverage general intellectual functioning."[313]

Third, an offender was "an adult, or a minor under eighteen (18) years of age who was tried as an adult and was convicted, found guilty or entered a plea of guilty for a crime and is subject to sentencing" under this statute.[314]

Fourth, in the 1991 bill, "significantly subaverage intellectual functioning" was defined as "an intelligence quotient (I.Q.) of seventy (70) or below."[315] In the 1992 bill, this specific definition was eliminated.[316] The remainder of both bills are identical.

Following the definitions, the prohibition of executions of persons with mental retardation is simply stated as: "no mentally retarded defendant shall be put to death."[317]

Procedures for the determination of mental retardation state that "[t]he state, the defendant or the court may raise the issue of whether the defendant is mentally retarded."[318] This feature of Idaho's proposed legislation is unique among the states. In most instances, if the issue of who raises the question of the defendant's mental limitations is addressed at all, it is the defense's responsibility to do so. By allowing the court or prosecution to raise the question, Idaho guarded against defense attorneys who might not be well-versed in the area of mental handicaps and their relationship to criminal responsibility. This provision offered a broader protection to defendants with mental retardation than making the defense attorney solely responsible for the presentation of evidence of the defendant's mental retardation. It also reduced the chances of appeals on the basis of incompetency of defense counsel when the defense has failed to raise the issue of the defendant's diminished intellectual capacity at trial, and possible mental retardation is discovered in later stages of the legal process.

Once the issue of the defendant's alleged mental retardation had been raised, then "the determination of whether a defendant is mentally retarded . . . shall be made by the court prior to imposition of sentence and shall be set forth in written findings."[319] The process is somewhat vague in comparison to that of some states. No separate hearing, evaluation or submission of evidence was required. No standard of proof, such as the preponderance of the evidence which is so common in his type of legislation, must be met. The issue of mental retardation must simply be raised by any involved legal party, whereupon the court would make the determination based on its interpretation of the definition of a defendant with mental retardation.

Timing was also vague. The bills contained no time frames such as the requirement for submission of evidence thirty days prior to the trial and the issuance of a court ruling within ten days prior to trial as is contained in Kentucky's mental retardation death penalty statute.[320] The only certainty was that the court must issue its written finding prior to sentencing. Thus the determination could be made either during the trial, after conviction while the defendant is awaiting sentencing, or during the penalty hearing before the final sentence determination.

Once a determination has been made that the defendant has mental retardation, and the defendant had been convicted, then he or she could be sentenced "to any other sentence than death authorized by law for a crime which is a capital offense."[321] Thus the offender can be sentenced to life with or without parole.

The proposed statute contained no effective date. Nor was the issue of retroactivity to offenders with mental retardation already under sentence of death addressed.

In 1991 and 1992, neither of Idaho's two bills received a full hearing on the Senate floor. Both were referred to the Senate Judiciary and Rules Committee, where they were held through the end of their respective legislative sessions.[322]

ILLINOIS

In 1989, Illinois came close to being the third state (after Georgia and Maryland) to ban executions of offenders with mental retardation completely. However, its attempt to do so followed a path similar to that of South Carolina's H.B. 3095.[323] What started out to be an absolute ban on executions of persons with mental retardation ended up as a simple addition of mental retardation to the list of mitigating factors in capital cases.

Senator William Marovitz (D-Chicago) introduced Senate Bill 956[324] early in April, 1989.[325] A major and well-respected proponent of the bill, Dolly Hallstrom, spoke persuasively to the legislature in support of the bill.[326] Her name was used throughout the debate to gain legislative support for the measure.[327]

The bill itself contained a definition of mental retardation with some elaboration on the standard definition features. It stated that both:

'mentally retarded' and 'mental retardation' mean significantly subaverage general intellectual functioning existing concurrently with deficits in adaptive behavior and manifested during the developmental period, as determined by a test or tests which are standardized and sufficiently established and reliable to have gained general acceptance in the mental health profession and which are administered and interpreted by a professional trained in the administration and interpretation of such tests.[328]

Thus the determination of at least two of the facets of mental retardation, low intelligence and impaired adaptive behaviors, required strict standards of measurement. The bill required that they be verified by standardized and generally accepted measurement tests. Clinical professionals who have the appropriate training were required to administer them.

Further, the developmental period was defined as "the period of growth and maturation that occurs prior to the age of 18 years."[329] Thus Illinois' definition required true professional verification of mental retardation and went well beyond such proposals which do not indicate how the three elements of mental retardation shall be measured.

Illinois' legislative attempt to prohibit executions of offenders with mental retardation was added to its first degree murder and capital punishment statute.[330] A somewhat negative statement of the prohibition of executions of people with mental retardation was contained in the section that delineates aggravating factors. It stated that "a defendant who at the time of commission of the offense . . . who is not mentally retarded and who has been found guilty of first degree murder may be sentenced to death. . . ."[331] Since only those convicted persons who do not have mental retardation can be executed, by implication those with mental retardation cannot.

The standard for proving that the defendant has mental retardation was the preponderance of the evidence standard, and the defense carried the burden of proof.[332]

The bill passed both houses of the Illinois legislature. After the Senate passed the bill the first time, the House added an amendment to place the burden of proof on the defense. The bill was then returned to the Senate, and after two tries, finally received the three-fifths majority required to pass such a bill.[333]

The bill than went to Governor James Thompson for signature. However, the Governor used his amendatory veto power to strike the proposed bill and substitute mental retardation as a mitigating factor for the absolute ban on executions of people with mental retardation.[334] The bill then went back to the Senate where Senator Marovitz once again tried to lead the Senate to victory. To override the Governor's veto, three-fifths of the Senate would have had to vote for the measure. Although a majority supported the override (the vote was twenty-nine in favor and twenty-five against), the bill failed to receive the necessary three-fifths majority.[335]

In 1991, Illinois once again attempted to pass an outright prohibition of executions of persons with mental retardation. SB 287 would have prohibited defendants with mental retardation from being sentenced to death for first degree murder. This bill was introduced on March 29, 1991 and referred to the Senate Committee on the Judiciary II the next day. However, it went no further than that during the legislative session.[336]

INDIANA

The State of Indiana first attempted to prohibit executions of offenders with mental retardation in 1990. Representative William Crawford of Indianapolis was the sponsor of House Bill 1009 introduced in the 1990 General Assembly[337] and a virtually identical bill, H.B. 1427, introduced in 1991. Neither of these bills succeeded in passing the Indiana legislature.[338]

The Indiana draft legislation was similar in concept to that of Georgia in that it combined the mental retardation defense for capital offenses with the guilty but mentally ill provisions[339] and provided for an evaluation of the defendant's mental condition.[340] However, it did not require a separate evidentiary hearing on the issue of mental retardation.

Indiana's provisions differed from those of Georgia in that they did not permit a guilty but mentally retarded verdict nor provide for treatment of mentally retarded offenders outside of prison. Also unlike Georgia, Indiana coupled its mental retardation provisions with its general death penalty statute.[341]

When the prosecution has filed a warrant seeking the death penalty in a capital case, the bill allowed the defense to allege that the individual has mental retardation in either the trial or penalty hearing.[342] If the defendant had been convicted and a death warrant had been filed, and if the defendant was alleged to be an individual with mental retardation, then the court must order an evaluation of the defendant's condition.[343] This evaluation would entail investigation of all three elements of the definition of mental retardation contained in the bill - an I.Q. score of seventy or less on an individually administered I.Q. test as evidence of significantly subaverage intellectual functioning, adaptive behavior impairment, and onset prior to age twenty-two.[344] Thus Indiana would have required substantive evidence of mental retardation rather than simply relying on the adversarial process in an evidentiary hearing as do Kentucky and New Mexico.[345]

If, based on the evaluation, the defense proved by the preponderance of the evidence in the sentencing hearing that the defendant is a mentally retarded individual,[346] then the jury could not recommend a death sentence,[347] nor could the court impose such a sentence.[348] Indiana is one of the few states which legislatively requires that the judge impose the sentence in capital cases and relegates the jury to the lesser role of mere sentence recommendation.[349] Indiana's mental retardation procedures accommodated these unique features of the Indiana capital sentencing process.

LOUISIANA

By rights, the State of Louisiana should have been one of the first to ban executions of persons with mental retardation. It has executed three offenders with mental retardation, more than any other state.[350] The execution of Dalton Prejean received national publicity[351] as has the impending execution of Robert Wayne Sawyer, a dually diagnosed murderer with mental retardation and mental illness.[352]

The reaction to capital punishment and offenders with mental retardation in Louisiana has not been as great as that in Georgia or Maryland where condemned murderers with mental retardation have propelled the issue into the public consciousness and onto the legislative agenda. The initial attempt to deal with the issue came from Senator Dennis Bagneris, (D-New Orleans) with the introduction of Senate Bill No. 687 in 1991. This bill would have required the court to conduct a special hearing after conviction for first degree murder and before the sentencing hearing to receive evidence concerning the offender's possible mental retardation.

Should the evidence show that the offender did in fact have mental retardation, then he or she would automatically be sentenced to life in prison.[353]

However, an amendment to the bill by the Senate Committee on Judiciary C removed the procedures for determining mental retardation as well as the complete ban on executions of offenders with mental retardation. It simply added mental retardation "at the time of the sentencing hearing which manifest during the developmental period" to the list of mitigating factors already required to be considered in determining the sentence in capital cases.[354]

In 1992, Representative Haik introduced House Bill No. 29, a bill similar to the original S.B. 687.[355] This bill contained the usual definition of mental retardation. It stated that:

. . . 'mentally retarded' means significantly subaverage general intellectual functioning, which exists concurrently with deficits in adaptive behavior that are manifested during the developmental period. An intelligence quotient of seventy or below on a reliably administered intelligence quotient test shall be presumptive evidence that a person is mentally retarded.[356]

The provision prohibiting executions of persons with mental retardation stated that "Notwithstanding any other provision of law to the contrary, a sentence of death shall not be imposed on any person who is mentally retarded."[357]

Procedures for making a determination of mental retardation required that, after a defendant had been convicted and before the penalty hearing, if the defense filed a motion to request it, the court should hold a special hearing to consider the issue. During this time the jury would remain sequestered.[358]

The defense had the burden of proving by the preponderance of the evidence that the defendant has mental retardation.[359]

Additional procedures not ordinarily included in this type of legislation stated that "the hearing shall be conducted according to the rules of evidence," and, "insofar as applicable, the procedure at the hearing to determine mental retardation shall be the same as that provided for trial" under Louisiana law. The defendant was permitted to "testify in his own behalf," and "in the event of retrial the defendant's testimony shall not be admissible except for purposes of impeachment."[360] Thus the hearing on the issue of mental retardation was made as similar as possible to ordinary court procedures.

If the court found that the defendant in fact has mental retardation, then no additional sentencing hearing would be conducted, and the court was required to sentence the defendant to "life imprisonment without benefit of probation, parole, or suspension of sentence."[361]

If the court found that the defendant does not have mental retardation, then the ordinary sentencing hearing would proceed, and the jury would not be told of the court's ruling. The defendant would be free to offer evidence of mental retardation as a mitigating factor in the regular penalty hearing.[362] Thus the bill provided a check on the court's singular determination of the mental retardation issue, and the jury's review of the evidence would provide the defendant with a second chance to have evidence of his mental retardation mitigate his sentence.

H.B. 29 fared little better than S.B. 687. It was referred to the House Committee on Administration of Criminal Justice on March 30, 1992,[363] where it died without ever being heard or debated.[364]

MISSISSIPPI

A bill has been introduced to ban the death penalty for people with mental retardation in the Mississippi House of Representatives in each of three successive years. House Bill 444 in 1990,[365] House Bill 303 in 1991,[366] and House Bill 995 in 1992[367] were identical except for the effective date which was moved forward to July 1 of each successive year.[368] None of the three bills proceeded in the legislative process beyond the House Judiciary Committee to which each was initially referred.[369]

The bills would have amended the capital sentencing process after a person had been convicted of "capital murder or other capital offense."[370] The law required the sentencing hearing to be conducted before a jury.[371] Consequently, the jury would also make the determination of mental retardation.

"For the jury to impose a sentence of death, it must unanimously find in writing," along with the usual determination of aggravating circumstances, "that the defendant is not mentally retarded."[372] By implication, if the jury fails to find unanimously that the defendant is not mentally retarded, then he or she is mentally retarded and cannot be sentenced to death. Thus one hold out juror who would not certify that the defendant is not mentally retarded could prevent the imposition of the death penalty.

The capital sentencing process was further modified by a statement that "No person who is mentally retarded . . . shall be sentenced to death or executed."[373] Mentally retarded was defined, for the "purposes of this act," as "significantly subaverage general intellectual functioning which exists concurrently with defects in adaptive behavior and which is manifested during the developmental period."[374]

MISSOURI

The State of Missouri introduced bills in 1991 and 1992 which would have prohibited executions of persons with mental retardation. The first of these, House Bill No. 188, provided that life imprisonment without parole is the punishment for a mentally retarded person convicted of murder in the first degree.[375]

The second bill, House Bill No. 1213 which was introduced on January 8, 1992, had similar provisions. It stated that the punishment for murder in the first degree

shall be either death or imprisonment for life without eligibility for probation or parole, or release except by act of the governor; except that, if a person has not reached his sixteenth birthday at the time of commission of the crime or is mentally retarded as defined [elsewhere in the Missouri statutes], the punishment shall be imprisonment for life without eligibility for probation or parole, or release.[376]

The referenced definition of mental retardation states that it is "significantly subaverage general intellectual functioning which originates before age eighteen; and is associated with a significant impairment in adaptive behavior."[377]

Neither of the Missouri proposals contained procedures for determination of mental retardation. Neither did either of the bills go very far in the legislative process. In 1991, H.B. 188 was introduced on January 9, 1991 and referred to the House Committee on the Judiciary later that month. No action was taken on it subsequently.[378]

In 1992, H.B. 1213 was referred to the House Committee on Civil and Criminal Law and died there upon adjournment of the General Assembly on May 15, 1992.[379]

NEBRASKA

The impetus for Nebraska's 1989 attempt to no longer permit persons with mental retardation to be executed came from several related events which had recently occurred on the national scene. According to the statement of intent of the sponsor of Legislative Bill 464, Senator Ernie Chambers, he was proposing the bill because the federal Anti-Drug Abuse Act of 1988 contained "such a prohibition," the American Bar Association had passed a resolution opposing executions of persons with mental retardation, and the State of Georgia had enacted a similar statute after the execution of Jerome Bowden.[380] In addition, Senator Chambers used the "anti-child execution" argument.[381] He stated that "the mental age of a person falling within the definition is under 13."[382]

L.B. 464 was introduced on January 17, 1989 and referred to the Judiciary Committee the next day. That committee held a public hearing on the bill on February 22, 1989, but the bill was never voted out of Committee. It died there at the end of the legislative session.[383]

Nebraska's Legislative Bill 464 was tersely stated in three sections which were unrelated either to Nebraska's general capital punishment or mental illness statutes. First, the bill stated that, "Notwithstanding any other provision of law, the death penalty shall not be imposed upon a person with mental retardation."[384]

The second section, the definition of mental retardation is also stated simply. " . . . [P]erson with mental retardation shall mean a person who has significantly sub-average general intellectual functioning existing concurrently with deficits in adaptive behavior and manifested during the developmental period."[385]   No delineation of I.Q. score or definition of developmental stage was given. No method of determination by testing, hearing or evaluation was required. No designation of whether judge or jury should make the determination or in what stage of the criminal proceedings the determination should take place was listed.

The third section required that "[t]he burden of proof shall be on the defendant to show that he or she is a person with mental retardation."[386] No standard of proof by which the evidence of mental retardation should be weighed was contained in the bill. This deficiency was noted at the public hearing on the bill held by the Judiciary Committee. One person who testified in favor of adoption of the bill asked for a clarification of what standard would be used and whether it would be the "beyond a reasonable doubt" burden of proof. He also argued that even the preponderance of the evidence standard, "the least burden that the law recognizes," is "too heavy" for this type of case.[387]

Beyond these three sections, L.B. 464 contained no effective date nor provisions for dealing with offenders with mental retardation already sentenced to death. Senator Pirsch implicitly referred to the lack of a resolution of this issue during the public hearing held on the bill. The Senator asked three different witnesses testifying in favor of the bill whether those persons already on Nebraska's Death Row had been evaluated.[388] He also questioned if the witnesses knew if any of the Death Row inmates had mental retardation,[389] and whether any persons with mental retardation had been executed in Nebraska.[390]

The witnesses responded that, to their knowledge, Death Row inmates had not been evaluated.[391] They also stated that they didn't know whether any of the condemned had mental retardation.[392] One witness answered that no people with mental retardation had been executed in Nebraska.[393]

The definition of mental retardation contained in the bill was also questioned. A witness testifying against the bill argued that mental retardation was "improperly defined," and that it was importantly divergent from the definition in the *Diagnostic and Statistical Manual (DSM-III)*.[394] No definitive resolution of the definition issue resulted from the discussion.

Thus, the Nebraska bill had several ambiguities which were pointed out to the Judiciary Committee during the public hearing. These included a lack of a standard of proof, a questioned definition of mental retardation, no knowledge of whether any existing inmates sentenced to death has mental retardation, and if any did, how the bill would affect them.

Failure to resolve these ambiguities to the satisfaction of the committee members may have contributed to the committee's failure to move the bill out of committee during this legislative session. Impetus in Nebraska for pushing the ban on executions of persons with mental retardation was lost, and no new attempts to pass such legislation have occurred there since L.B. 464.

NEW JERSEY

The State of New Jersey has attempted to pass bills which ban executions of persons with mental retardation in two successive years. The first attempt, A-4631, was proposed in 1989.[395] The second bill, A-3024, was introduced in 1990 and was exactly the same as the first.[396]

These bills would have amended the New Jersey capital punishment statute by adding a new section to the existing law. This section stated that any "person who suffers from mental retardation shall not be sentenced for murder in the first degree pursuant to the provisions" which require the jury or court to "sentence the defendant to death"[397] when aggravating factors outweigh mitigating ones.[398]

Instead, the person with mental retardation would be sentenced according to the provisions which require the offender to be sentenced to prison, either for a term of thirty years "during which the person shall not be eligible for parole," or to a term "between 30 years and life imprisonment" with a requirement that at least the first thirty years be served before the offender becomes parole eligible.[399] Thus New Jersey avoided the issue of holding a separate hearing on the defendant's mental retardation by linking the determination of mental retardation and the execution prohibition based on it to the penalty hearing.

Mental retardation was defined as "a state of significantly sub-average general intellectual functioning existing concurrently with deficits in adaptive behavior and manifested during the developmental period."[400]

The act was to take effect immediately upon passage.[401]

The bill synopsis stated that the "sponsor believes that the philosophy which grants a juvenile offender an exemption from the death penalty should also encompass an adult defendant who has the mind of a child."[402]

Both A-4631 and A-3024 expired without passage, and no further attempts have been made to date in the New Jersey legislature to ban capital punishment for persons with mental retardation.[403]

NORTH CAROLINA

In March of 1989, Representative Locks introduced House Bill 968 into the North Carolina General Assembly. More than twenty of Lock's colleagues joined as co-sponsors for the bill. H.B. 968 would have prohibited the death penalty for persons with mental retardation.[404]

The bill defined mental retardation by using a definition already contained in North Carolina law.[405] In this way the bill's drafters avoided subjecting the bill to attacks for having a too vague, and therefore unacceptable, definition of who would be exempted under its provisions.

The existing North Carolina statutory definition states that mental retardation is:

significantly subaverage general intellectual functioning existing concurrently with deficits in adaptive behavior and manifested before age 22.[406]

The restriction in H.B. 968 on executions of persons with mental retardation was combined with similar restrictions for two other classes of persons. These included, first, the mentally ill, when their illness is "severe and persistent" and results in impaired emotional or behavioral functioning interfering with "their capacity to remain in the community without supportive treatment or services of a long-term or indefinite duration."[407]

Second, those persons were exempted from execution who otherwise fit the cognitive and behavioral definition of mental retardation, but whose condition exists "as a result of organic brain injury or impairment and regardless of age of onset."[408] In this way, persons who did not meet the third part of the generally accepted definition of mental retardation, that is, their condition began during the developmental period, were included under the aegis of the mental retardation provision. Persons whose intellectual capacities were impaired in adulthood by such events as head trauma, disease or substance abuse would also be spared.

The bill contained procedures for determining that the accused suffered from developmental mental retardation, mental illness or adult mental retardation. The burden of raising the issue was placed on the defendant. Upon submission of a defense motion to the court, the court would be required to "conduct a hearing to determine whether the defendant suffers from any" of the three enumerated conditions.[409] The bill was unclear as to what stage in the trial process this hearing would occur, but by implication, it would be held prior to trial. At a minimum, it would of necessity have to be held prior to any penalty hearing.

The burden of proof was presented negatively and placed on the State. The bill required the prosecution "to prove beyond a reasonable doubt that the defendant does not suffer from" any of the three conditions. If the court found that the State failed to do so, then the defendant would not be "eligible for the death penalty."[410]

A finding that the defendant did in fact suffer from one of the three debilitating conditions would result in a judicial declaration that the case was "noncapital." Thereafter, the prosecution would be prohibited from seeking "the death penalty against the defendant."[411]

Should the Court deny relief under these proceedings, such a denial would be "without prejudice to the defendant's right to rely on this defense at trial." Further, ". . . no reference to the hearing" could "be made at the trial, and recorded testimony or evidence" would be inadmissible as evidence.[412] Thus, evidence of developmental or adult mental retardation could be presented *de novo* in mitigation of the punishment in a separate death penalty proceeding.

Upon introduction, H.B. 968 was referred to the House Committee on the Judiciary. Later in the 1989 session, it was withdrawn from that committee and referred to the Joint Committee on Civil Procedure where it remained dormant until the end of the legislative session.[413]

In 1991, Representative Milton F. Fitch, Jr. (D), one of the co-sponsors of H.B. 968, became the lead sponsor of another attempt to prohibit the death penalty for mentally retarded persons. This bill, House Bill 1005, was introduced in April, 1991 and referred to the House Committee on the Judiciary I. It went no further than that in the 1991 legislative session.[414]

OHIO

Ohio's effort to pass legislation barring executions of offenders afflicted with mental retardation was introduced into the 1991 regular session of the 119th General Assembly. The bill, House Bill 342, was referred to the House Committee on the Judiciary and Criminal Justice in April, 1991. The bill lay dormant there throughout the 1991 legislative session and carried over into 1992. On June 17, 1992, it was released from committee and "recommended as substituted." However, it proceeded no further in that legislative session.[415]

H.B. 342 proposed to modify Ohio's death penalty statute as it applies to aggravated murder.[416] The definition of mental retardation was added to the definition's section of the statute. A "mentally retarded person" was defined as one "having significantly subaverage general intellectual functioning existing concurrently with deficiencies in adaptive behavior and manifested during the developmental period."[417]   There was no I.Q. definition nor age for a cutoff in the developmental period.

The provision barring a person convicted of aggravated murder from the death penalty stated that "no person who asserts that he is a mentally retarded person . . . and who is found to be a mentally retarded person shall suffer death."[418]

The bill required that the issue of the defendant's mental retardation be raised at trial when the defendant is charged with aggravated murder rather than at any separate hearing prior to the determination of guilt or innocence.   At trial, the defense "may present evidence of his mental retardation," and "the burdens of asserting mental retardation and of going forward with the evidence relating to the matter of mental retardation" were placed "upon the defendant."[419]

Although the defense must raise the issue and present the evidence, it is up to the prosecution to prove that the defendant is not a mentally retarded person, just as in Ohio's proposed legislation.   "The prosecution shall have the burden of proving, by proof beyond a reasonable doubt, that the defendant is not a mentally retarded person."[420]   This process considerably favored the defendant over the prosecution in comparison to those bills which require the defense to carry the burden of proving that the defendant is mentally retarded by the preponderance of the evidence.

If the defendant is found guilty of aggravated murder and the issue of mental retardation has been raised at trial, the verdict in the case must "separately state whether the offender is a mentally retarded person" as that is so defined.[421]

The death penalty exclusion for mentally retarded persons is reinforced again elsewhere in the bill.   "Death may not be imposed as a penalty for aggravated murder if the offender . . . asserted that he is a mentally retarded person and was found at trial to be a mentally retarded person."[422]

Finally, the bill's provisions were made retroactive to mentally retarded persons already sentenced to death.   Any person condemned to death but not yet executed can file a motion with the court of common pleas that imposed the death sentence.   That court must conduct a hearing if the offender alleges he was a mentally retarded person and this was not previously alleged at trial.   If the prosecution "does not prove beyond a reasonable doubt that the offender . . . is not a mentally retarded person," then the court must "vacate the sentence."[423]   This provision provided for equal protection for mentally retarded persons already on Ohio's Death Row.

OKLAHOMA

The State of Oklahoma has made one attempt to pass legislation to prohibit executions of persons afflicted with mental retardation. Senate Bill 812 was introduced in the Oklahoma Senate on February 5, 1992 during the Forty-Third Legislature's second regular session. The bill would have prohibited the execution of "a seriously mentally retarded person sentenced to death." It would have required life imprisonment without permitting any other sentence for capital offenses. If passed, the bill would have taken effect on July 1, 1992.[424]

The bill was referred to the Senate Committee on the Judiciary which moved it out to the Senate floor for a vote on February 18, 1992. It failed to pass the Senate.[425]

OREGON

Senate Bill 707, Oregon's endeavor to ban the death penalty for mentally retarded persons, was introduced into the Legislative Assembly in February, 1991. It was referred to the Senate Judiciary Committee.[426] That Committee amended the bill to provide for a pretrial hearing at which the defense must establish by the preponderance of the evidence that the defendant is mentally retarded.[427]

In a public hearing held on the bill on April 26, 1991, Professor James Ellis, renowned expert on the legal aspect of offenders with mental retardation, testified in favor of the bill. He discussed the *Penry* decision and how it placed the responsibility on the states to prohibit executions of such persons as Penry.[428]

A representative from the Oregon District Attorney's Association testified against the bill. He argued that the bill was not needed because no Death Row inmates in Oregon were mentally retarded.[429]

Subsequent to the hearing, the Committee unanimously endorsed the bill and moved it out to the Senate floor. On June 4, 1991, the bill sailed through the Senate by a twenty-seven to two vote.[430]

In the House, the bill was referred to the Judiciary Committee. It died there upon legislative adjournment on June 30, 1991 without further movement.[431] Since the Oregon legislature meets only every other year, it was not in session in 1992,[432] and no additional action has been taken on this issue.

The definition of mental retardation in the proposed legislation was that contained in Oregon's statute that deals with the mentally retarded generally, rather than a new definition made specifically for this section of the law. Mental retardation as defined there means "significantly subaverage general intellectual functioning existing concurrently with deficits in adaptive behavior and manifested during the developmental period."[433] Specifically, the person must have an "intelligence quotient of 70 [seventy] or below, the mental disability must exist concurrently with behavioral difficulties, and this disability must have occurred before the age of 18 [eighteen]."[434]

S.B. 707 joined the ban on mentally retarded executions to Oregon's capital crimes statute. The bill contained procedures for the establishment of mental retardation in aggravated murder cases. "When a defendant charged with aggravated murder intends to assert that [he or she is mentally retarded as defined in Oregon's mental retardation statute,] "as a bar to the imposition of the death penalty in the event the defendant is convicted, the defendant" is required to notify the court to that effect.[435] The court then is required to hold a hearing to determine whether the person has mental retardation. The defense carries the burden of proof "by the preponderance of the evidence."[436] If the court finds that the accused is mentally retarded, then it is required to enter "an order to that effect."[437]

If the accused has been found to be mentally retarded in this separate pretrial hearing, then the State is permitted to appeal the ruling to the Court of Appeals.[438]

Should the appeal be unsuccessful and the accused is "found guilty of aggravated murder," then no sentencing hearing can be held to consider a death sentence.[439] Instead, a sentencing hearing must be held to consider the more limited punishments of "life imprisonment without the possibility of release or parole . . . or life imprisonment" with this possibility.[440]

In sum, Oregon's proposed legislation skillfully dealt with the issue of defining mental retardation by using the existing statutory definition. It provided for a pretrial determination of the offender's mental retardation in a separate hearing held specifically for this purpose, and for the state to appeal from this determination. It provided for a sentencing hearing to determine whether the sentence should be life or life without the possibility of release. Oregon's legislation could not be faulted on technical grounds, and the bill died for want of time to get it through the entire legislative process.

PENNSYLVANIA

Legislators in Pennsylvania have twice introduced legislation to prevent offenders with mental retardation from being executed. In August, 1989, Senators Edward W. Helfrick and Roxanne H. Jones introduced Senate Bill 1198. The bill was referred to the Senate Judiciary Committee.[441]

To the statutes which set out the "sentencing procedure for first degree murder," S.B. 1198 would have added the simple statement that "A sentence of death shall not be imposed upon any person who establishes by a preponderance of the evidence that he was, at time the offense was committed, mentally retarded.[442]

The bill also contained a standard definition of mental retardation:

'Mentally retarded' means the individual has significantly subaverage intellectual functioning as evidenced by an intelligence quotient of 70 or below on an individually administered intelligence quotient test and impairment in adaptive behavior manifested before the individual attains the age of 22.[443]

Pennsylvania is one of the few states that interprets the developmental period to extend to twenty-one years of age.

The effective date of the bill was sixty days from enactment.[444]

In 1991, Senators Helfrick and Jones introduced Senate Bill 331 which was identical to the 1989 bill.[445] This time the legislation was submitted in January, cleared the Senate Judiciary Committee in November, and passed the Senate in December. When it moved over to the House, it was referred to the House Committee on the Judiciary. It remained there without movement for the remainder of the 175th General Assembly.[446]

South Carolina

South Carolina began its attempt to pass legislation to ban mentally retarded executions as early as 1989.[447] The initial 1989 bill was sponsored by a coalition of Democrats and Republicans who comprised "a rare collaboration of philosophical and political opposites."[448] South Carolina's proximity to Georgia made policy makers and the public well aware of the implications of these executions. Consequently, the legislative effort initially enjoyed broad support.

Several other factors besides South Carolina's geographic location next to Georgia contributed to thrusting the issue onto the legislative agenda.

One of the most knowledgeable and articulate capital case defense attorneys, David Bruck, maintains a legal practice in South Carolina. His expert defense of mentally retarded defendants and his writings on the subject are widely known throughout the nation.[449] Attorney Bruck spoke out in favor of this legislation and was frequently quoted in the press to that effect.[450] For example, he stated that it wasn't "good enough for the legislature" to allow the issue to be resolved on a case-by-case basis. Even though a defendant's mental state could be considered as a mitigating factor in capital cases in South Carolina,[451] the fact that judges and juries were "still free to sentence retarded offenders to death" if an aggravating factor existed was called a "loophole"[452] and an "ethical and legal flaw"[453] in the state's capital punishment law.

A local newspaper in the state capital of Columbia frequently quoted Mr. Bruck and wrote editorials favoring the legislation.[454] One argument presented was that the bill takes some of the pressure off jurors who are under a great deal of stress in capital cases.[455] It relieves them of the heavy responsibility of determining if a person with mental retardation should be put to death.

Ultimately, the question was phrased in moral terms. That the legislature was considering the ban on executions of offenders with mental retardation was called "heartening."[456] The legislature was urged to "take the high moral ground"[457] and "to seize the initiative" and pass the legislation as a "matter of conscience and in the interest of justice."[458] The newspaper made such statements as, "No state in good conscience can sanction the execution of someone with the mind of an 11-year-old."[459]

The state Supreme Court also took an activist role in the issue of reviewing death sentences, particularly those of defendants with limited intelligence. In 1988, the Court remanded the well-publicized case of Limmie Arthur back to the trial court because the trial judge had failed to question him thoroughly on his waiver of a jury trial, and it was unlikely that Arthur had understood what he was doing.[460] Arthur's life was subsequently spared when the prosecutor decided not to retry the case.[461]

In 1990, the same court ordered a new trial for Horace Butler, an offender with mental retardation and severe mental illness. Butler has an I.Q. of sixty-one and was hospitalized multiple times with psychiatric problems during the more than ten years that he was on Death Row in South Carolina.[462] Although the court stopped short of holding capital punishment of mentally retarded offenders to be cruel and unusual punishment in these cases, it carefully scrutinized each case and frequently remanded them when the intellectual limitations of the defendant were not made clear to the jury or when there was doubt that the defendant understood court proceedings enough to participate in his own defense.[463] This was the case in Butler's trial.

In 1991, the Supreme Court ordered a new trial for Ronald J. Orr, a man with an I.Q. less than sixty, because it was uncertain that the defendant fully knew what he was doing when he gave up his right to testify in his own defense.[464] Trial judges were urged to be especially "vigilant" in insuring that defendants with mental retardation understood their legal rights.[465]

In sum, factors which contributed to South Carolina's efforts to pass this legislation included a prominent spokesperson for the bill, at least two mentally retarded offenders with death sentences whose cases were well publicized, media backing for the bill, and a supportive state judiciary.

The bill that finally became law in 1992 was a disappointment. Although three bills were introduced in January, 1991 which would have provided a total ban on mentally retarded executions (S.B. 241, S.B. 435, and H.B. 3095)[466] the bill that finally passed, H.B. 3095, was a watered down version of the original concept.[467] As the bill proceeded through the various stages of the legislative process, its prohibitive features were amended away, so that, instead of forbidding executions of offenders with mental retardation as originally designed, the final version merely added mental retardation to the list of mitigating factors that can be considered in determining the sentence in capital cases. This mental retardation mitigation bill became effective with Governor Carroll A. Campbell, Jr.'s signature on July 1, 1992.[468]

TEXAS

In the State of Texas where John Paul Penry has twice been sentenced to death, the issue of mental retardation and the death penalty has been filtered by the *Penry* decision's requirement that mental retardation be considered as a mitigating factor in capital sentencing. Legislatively, the state has not gone beyond the mitigation issue to address the more substantive total ban on executions of mentally retarded persons like Penry.

In 1989, two bills were introduced in the Texas legislature to make mental retardation a specific mitigating factor in capital sentencing. House Bill 55 was introduced in the Regular Session of the Seventy-First Legislature in 1989 and referred to the House Criminal Jurisprudence Committee. That Committee held four public hearings on the bill in April and May of that year, but the bill failed to pass.[469]

H. B. 55 would have added mental retardation as a fourth special issue to be considered by Texas juries in determining the sentence in capital cases. Besides consideration of the defendant's future dangerousness, deliberateness in causing the victim's death, and the reasonableness of the response to victim provocation, juries would be required to consider, "if raised by the evidence, whether the defendant is unimpaired by mental retardation as that term is defined by the Mentally Retarded Persons Act of 1977. . . ."[470] The definition states that a person with mental retardation is:

> a person, other than a person with a mental disorder, whose mental deficit requires the person to have special training, education, supervision, treatment, care or control in the person's home or community or in a state school.[471]

House Bill 89 was introduced in the First Called Session of the Seventy-First Legislature. It was on the agenda for review at a "formal meeting" held June 29, 1989 put went no further in the legislative process.[472]

H.B. 89, like the earlier version of the measure, would have required a fourth issue to be put before the jury in the penalty hearing in capital cases. "If raised by the evidence," the jury would be required to consider "whether there are no mitigating circumstances that would render a sentence of death for the defendant disproportionate to the conduct of the defendant that caused the death of a person."[473] Mitigating circumstances would include "the defendant's mental retardation as . . . defined by the Mentally Retarded Persons Act of 1977."[474]

Thus Texas, as the State where the Supreme Court case originated that began the national movement in the state legislatures to ban the death penalty for offenders with mental retardation, Texas, the State most in need of such a measure, was unable to pass even a requirement to have juries consider mental retardation as a mitigating factor. This issue has not been addressed legislatively in Texas again since these abortive attempts in 1989.

UTAH

In 1990, the State of Utah proposed House Bill No. 112, An Act Relating to Criminal Law, Amending the Penalties for Capital Crimes to Exempt Persons Having Mental Retardation from the Death Penalty.[475] This bill ties the exclusion from execution of mentally retarded offenders to the sections of Utah's law that deal with capital felony sentences[476] and capital felony sentencing procedures.[477]

In the capital felony sentence delineation section, the bill states, "If the trier of fact finds a person convicted of a capital felony has mental retardation, the person shall be sentenced to life imprisonment. The person is not subject to proceedings regarding the death penalty and may not be sentenced to death."[478] Thus the court must make the determination of mental retardation during the guilt/innocence phase of the trial. However, no party to the procedure (defense, court or prosecution) is required to raise the issue, no delineation of the type of evidence is listed, no separate hearing nor evaluation is required, and no standard of proof is adopted. As is typical in legislation proposed in the western states, procedures for determination of mental retardation are not spelled out.

The bill contains a peculiar retroactive clause which requires that persons previously sentenced to death who have mental retardation be brought back to the court which has "jurisdiction over them."[479] That court is required to sentence them "to life imprisonment or life in prison without parole."[480] Utah is one of the few states to address the issue of retroactivity directly and to opt for applying the death penalty exemption to existing Death Row offenders who have mental retardation.

The definition of mental retardation in Utah's bill is in part standard. "'Mental retardation' means significantly subaverage general intellectual functioning existing concurrently with deficits in adaptive behavior and manifested during the developmental period. . . ."[481] However, a unique feature of the definition is that it is linked to the *DSM III*, that is, "significantly subaverage intellectual functioning . . . as defined in the current edition of Diagnostic and Statistical Manual of Mental Disorders, published by the American Psychiatric Association."[482] Thus, should the generally accepted definition of mental retardation change, the law would automatically account for such changes.

In the section of existing law that deals with sentencing procedures,[483] the bill further elaborates on the previous provision which requires a determination of mental retardation by the trier of fact. This section precludes a convicted offender from a sentencing hearing by stating that the requirement for such a hearing "does not apply to a defendant who has been found to have mental retardation."[484]

Utah's attempt to ban executions of offenders with mental retardation was introduced in the House of Representatives on January 8, 1990 and referred to the House Rules Committee, but no further action was taken on it after this date.[485]

VIRGINIA

In 1989, Senator Emilie F. Miller (D-Fairfax) and Delegate Warren G. Stambaugh (D-Arlington) introduced twin bills in the Virginia General Assembly to ban executions of offenders with mental retardation. These bills would have required that offenders with mental retardation convicted of capital crimes be sentenced to life imprisonment instead of being executed.[486]

The strategy for passage of the measures had the sponsor of the House of Delegate's bill waiting for the Senate Courts of Justice Committee to act.[487] The Senate bill was heard in the Senate Courts Committee in February, 1989 but was defeated by a vote of ten to five.[488] Few were willing to act favorably on this kind of measure "in an election year."[489]

In 1990, both Senator Miller and Delegate Stambaugh reintroduced their bills simultaneously in both houses as Senate Bill 210 and House Bill 457, respectively. This time the Senate and the House Courts of Justice Committees both voted down the bills.[490]

S.B. 210 would have prohibited imposition of the death penalty in capital cases where the defendant moved for a hearing on the issue after a guilty verdict, and the court found the defendant to have mental retardation by the preponderance of the evidence. No penalty hearing would be held.[491]

Should the court find that "evidence of diminished intelligence introduced by the defense does not preclude the death penalty," then this evidence could still be introduced in mitigation of the sentence in the death penalty hearing. Should the penalty hearing be held before a jury, the jury would not be told of the court's earlier negative ruling on the mental retardation issue so that it would not be prejudiced against accepting this evidence of mitigation.[492]

Mental retardation was defined as "significantly sub-average general intellectual functioning, existing concurrently with deficits in adaptive behavior and manifested during the developmental period."[493] Although the bill contained no delineation of sub-average intellectual functioning, the intent of the legislator, Senator Miller, clearly was to have it apply to offenders with I.Q.s in the range of fifty to seventy.[494]

A companion bill to S.B. 210 and H.B. 457 introduced by Delegate Stambaugh, House Bill 458, added mental retardation to the list of factors admissible in mitigation when a defendant is found guilty of an offense punishable by death. In lieu of passing the broader total ban on executions of offenders with mental retardation, both houses passed this bill, and the Governor signed it into law on April 9, 1990.[495]

No attempt has been made legislatively in Virginia since 1990 to ban mentally retarded executions completely.

WASHINGTON

The State of Washington has taken the issue of banning executions of persons afflicted with mental retardation very seriously. Bills to this effect were filed in the Washington legislature for three consecutive years (1989,[496] 1990[497] and 1991[498]). The 1991 bill also carried over into, and was worked in, the second session of the Fifty-Second Legislature in 1992.[499]

The initial 1989 bill, S.B. 5940, provided a definition of mental retardation, prohibited the death penalty for offenders with mental retardation, and included a provision for retroactivity. It required the state Supreme Court to conduct a sentence review to determine if the defendant was mentally retarded and, should it make such a determination, to remand the case for resentencing. S.B. 5940 was introduced in February, 1989 and referred to the Senate Committee on Law and Justice. No further action was taken on it.[500]

In 1990, S.B. 6489 defined mental retardation and provided that a death sentence could not "be imposed on person afflicted with mental retardation," under the definition of having an I.Q. of seventy or below.[501] It substituted life imprisonment without any release as the sentence. This bill was also referred to the Senate Committee on Law and Justice where it died without further action.[502]

In 1991, proponents of this legislation took a different tack. They introduced the bill in the House first. Representative Cal Anderson (D-Seattle)[503] was the primary sponsor of H.B. 1234. Thirty-two of his colleagues joined him as co-sponsors.[504]

The definition of mental retardation included in the initial version of H.B. 1234 contained a reference to the American Association on Mental Retardation's definition of mental retardation. This was deleted in a substitute house bill.[505]

The original version of H.B. 1234 also didn't make clear that "significantly subaverage general intellectual functioning" and "deficits in adaptive behavior" must exist concurrently and must have "been manifested during the developmental period." This ambiguity was clarified in the substitute house bill.[506]

Substitute House Bill 1234 tied the mental retardation provisions to Washington's aggravated first degree murder and death penalty statute. That statute states that, "If . . . the trier of fact finds that there are not sufficient mitigating circumstances to merit leniency, the sentence shall be death."[507]

Immediately following, S.H.B. 1234 would have added statements to the effect that, "In no case, however, shall a person be sentenced to death if the person was mentally retarded at the time the crime was committed, under the definition of mental retardation set forth" in this statute.[508] The prohibition against executing persons afflicted with mental retardation was further enforced by adding the statement that "a person found to be mentally retarded . . . may in no case be sentenced to death"[509] to the section of the existing statute listing mitigating and aggravating factors. The prohibition was linked to the factor which states that the sentencer should consider whether "at the time of the murder, the capacity of the defendant to appreciate the wrongfulness of his or her conduct or to conform his or her conduct to the requirements of law was substantially impaired as a result of mental disease or defect" in making its decision whether or not to impose the death penalty.[510]

Further, mental retardation was to be determined by a "diagnosis of mental retardation . . . documented by a licensed psychiatrist or a licensed psychologist expert in the diagnosis and evaluation of mental retardation."[511]

The burden of proof fell on the defendant. "The defense must establish mental retardation by a preponderance of evidence."[512]

The definition of a mentally retarded individual is one who "has: (i) significantly subaverage general intellectual functioning; (ii) existing concurrently with deficits in adaptive behavior; and (iii) both . . . [of these] . . . were manifested during the developmental period."[513]

Further, the bill specifically defined each term of the definition:

'General intellectual functioning' means the results obtained by assessment with one or more of the individually administered general intelligence tests developed for the purpose of assessing intellectual functioning.

'Significantly subaverage general intellectual functioning' means intelligence quotient [of] seventy or below.

'Adaptive behavior' means the effectiveness or degree with which individuals meet the standards of personal independence and social responsibility expected for age and cultural group.

'Developmental period' means the period of time between conception and the eighteenth birthday.[514]

This definition of mental retardation was one of the clearest and best stated in any state's attempt to ban executions of persons with mental retardation legislatively.

Finally, the bill provided that the State of Washington's Supreme Court should automatically review the determination of mental retardation[515] along with its proportionality review and automatic review of such other considerations as whether the sentence was imposed "through passion or prejudice."[516]

In sum, this version of Washington's prohibition of executions of offenders with mental retardation was one of the most comprehensive, thorough, definitive and well-written pieces of legislation in any state.

The Washington House of Representatives passed S.H.B. 1234 on March 4, 1991. The vote was sixty-seven to thirty. The bill then went to the Senate where it was referred to the Law and Justice Committee.[517]

Support in the Senate for the concept did not approach that in the House. On April 3, 1991, the Senate's Law and Justice Committee substantially "gutted" the House version of the bill.[518] Its amendments to S.H.B. 1234 removed the definition of mental retardation, the procedures for its determination, and the automatic appellate review of the determination. It substituted instead questionable procedures which are unique to the State of Washington.

The Law and Justice Committee's amendment referred to general sentencing procedures in capital cases. If the prosecutor intended to seek the death penalty when the defendant "is charged with aggravated first degree murder," he or she must "file written notice of a special sentencing proceeding," and the intent to seek the death penalty.[519] In the mental retardation procedures, the bill stated that prior to filing this notice, the prosecutor "shall seek written advice" from defense counsel "as to whether or not evidence tending to show mitigating circumstances is available. . . . For crimes committed on or after July 1, 1992, the prosecuting attorney shall request that the defense provide any evidence tending to show that the defendant is mentally retarded."[520]

Thereafter, the prosecutor had the sole discretion to determine whether or not the defendant has mental retardation. No examination, evaluation of the defendant or hearing on the merits of the evidence was required. No procedures or standard of proof for this determination were listed. The bill simply stated that, "if the review of any evidence supplied by the defense or otherwise available establishes, *to the prosecuting attorney's satisfaction,* that the defendant is mentally retarded"[521] then the prosecuting attorney should not seek the death penalty. Thus one person would make the determination of mental retardation. He or she could be completely arbitrary and capricious in making this determination and by proceeding to seek the death penalty despite overwhelming evidence of mental retardation.

Lest the prosecution should abuse this discretion, some small check on the prosecutor was included. If the prosecutor determined to go ahead with a separate sentencing hearing seeking the death penalty, then evidence of mental retardation could still be offered as mitigating evidence in the penalty hearing. However, if the jury found it to be "insufficient" [to preclude the death penalty,] then this "shall not create any right to assert a claim for relief,"[522] that is, it would not create grounds for appeal.

The Law and Justice Committee's amended bill was exceedingly bad legislation which did not deserve to pass. Nonetheless, it was returned to the House and again passed there in January, 1992. This time the favorable vote was by a slightly smaller margin, sixty-one in favor and thirty-four against.[523]

Back in the Senate, after once again going through the Law and Justice Committee, the Rules Committee returned the bill to the House for a third reading. The bill deservedly died there at the end of the 1992 legislative session.[524]

CONCLUSIONS

CRITICAL ELEMENTS OF THE LEGISLATION

The analysis in this chapter of proposed bills to ban executions of offenders suffering from mental retardation shows that there are certain elements which are vital to this kind of legislation. Although different approaches to including these key elements can be used, failure to address them in one fashion or another can seriously jeopardize the legislation's chances of success. However, it must be recognized that, under the pressure of some legislative circumstances, the price of achieving a prohibition against putting mentally retarded offenders to death may be the modification or even the sacrifice of one or more of these elements.

Components of good legislation include a definition of mental retardation, a procedure for determining if the defendant is mentally retarded, a standard of proof, a statement of the death prohibition, a designation of the appropriate sentence(s) other than the death penalty, provision for the care and treatment of the offender during imprisonment, provision for alternative use of the evidence as a mitigating factor, an effective date for the legislation, a method for determining how existing Death Row inmates who are mentally retarded, if any, should be handled, and an appeals process. Non-content factors which can contribute to the passage of the legislation include timing, sponsorship and supporting characters.

Definition. Critical to any legislation which seeks to ban the death penalty for offenders with mental retardation is a clear and precise definition. The definition should be specific enough to allay fears and answer the antagonists who argue that non-mentally retarded murderers will somehow slip through under the definition and escape their justly deserved execution. Several states use a reference to the definition of mental retardation contained in their mental retardation statute. This is an ideal way to handle the issue of how mental retardation is to be defined because it uses a definition that already has statutory authority and legitimacy.

Procedures. Proposed legislation should contain specific and adequate procedures for making the determination as to whether the accused is mentally retarded under the definition. Ideally, procedures should include adequate documentation through professional testing and evaluation.

The evidence of mental retardation can be introduced at a separate pretrial hearing on the issue, in the guilt/innocence phase of the trial, in a separate hearing after conviction, or in the penalty hearing itself. The defense can be required to make a motion for determination of mental retardation under the procedures, which is the most frequent method for raising the issue. Idaho's procedure is better. It allows the prosecution, the court or the defense to raise the issue.

The court or jury can make the determination as to whether the defendant is mentally retarded. The determiner should be required to issue its finding in writing. This determination should never be placed in the hands of the prosecution as occurred in the State of Washington's proposal.

Standard of Proof. The bill should require that a standard of proof be used to make the determination of mental retardation. The most frequently proposed standard is the "preponderance of the evidence." The more stringent "beyond a reasonable doubt" standard is not advisable, unless it is used in the negative sense of requiring the prosecution to prove that the defendant is not mentally retarded beyond a reasonable doubt. Failure to include such a standard causes ambiguity which may reduce the bill's chances of passing.

Death Prohibition. The proposed legislation should contain a positive statement to the effect that a person who has been determined to be mentally retarded under the procedures and definition should not be subject to the death penalty and should not be executed.

Legitimate Sentences. What the sentence should be, other than the death sentence, should also be stated. This can be life without parole, life with parole after a specified number of years such as twenty-five or thirty, or any other sentence than death which is authorized by the existing capital sentencing statute. Delineation of the sentence makes clear that the murderer with mental retardation will be severely punished. It states to the court, the jury and the public that the murderer will not be set free, although he or she will not be executed.

Treatment. Although not required but in the "nice to have" category, the bill may provide for the adequate care and treatment of the offender with mental retardation throughout his or her life imprisonment.

Evidence of Mitigation. If the procedures allow for a determination to be made that the defendant does not have mental retardation prior to the ordinary penalty hearing, then the proposed legislation should contain a statement to the effect that the evidence of diminished mental capacity can be used again as a mitigating circumstance in the penalty hearing.

Effective Date and Retroactivity. Bills should contain an effective date. This may be for offenses, trials, or sentencings occurring on or after this date. Some provision for retroactivity to offenders already sentenced to death can be provided if it is known that there are offenders with mental retardation on Death Row, or if it is not known with certainty that there are none. In this way, equal protection of the laws is assured, and appeals from existing condemned inmates are avoided.

Appeals Process. The bill ideally should contain appeals procedures which permit both parties, the prosecution and the defense, to appeal from the finding that the defendant does or does not have mental retardation.

In sum, it is important that any such bill must be skillfully drafted and without technical flaws.

Timing. From a broader perspective than bill content, timing of the measure is all important in getting the legislation passed. The issue of an execution of a person with mental retardation must be real rather than theoretical. When an offender with mental retardation is either on the verge of being executed (as in Maryland) or actually executed (as occurred in Georgia), there is a greater reason to pass the legislation than if there are no such offenders currently affected. An execution of a offender who does not have mental retardation, after a long hiatus from executions in a state, may also be an impetus for passage. However, it is not as strong as when a proven mentally retarded person is executed. Alternatively, if no offenders with mental retardation are on Death Row currently nor approaching trial, proponents can argue that the bill is not necessary. They can and have used this fact to oppose the measure effectively.

Supporting Characters. A second key non-content element is the support or sponsorship of a popular, respected and influential legislator or local leader. One prominent, determined and outspoken person can make all the difference in passage. Rallying of church, human and civil rights groups to testify for the bill also helps, as does media support, particularly editorial support in the major newspapers of the state and region.

Notes

[1]*See* "Retarded Killer Dies in Georgia Chair," *Chicago Tribune*, 25 June 1986.

[2]*See* Chapter 1. THE *PENRY* CASE, *supra*.

[3]492 U.S. 304, 106 L.Ed. 2d 256, 109 S.Ct. 2934 (1989).

[4]*See* Chapter 2. THEORETICAL ARGUMENTS, FEDERAL STATUTES, *supra*.

[5]California became the nineteenth executing state on April 21, 1992 when it executed Robert Alton Harris. *See* Chapter 3. THE EXECUTED, *supra*.

[6]408 U.S. 238, 92 S.Ct. 2726, 33 L.Ed.2d 346 (1972).

[7]Gregg v. Georgia, 428 U.S. 153, 179 (1976).

[8]428 U.S. 153, 49 L.Ed.2d 859 (1976).

[9]GA. CODE ANN., s. 26-1005 (Supp.1971) effective prior to July 1, 1969, GA. CODE ANN., s. 26-1302 (Supp.1971) effective prior to July 1, 1969, quoted in ibid., 239.

[10]VERNON'S TEX. PENAL CODE, Art. 1189 (1961) quoted in ibid., 239.

[11]Ibid., 252-253, also "father of six" reference.

[12]Ibid., 253.

[13]Ibid., 252.

[14]Ibid., 240-249.

[15]Ibid., 253.

[16]McCleskey v. Kemp, 481 U.S. 279, 107 S.Ct. 1756 (1987).

[17]Ibid., 245.

[18]The President's Commission on Law Enforcement and Administration of Justice, *The Challenge of Crime in a Free Society*, 143 (1967) quoted in ibid., 250.

[19]Ibid., 286.

[20]Ibid., 274, 289.

[21]Ibid., 293.

[22]Ibid., 296-300.

[23]Ibid., 300-305.

[24]Ibid., 305.

[25]Ibid.

[26]Ibid., 309.

[27]Ibid., 310.

[28]Ibid., 309-310.

[29]Ibid., 313.

[30]Ibid., 322-329.

[31]Trop v. Dulles, 356 U.S. 86, 101 (1958), Weems v. U.S., 217 U.S. 349, 373 (1910), Robinson v. California, 370 U.S. 660,666 (1962), quoted in ibid., 329.

[32]Ibid., 330.

[33]Ibid., 331.

[34]Ibid.

[35]Ibid., 332.

[36]Ibid., 341.

[37]Ibid., 342.

[38]These were "retribution, deterrence, prevention of repetitive

criminal acts, encouragement of guilty pleas and confessions, eugenics, and economy." Ibid.

[39]Ibid., 345.
[40]Ibid., 353.
[41]Ibid., 354.
[42]Ibid., 355.
[43]Ibid., 356.
[44]Ibid., 357.
[45]Ibid.
[46]Ibid., 358.
[47]Ibid., 360.
[48]Gregg, 179-180.
[49]Furman, 248.
[50]American Law Institute, *Model Penal Code*, s. 201.6, Comment 5, 74-75 (Tent. Draft No. 9, 1959), quoted in Gregg, 191.
[51]Gregg, 196.
[52]Ibid. *See also* American Law Institute, *Model Penal Code*, s. 201.6, Comment 3, 71 (Tent. Draft No. 9, 1959), quoted in Gregg, 193.
[53]Ibid., 195, 196.
[54]Ibid.
[55]Gregg v. Georgia, 428 U.S. 153, 96 S.Ct. 2909, 49 L.Ed.2d 859 (1976).
[56]Ibid., 169.
[57]Ibid., 158-160, 212-213.
[58]GA. CODE ANN. ss. 27-2503, 2534 ff., quoted in ibid., 195-196, and 196, n. 9.
[59]Ibid., 169, and 169, n. 14.
[60]Ibid., 169, and 169, n. 13.
[61]Ibid., 169, and 169, n. 15.
[62]Ibid., 162, 221.
[63]Ibid., 164.
[64]The Supreme Court had long upheld this principle as necessary in capital sentencing. *See* Pennsylvania ex rel. Sullivan v. Ashe, 302 U.S. 51, 55 (1937), quoted in Gregg v. Georgia, 428 U.S. 153, 188, (1976).
[65]Ibid., 166.
[66]Ibid.
[67]481 U.S. 279, 107 S.Ct. 1756 (1987).
[68]Ibid., 282.
[69]Ibid., 283.
[70]Ibid., 279.
[71]Ibid., 287.
[72]David C. Baldus, Charles Pulaski and George Woodworth, "Comparative Review of Death Sentences: An Empirical Study of Georgia Experience," *Journal of Criminal Law and Criminology* 74 (1983), quoted in ibid., 279 ff.
[73]McCleskey, 312.
[74]Singer v. U.S., 380 U.S. 24, 35 (1965), quoted in McCleskey, 313.
[75]McCleskey, 302-303.
[76]Ibid., 298.
[77]Ibid., 279-280, 298.

[78]Ibid., 280-282.

[79]Samuel Gross, University of Michigan Law School, and Robert Mauro, University of Oregon psychologist, quoted in Mark Hansen, "Final Justice," *ABA Journal* (March 1992):66.

[80]Ibid.

[81]One was Black, the other Asian.

[82]National Coalition to Abolish the Death Penalty, "United States Executions," 25 September 1991, 2-5.

Add Georgia Code cites here.

[83]*ABA Criminal Justice Mental Health Standards*, (1984), 4.

[84]*See* Emily F. Reed, "Legal Rights of Mentally Retarded Offenders: Hospice and Habilitation," *Criminal Law Bulletin* 25 (September-October 1989):430-436.

[85]*Fleming v. Zant*, 250 GA 687, 386 S.E.2d 339, (1989). *See also* Chapter 2. THEORETICAL ARGUMENTS, ANTI-GEORGIA ARGUMENTS, *supra*.

[86]GA. CODE ANN., s. 17-7-131 (1988 Supp.)

[87]Ibid., s. 17-7-131(b)(1)(C).

[88]Ibid., s. 17-7-131(b)(1)(D).

[89]Ibid., s. 17-7-131(d).

[90]Ibid., s. 17-7-131(b)(2).

[91]Ibid., s. 17-7-131(b)(3)(A)(B).

[92]Ibid., s. 17-7-131(d)(e)(f)(g)(h)(i).

[93]Ibid., s. 17-7-131(d)(e)(f)(g).

[94]Ibid., s. 17-7-131(b)(1)(E).

[95]Ibid., s. 17-7-131(a)(3).

[96]Ibid., s. 17-7-131((b)(1)(A)(B)(C)(D)(E).

[97]Ibid., s. 17-7-131(b)(2).

[98]Ibid., s. 17-7-131(b)(3).

[99]Ibid., s. 17-7-131(c).

[100]Ibid., s. 17-7-131(c)(1)(2)(3).

[101]Ibid., s. 17-7-131(c)(3).

[102]The Georgia Supreme Court later held that in cases in which the defendant had been sentenced to death prior to the enactment of this statute and a new jury trial is held to determine if the defendant has mental retardation, the defense need only hold to a preponderance of the evidence standard of proof. *See* Zant v. Foster, 406 S.E.2d 74, 76 (1991).

[103]GA. CODE ANN., s. 17-7-131(b)(3)(C).

[104]State v. Patillo, 1992 W.L. 136167 (GA)

[105]Ibid., s. 17-7-131(g)(1).

[106]Ibid., s. 17-7-131(j).

[107]Ibid., s. 17-7-131(g)(1).

[108]Ibid.

[109]Ibid., s. 17-7-131(g)(2) (1988 Supp.)

[110]Dewey Dempsey, Georgia Department of Corrections, "Georgia Programs for Mentally Retarded Offenders," *Summary Minutes of the Delaware Criminal Justice Council Meeting*, Dover, DE: 7 December 1988, quoted in Reed, "Legal Rights," 432.

[111]GA. CODE ANN., s. 17-7-131(g)(3).

[112]Ibid., s. 17-7-131(g)(4).

[113]Fleming v. Zant, 386 S.E.2d 339, 343 (1989).
[114]Ibid., 340-341.
[115]Jeanne Cummings, "Court Extends Execution Ban for Retarded," *Atlanta Constitution*, 2 December 1989, sec. C.
[116]Fleming v. Zant, 340-341.
[117]Ibid., 341.
[118]Ibid.
[119]Ibid.
[120]Ibid.
[121]Ibid.
[122]Ibid., 341-342.
[123]Ibid., 341.
[124]Ibid., 342.
[125]Ibid.
[126]Ibid., 342, and 342, n. 3.
[127]Ibid.
[128]Ibid., 342.
[129]Ibid.
[130]Ibid.
[131]Ibid.
[132]Ibid.
[133]Ibid., 343.
[134]Ibid., 342-343.
[135]Ibid., 343.
[136]Patillo, 136, 167.
[137]Ibid, n. 1.
[138]Fleming, 342-343.
[139]Jeanne Cummings, "Court Extends Execution Ban," sec. C.
[140]Tom Teepen, "Georgia's Decision Not to Execute the Mentally Retarded is Working," *Atlanta Constitution*, 14 July 1988, sec. A.
[141]"Georgia News Briefs," United Press International, Dateline: Pembroke, GA, 16 August 1988.
[142]"Court Says Retarded Man Unfit To Confess," United Press International, Dateline: Atlanta, GA, 27 August 1988.
[143]"One Defendant Gets Life, Other to be Executed," United Press International, Dateline: Greenville, GA, 6 December 1988.
[144]Zant v. Beck, 386 S.E.2d 349, 351 (1989).
[145]"Lawton Gets Five Consecutive Life Sentences for Double Slaying," United Press International, Dateline: Savannah, GA, 28 April 1990.
[146]Zant v. Foster, 406 S.E.2d 74, (1991).
[147]State v. Patillo, 1992 W.L. 136167 (GA). *See also* Patillo v. State, 368 S.E.2d 493 (1988).
[148]Jeanne Cummings, "Ban on Execution of Retarded Kept Intact," *Atlanta Constitution*, 27 February 1990, sec. B.
[149]Teepen, "Georgia's Decision," sec. A.
[150]P.L. 100-690, 102 Stat.4387 (1988). *See also* Chapter 2, THEORETICAL ARGUMENTS, FEDERAL STATUTES, *supra* for an elaboration of this section.
[151]Sara Fritz, "House Votes Death Penalty for Drug-Related Killings," *Los Angeles Times*, 9 September 1988, sec. 1.

[152]Ibid.

[153]*See* Chapter 2, THEORETICAL ARGUMENTS, PUBLIC OPINION POLLS, *supra.*

[154]Ibid. *See also* Irvin Molotsky, "House Gets a Sweeping Bill to Combat Drugs," *The New York Times,* 12 August 1988, sec. B.

[155]"Death Penalty Added to Drug Bill," *The Chicago Tribune,* 21 October 1988, sec. News.

[156]Fritz, "House Votes," sec. 1.

[157]Ibid.

[158]Ibid.

[159]P.L. 100-690, Title VII, Subtitle A, sec. 7001(e)(1)(A).

[160]Ibid.

[161]Ibid. *See also* "Death Penalty Added," sec. News.

[162]Ibid., (e)(1)(B). *See also* "Death Penalty Added," sec. News.

[163]Molotsky, sec. B. *See also* Fritz, "House Votes," sec. 1.

[164]Ibid.

[165]Ibid.

[166]Ibid.

[167]P.L. 100-690, Title VII, Subtitle A, sec. 7001(l).

[168]*See* Chapter II, THEORETICAL ARGUMENTS, ANTI-DRUG ABUSE ACT OF 1988 for a fuller discussion of this debate.

[169]Congressional Record - H1259-02, 8 September 1988.

[170]P.L. 100-690, Title VII, Subtitle A, sec. 7001(l)(1-2).

[171]The vote was 299 for and 111 against. Fritz, "House Votes," sec. 1.

[172]"Death Penalty Added," sec. News.

[173]Sara Fritz, "Congress Passes Anti-Drug Bill, Then Adjourns," *Los Angeles Times,* 22 September 1988, part 1.

[174]Ibid.

[175]MD. CRIM. LAW CODE ANN., Art. 27, s. 412 (1989).

[176]Jo-Ann Armao, "Ban on Md. Death Penalty for Retarded Voted," *The Washington Post,* 15 March 1989, sec C.

[177]*See for example* ibid.; Jo-Ann Armao, "Executing the Retarded Prompts Debate in Md.," *The Washington Post,* 3 February 1989, sec. C.; and John Lancaster, "Md. Bill Banning Execution of Mentally Retarded Gains," *The Washington Post,* 19 March 1989, sec. D.

[178]Ibid.

[179]Armao, "Ban on Md. Death Penalty," sec. C. Armao, "Executing the Retarded," sec. C.

[180]Howard Schneider, "Md. Panel's Death Penalty Vote Called Unfair," *The Washington Post,* 25 February 1989, sec. B.

[181]Jo-Ann Armao, "Md. Panel Revives Death Penalty Bill," *The Washington Post,* 4 March 1989, sec. B.

[182]Ibid.

[183]Jo-Ann Armao, "In Md., a Masterly 34 Years in Politics: At 84, Sen. Schweinhaut Looking Ahead to Next Campaign," *The Washington Post,* 20 March 1989, sec. D.

[184]Armao, "Ban on Md. Death Penalty," sec. C.

[185]Armao, "In Md., a Masterly 34 Years," sec. D.

[186]Armao, "Ban on Md. Death Penalty," sec. C.

[187]Armao, "In Md., a Masterly 34 Years," sec. D.

[188]Lancaster, "Md. Bill," sec. D.

[189]"Measure to Ban Execution of Retarded Slayers Clears House, Goes to Conference," *The Washington Post*, 25 March 1989, sec. B. The vote was ninety-nine to twenty-seven.

[190]Ibid.

[191]"Death Penalty Exemption," *The Washington Post*, 8 April 1989, sec. B. The vote was thirty to twelve.

[192]Armao, "Md. Panel," sec. B.

[193]Ibid.

[194]Armao, "Executing the Retarded," sec. C.

[195]Lancaster, "Md. Bill," sec. D.

[196]Ibid.

[197]Armao, "In Md., a Masterly 34 Years," sec. D.

[198]MD. CRIM. LAW CODE ANN., Art. 27, s. 412 (1989).

[199]Ibid., s. 412(e)(3).

[200]GA. CODE ANN., s. 17-7-131(a)(3).

[201]MD. CRIM. LAW CODE ANN., Art. 27, s. 412(f)(1).

[202]GA. CODE ANN., s. 17-7-131(c)(3).

[203]*See generally* ibid., s. 17-7-131.

[204]"Life Sentence Returned for Test Death Penalty Case, "United Press International, Dateline: Towson, MD, 15 December 1989.

[205]Trimble V. Maryland, 321 Md. 248, 582 A.2d 794, 800-802 (1990).

[206]Ibid., 802-803.

[207]Ibid., 803.

[208]Sue Allison, "Senate Passes Pornography Bill," United Press International, Dateline: Nashville, TN, 5 April 1990.

[209]Sue Allison, "Lawmakers Exclude Mentally Retarded from Capital Punishment," United Press International, Dateline: Nashville, TN, 13 April 1990.

[210]Ibid.

[211]TENN. PUB. ACTS, s. 39-13-303 (1990).

[212]Allison, "Senate Passes Pornography Bill," UPI, 5 April 1990.

[213]Allison, ""Lawmakers Exclude Mentally Retarded," UPI, 13 April 1990.

[214]Ibid.

[215]TENN. PUB. ACTS, s. 39-13-303(a)(1-3).

[216]Ibid., s. 39-13-303(b).

[217]Ibid., s. 39-13-303(c).

[218]Ibid., s. 39-13-303(d).

[219]Ibid.

[220]Ibid.

[221]Ibid., s. 39-13-303(e).

[222]Senate Bill No. 1851, An Act to Amend Tennessee Code Annotated, Title 39, Chapter 13, Part 2, Prefiled for Introduction on 1/11/90.

[223]No evidence could be found that any of Tennessee's condemned have appealed their death sentences as did Son Fleming in Georgia.

[224]KY. REV. STAT., s. 532.140 (1990).

[225]Ibid., s. 532.130(1).

[226]Ibid., s. 532.140(1).

[227]Ibid., s. 532.130(2).

228Ibid.

229Ibid., s. 532.135(1-2).

230Ibid., s. 532.135(4).

231Ibid., s. 532.140(1).

232Ibid., s. 532.140(3)(2-3).

233Ibid., s. 532.140(3).

234NEW MEX. STAT. ANN. s. 31-20A-2.1 (1991).

235Senate Bill 148, 1991 NM S.B. 148, New Mexico Bill Tracking, Statenet, Information for Public Affairs, Inc., 1991. This source lists the date of introduction as January 24, 1991 and the date of the governor's signature as March 29, 1991.

236NEW MEX. STAT. ANN., s. 31-20A-2.1(A).

237Ibid.

238Ibid., s. 31-20A-2.1(C).

239Ibid., s. 31-20A-2.1(B).

240Ibid., s. 31-20A-2.1(C).

241Ibid.

242Ibid.

243Ibid.

244William F. Rawson, "Partial Death Penalty Repeal Advances," *The Phoenix Gazette*, 27 March 1992, sec. Metro.

245Senate Bill 1472 and House Bill 2237, Arizona Bill Tracking, Statenet, Information for Public Affairs, Inc., 1992.

246Pamela Manson, "Death Penalty Foes Fight State Law, Public Opinion," *The Arizona Republic*, 30 March, 1992, sec. Front.

247Ben Winton, "Vigil Held to Prevent Execution - Groups Aim to Ban Capital Punishment," *The Phoenix Gazette*, 31 March 1992, sec. Front.

248Rawson, "Partial Death Penalty Repeal," sec. Metro.

249See Chapter 6. LEGISLATIVE INITIATIVES TO ABOLISH THE DEATH PENALTY FOR OFFENDERS WITH MENTAL RETARDATION, Other State Statutes, MARYLAND, *supra*.

250Randy Kull and Pat Flannery, "Gas, Lethal Injection or Nothing? Harding's Slow Death Renews Penalty Debate - Panel OKs Bill to Exempt Minors, Retarded," *The Phoenix Gazette*, 7 April 1992, sec. Front.

251Bob Baker and Laura Laughlin, "Arizona Executes Killer; State Gripped by Grisly Accounts," *Los Angeles Times*, 7 April 1992, part A.

252Senate Bill 1472, Arizona Bill Tracking, Statenet, Information for Public Affairs, Inc., 1992.

253Kull and Flannery, "Gas," sec. Front.

254Senate Bill 739, Arkansas Bill Tracking, Statenet, Information for Public Affairs, Inc., 1991.

255Senate Bill 55, Second Regular Session, Fifty-Eighth General Assembly (1992), The State of Colorado Bill Text, Statenet, Information for Public Affairs, Inc., 1992.

256See Chapter 6. LEGISLATIVE INITIATIVES TO ABOLISH THE DEATH PENALTY FOR OFFENDERS WITH MENTAL RETARDATION, Other State Statutes, NEW MEXICO, *supra*.

257S.B. 55, sec. 1, 16-9-401(2).

258Ibid., sec. 1, 16-9-402(1-2).

259Ibid., sec. 1, 16-9-402(2).

[260]Ibid., sec. 1, 16-9-403(2).

[261]Ibid., sec. 2, 16-11-103(1)(a).

[262]Ibid., sec. 3.

[263]House Bill 1020 b, Second Extraordinary Session, Fifty-Eighth General Assembly (1991), The State of Colorado, Bill Text, Statenet, Information for Public Affairs, Inc., 1992.

[264]Ibid., sec. 1, 16-9-401(2-3).

[265]Ibid., sec. 1, 16-9-402, 16-11-103.

[266]House Bill 1020 b (1991), South Carolina Bill Tracking, Statenet, Information for Public Affairs, Inc., 1992.

[267]Proposed Bill No. 5083, Referred to Committee on Judiciary, Introduced by Rep. Adamo, 116th District, Rep. Dargan, 115th Dist., General Assembly, January Session, A.D., 1991, sec. 1.

[268]House Bill 5083 (1991), Connecticut Bill Tracking, Statenet, Information for Public Affairs, Inc., 1991.

[269]Senate Bill No. 481, "An Act to Amend Chapter 4, Title 11, Section 408, Delaware Code Relating to Defense to Criminal Liability," Delaware State Senate, 135th General Assembly, 14 June 1990.

[270]GA. CODE ANN., s. 17-7-131 (1988 Supp.).

[271]See "Preliminary Draft, Guilty but Mentally Retarded Act of 1990," revised, 21 November 1989 sec. 408a(f)(1).

[272]S.B. 481, 14 June 1990.

[273]DEL. CODE ANN., title 11, sec. 408 (1974).

[274]S.B. 481, sec. 1, 408a(a)(1-3).

[275]Ibid., sec. 1, 408a.

[276]Ibid., sec. 1, 408a(b).

[277]"Preliminary Draft, Guilty but Mentally Retarded Act of 1990," revised, 21 November 1989 sec. 408a(c)(1).

[278]The author was the drafter of the initial versions of the bill and made the changes in them as multiple parties stated objections to various parts. Her intent was to develop a compromise bill that would have some acceptance and support from professionals in the field.

[279]DEL. CODE ANN., title 11, secs. 6580-6581 (Revised 1985).

[280]Delaware Superior Court Judges Sentencing Worksheet (1990).

[281]Summary Minutes of the Meeting of the Sentencing Accountability Commission, Dover, DE: 4 June 1990.

[282]House Bill No. 192 and Senate Bill No. 101, "An Act to Amend Chapter 4, Title 11, Section 408, Delaware Code Relating to Defenses to Criminal Liability," Delaware State Senate, 135th General Assembly, 25 & 24 April 1991 (respectively).

[283]Ibid., sec. 1, 410(b)(1-3).

[284]Ibid., sec. 1, 410(a).

[285]House Bill No. 192 and Senate Bill No. 101, "An Act to Amend Chapter 4, Title 11, Section 408, Delaware Code Relating to Defenses to Criminal Liability," Delaware State Senate, 135th General Assembly, 25 & 24 April 1991 (respectively).

[286]Thomas Peele, "Input Sought on Barring Execution of Retarded," Delaware State News, 9 May 1991, sec. 1.

[287]Thomas Peele, "Execution Ban for Retarded Called Biased," Delaware State News, 15 May 1991, sec. 1.

[288]"Ban Execution of Retarded - Four Other States Considering It," *Miami Herald*, 17 March 1990, sec. Local.
[289]Ibid.
[290]Ibid.
[291]Ibid.
[292]FLA. STAT., sec. 922.07.
[293]H.B. 3092, "A Bill to Be Entitled An act Relating to Capital Felonies; Amending s. 921.141, F.S.; providing that a defendant who establishes by a preponderance of the evidence that he meets the definition of retardation shall not be punished by death; amending s. 922.07, F.S.; providing proceedings to be used when a person under sentence of death appears to be retarded; providing an effective date," Florida House of Representatives (1990), sec. 1, 921.141(1).
[294]FLA. STAT., sec. 393.063.
[295]H.B. 3029, sec. 1, 921.141(1).
[296]Ibid., sec. 2, 922.07(1).
[297]Ibid., sec. 2, 922.07(2)(3).
[298]H 3029, 1990 Session, General Bill by Sansom and others (Compare S 1242), Summary of Actions Taken, 13 March 1991.
[299]House Bill 657, Florida Bill Tracking, Statenet, Information for Public Affairs, Inc., 1990.
[300]Senate Bill 872, Florida Bill Tracking, Statenet, Information for Public Affairs, Inc., 1992.
[301]FLA. STAT., sec. 916.106.
[302]S.B. 872, The State of Florida, Bill Text, Statenet, Information for Public Affairs, Inc., 1992, sec. 3, 921.141(1)(A).
[303]Ibid.
[304]Ibid.
[305]Ibid., sec. 3, 921.141(1)(B); sec. 4, 924.079(k).
[306]Ibid., sec. 3, 921.141(1)(C).
[307]Ibid., sec. 5.
[308]S.B. 872, Florida Bill Tracking, Statenet, Information for Public Affairs, Inc., 1992.
[309]In the Senate, Senate Bill No. 1175, by Judiciary and Rules Committee, An Act Relating to Criminal Sentencing, Legislature of the State of Idaho, Fifty-first Legislature, First Regular Session, 1991.
[310]In the Senate, Senate Bill No. 1402, by Judiciary and Rules Committee, An Act Relating to Criminal Sentencing, Legislature of the State of Idaho, Fifty-first Legislature, Second Regular Session, 1992.
[311]S.B. 1175 and S.B. 1402, sec. 19-2515A, sec. 1(1)(a).
[312]Ibid., sec. 1(1)(b).
[313]S.B. 1402, sec. 19-2515A, sec. 1(1)(b).
[314]S.B. 1175 and S.B. 1402, sec. 19-2515A, sec. 1(1)(c).
[315]S.B. 1175, sec. 19-2515A, sec. 1(1)(d).
[316]S.B. 1402, sec. 19-2515A, sec. 1(1).
[317]S.B. 1175 and S.B. 1402, sec. 19-2515A, sec. 1(2).
[318]Ibid.
[319]Ibid.
[320]KY. REV. STAT., s. 532.135(1-2).
[321]S.B. 1175 and S.B. 1402, sec. 19-2515A, sec. 1(3).

[322]Letter from Diane L. DeChambeau, Assistant to the Speaker, House of Representative, State of Idaho, to the author, 20 July 1992.
[323]See Chapter 6. LEGISLATIVE INITIATIVES TO ABOLISH THE DEATH PENALTY FOR OFFENDERS WITH MENTAL RETARDATION, Legislation Pending in the States, SOUTH CAROLINA, *infra.*
[324]Dan Shamon, Jr., "Riverboat Gambling Sailing Again," United Press International, Dateline: Springfield, IL, 19 October 1989.
[325]Senate Bill 956, Illinois Bill Tracking, Statenet, Information for Public Affairs, Inc., 1989.
[326]Senate Transcript, Regular Session, 86th General Assembly, State of Illinois, 36th Legislative Day, 25 May 1989, 204.
[327]Ibid., 203, 204, 205; 55th Legislative Day, 26 June 1989, 119, 120; 59th Legislative Day, 30 June 1989, 157.
[328]SB 956 Enrolled, "An Act to add Section 2-10.2 to and amend Section 9-1 of the `Criminal Code of 1961,' approved July 28, 1961, as amended," (1989).
[329]Ibid.
[330]Ibid., sec. 9-1.
[331]Ibid., sec. 9-1(b).
[332]Ibid., sec. 9-1(f).
[333]Senate Transcript, 55th Legislative Day, 26 June 1989, 120; 59th Legislative Day, 30 June 1989, 157. *See also* Senate Transcript, 63rd Legislative Day, 18 October 1989, 80.
[334]Donald B. Ayers, "Governor Says Riverboat Gambling Depends on Rosemont Deals," United Press International, Dateline: Springfield, IL, 19 October 1989.
[335]Senate Transcript, 63rd Legislative Day, 18 October 1989, 80.
[336]Senate Bill 287, Illinois Bill Tracking, Statenet, Information for Public Affairs, Inc., 1991.
[337]House Bill No. 1009 (1990), Indiana Bill Tracking, Statenet, Information for Public Affairs, Inc., 1991.
[338]House Bill No. 1427 (1991), Indiana Bill Tracking, Statenet, Information for Public Affairs, Inc., 1992.
[339]Ibid., sec. 1, IC 35-36-2-5.
[340]Ibid., sec. 4, IC 35-36-2-9.5(b).
[341]Ibid., sec. 2, IC 35-36-2-1.5, sec. 3, IC 35-36-2-9, sec. 4, IC 35-36-2-9.5.
[342]Ibid., sec. 4, IC 35-36-2-9.5(a-b).
[343]Ibid., sec. 4, IC 35-36-2-9.5(b)(1-3).
[344]Ibid., sec. 2 , IC 35-36-2-1.5.
[345]See Chapter 6. LEGISLATIVE INITIATIVES TO ABOLISH THE DEATH PENALTY FOR OFFENDERS WITH MENTAL RETARDATION, Other State Statutes, TENNESSEE AND KENTUCKY, and NEW MEXICO, *supra.*
[346]H.B. 1427, sec. 4, IC 35-36-2-9.5 (1991).
[347]Ibid., sec. 4, IC 35-36-2-9.5(c)(1).
[348]Ibid., sec. 4, IC 35-36-2-9.5(c)(2).
[349]Ibid., sec. 3, IC 35-36-2-9(e)(f)(g). Florida, Alabama and Delaware also have judicial sentence determination in capital cases.
[350]See Chapter 3. A DEATH ROW DOZEN, SUMMARY, *supra.*

[351]Ibid., DALTON PREJEAN, *supra*.

[352]"Parole Board Votes Against Execution," *New Orleans Times Picayune*, 12 November 1991, sec. Metro-B; "Court Reviews La. Murderer's Death Sentence," *New Orleans Times Picayune*, 26 February 1992, sec. Metro-B.

[353]Ed Anderson and Jack Wardlow, "Bill to Protect Retarded from Execution Filed," *New Orleans Times Picayune*, 2 May 1991, sec. Metro-B.

[354]Senate Bill No. 687, by Senator Bagneris, "An Act to Amend and Reenact Code of Criminal Procedure Art. 905.5(h) and to enact Code of Criminal Procedure Art. 905.5(i), relative to sentencing in capital cases; to provide for mental retardation at the time of the sentencing hearing as a mitigating circumstances [sic]; and to provide for related matters," Regular Session, 1991.

[355]House Bill No. 29, by Representative Haik, "An Act to enact Code of Criminal Procedure Article 906, relative to capital punishment; to prohibit a mentally retarded person from being executed; to provide for definitions; to provide for a determination hearing; and to provide for related matters," Regular Session, 1992.

[356]Ibid., sec. 1(A).

[357]Ibid., sec. 1(B).

[358]Ibid., sec. 1(C).

[359]Ibid.

[360]Ibid.

[361]Ibid., sec. 1(D).

[362]Ibid.

[363]House Bill 29, Louisiana Bill Tracking, Statenet, Information for Public Affairs, Inc., 1992.

[364]"Note to Author Re: H.B. 29," Legislative Services, Louisiana House of Representatives, 24 July 1992.

[365]House Bill 444, "An Act to Amend Section 99-19-101, Mississippi Code of 1972, to Eliminate the Death Penalty for Individuals Who Are Mentally Retarded, and for Related Purposes," Mississippi Legislature, by Representative Percy W. Watson, Regular Session, 1990.

[366]House Bill 303, "An Act to Amend Section 99-19-101, Mississippi Code of 1972, to Eliminate the Death Penalty for Individuals Who Are Mentally Retarded, and for Related Purposes," Mississippi Legislature, by Representative Watson, Regular Session, 1991.

[367]House Bill 995, "An Act to Amend Section 99-19-101, Mississippi Code of 1972, to Eliminate the Death Penalty for Individuals Who Are Mentally Retarded, and for Related Purposes," Mississippi Legislature, by Representative Watson, Regular Session, 1992.

[368]H.B. 444, H.B. 303, H.B. 995, Sec. 2.

[369]House Bill 444, House Bill 303, House Bill 995, Mississippi Bill Tracking, Statenet, Information for Public Affairs, Inc, 1990, 1991, 1992.

[370]H.B. 444, H.B. 303, H.B. 995, Sec. 1, 99-19-101(1).

[371]Ibid.

[372]Ibid., Sec. 1, 99-19-101(3)(a-d).

[373]Ibid., Sec. 1, 99-19-101(8).

[374]Ibid.

[375]House Bill 188, Missouri Bill Tracking, Statenet, Information for

Public Affairs, Inc., 1991.

[376]House Bill No. 1213, Missouri 86th General Assembly, An Act to Repeal Mo. REV. STAT., Sec. 565.020, Supp. 1991, Relating to Certain Crimes, and To Enact in Lieu Thereof One New Section Relating to the Same Subject, with Penalty Provisions, sec. A(2) (1992).

[377]Mo. REV. STAT., Sec. 630.005(21) (1990).

[378]House Bill 188, Missouri Bill Tracking, Statenet, Information for Public Affairs, Inc., 1991.

[379]Legislative Library, Committee on Legislative Research, Jefferson City, State of Missouri.

[380]Senator Ernie Chambers, "Introducer's Statement of Intent, L.B. 464," Ninety-First Legislature, First Session, Legislature of Nebraska, 22 February 1989, 1.

[381]See Chapter 2. THEORETICAL ARGUMENTS AGAINST THE DEATH PENALTY FOR PERSONS WITH MENTAL RETARDATION, BEYOND MITIGATION, The Anti-Child Argument, *supra*.

[382]Chambers, "Introducer's Statement of Intent," 1.

[383]Legislative Bill 464, Nebraska Bill Tracking, Statenet, Information for Public Affairs, Inc., 1989.

[384]Legislative Bill 464, An Act Relating to Crimes and Punishments; to Amend Section 28-101, Revised Statutes Supplement, 1988; to Prohibit the Imposition of the death Penalty on Persons with Mental Retardation; to Harmonize Provisions; and to Repeal the Original Section; Legislature of Nebraska, Ninety-First Legislature, First Session, Read for the First Time, January 17, 1989, sec. 28-101(2)(1).

[385]Ibid., sec. 28-101(2)(2).

[386]Ibid., sec. 28-101(2)(3).

[387]Testimony of Bernie Glaser, "Summary Analysis L.B. 464," Committee on Judiciary, Legislature of Nebraska, 22 February 1989, 18.

[388]Senator Pirsch, ibid, 5, 9-10, 14.

[389]Ibid., 10, 14.

[390]Ibid., 9, 14.

[391]Testimony of Dwayne Knuth, ibid., 5, and Testimony of Donald Moray, ibid., 14..

[392]Knuth, ibid., 5, and Testimony of Timothy Shaw, ibid., 9-10.

[393]Testimony of Shaw, ibid., 10.

[394]Testimony of Sam Cooper, ibid., 19.

[395]A-4631, "An Act Concerning Capital Punishment and Amending N.J.S.2C:11-3," 1989.

[396]A-3024, "An Act Concerning Capital Punishment and Amending N.J.S.2C:11-3," 1990.

[397]Ibid., Sec. 1, 2C:11-3(h).

[398]Ibid., Sec. 1, 2C:11-3(c)(1)(a).

[399]Ibid., Sec. 1, 2C:11-3(b).

[400]Ibid., Sec. 1, 2C:11-3(h).

[401]Ibid., Sec. 2.

[402]Ibid., "Statement," 6.

[403]Scott J. Barstow, Public Information Assistant, Office of Legislative Services, New Jersey State Legislature, "Letter to Author," 7 August 1992.

[404]House Bill 968, "No Death Penalty/Mentally Retarded, An Act to

Prohibit The Death Penalty for Mentally Retarded Persons and Certain Mentally Ill Persons," General Assembly of North Carolina, Session 1989, 31 March 1989.

[405]Ibid., sec. 1, N.C. GEN. STAT. sec. 15A-2000(g)(1).

[406]N.C. GEN. STAT. 122C-3(22).

[407]H.B. 968, N.C. GEN. STAT. sec. 15A-2000(g)(2).

[408]Ibid., sec. 15A-2000(g)(3).

[409]Ibid., sec. 15A-2000(h)(1).

[410]Ibid., sec. 15A-2000(h)(2).

[411]Ibid., sec. 15A-2000(h)(1).

[412]Ibid.

[413]Story of House Bill 968, "No Death Penalty/Mentally Retarded," by Locks, North Carolina General Assembly, 1989.

[414]House Bill 1005, North Carolina Bill Tracking, Statenet, Information for Public Affairs, Inc. 1991.

[415]House Bill 342, Ohio Bill Tracking, Statenet, Information for Public Affairs, Inc., 1991.

[416]OHIO REV. CODE ANN., secs. 2929.01, 2929.02, 2929.022, 2929.023, 2929.03 and 2929.05, quoted in "Synopsis," The State of Ohio, Bill Text, Statenet, Information for Public Affairs, Inc., 1991.

[417]Ibid., sec. 2929.01(A).

[418]Ibid., sec. 2929.02(A).

[419]Ibid., sec. 2929.023(B).

[420]Ibid.

[421]Ibid., sec. 2929.03(B).

[422]Ibid., sec. 2929.03(D).

[423]Ibid., sec. 2929.05(C)(1)(2)(3).

[424]Senate Bill 812, Oklahoma Bill Tracking, Statenet, Information for Public Affairs, Inc., 1992.

[425]Ibid.

[426]S.B. 707, Calendar of Events, Legislative Administration Committee, Oregon Legislative Assembly (1991).

[427]Measure: S.B. 707-A, Oregon Legislative Assembly, Staff Measure Summary, Senate Judiciary Committee, 27 April 1991, 1.

[428]"Minutes," Senate Judiciary Committee, 26 April 1991, 6.

[429]Ibid.

[430]S.B. 707, Calendar of Events.

[431]Ibid.

[432]"Note to Author," Legislative Administration Committee, Oregon Legislative Assembly, c. 1 August 1992.

[433]OR. REV. STAT. 427.005(12).

[434]Measure: S.B. 707-A, Oregon Legislative Assembly, Staff Measure Summary, Senate Judiciary Committee, 27 April 1991.

[435]Senate Bill 707 A-Engrossed, 66th Oregon Legislative Assembly, 1991 Regular Session, sec. 2(1).

[436]Ibid., sec. 2(2).

[437]Ibid., sec. 2(3).

[438]Ibid., sec. 3(6).

[439]Ibid., sec. 1(3)(a)(A).

[440]Ibid., sec. 1(3)(a)(B)

[441]Senate Bill No. 1198, "An Act Amending Title 42 (Judiciary and Judicial Procedure) of the Pennsylvania Consolidated Statutes, further providing for imposition of the death sentence," Introduced by Helfrick and Jones, 28 August 1989.

[442]Ibid., sec. 1, sec. 9711(f).

[443]Ibid., sec. 1, sec. 9711(k).

[444]Ibid., sec. 3.

[445]Senate Bill 331, The State of Pennsylvania, Bill Text, Statenet, Information for Public Affairs, Inc., 1991.

[446]Senate Bill 331, Pennsylvania Bill Tracking, Statenet, Information for Public Affairs, Inc., 1991.

[447]Jeff Miller, "Death Penalty Ban for Retarded Has Support in Legislature," *Columbia State*, 13 March 1989, sec. B.

[448]"Life Terms for Retarded," *Columbia State*, 20 March 1989, sec. Editorial.

[449]*See for example* John Blume and David Bruck, "Sentencing the Mentally Retarded to Death: An Eighth Amendment Analysis," *Arkansas Law Review* 41 (1988):731; David Bruck, "Witness to An Execution," *Los Angeles Daily Journal*, 12 March 1987, sec. 1; David Bruck, "Banality of Evil," in Ian Gray and Moira Stanley, *A Punishment in Search of a Crime* (New York: Avon Books, 1989), 2.

[450]*See for example* Editorial, "Life Terms for Retarded," *Columbia State*, 20 March 1989, sec. A; Margaret O'Shea and John Allard, "Justices Overturn Verdict Retarded Inmate Granted New Trial by High Court," *Columbia State*, 21 June 1990, sec. Metro/Region.

[451]Editorial, "Life Terms," sec. A.

[452]"A Matter of Conscience," *Columbia State*, 5 March 1991, sec. Editorial.

[453]"No Debate for Death Penalty Bill," *Charlotte Observer*, 7 March 1991, sec. York Observer.

[454]"When Not to Execute," *Columbia State*, 20 January 1992, sec. Editorial.

[455]*See for example* Editorial, "Life Terms for Retarded," *Columbia State*, 20 March 1989, sec. A; Margaret N. O'Shea and John Allard, "Justices Overturn Verdict, Retarded Inmate Granted New Trial by High Court," *Columbia State*, 21 June 1990, sec. Metro/Region; "A Matter of Conscience," *Columbia State*, 5 March 1991, sec. Editorial; "IQs and Execution," *Columbia State*, 15 April 1991, sec. Editorial; "When Not to Execute," *Columbia State*, 20 January 1992, sec. Editorial.

[456]"Ban Execution of Retarded, Advocates Tell Senate Panel," *Columbia State*, 6 March 1991, sec. Metro/Region.

[457]"Life Terms for Retarded," *Columbia State*, 20 March 1989, sec. Editorial.

[458]"IQs and Execution," *Columbia State*, 15 April 1991, sec. Editorial.

[459]Editorial, "Life Terms for Retarded," *Columbia State*, 20 March 1989, sec. A.

[460]"A Matter of Conscience," *Columbia State*, 5 March 1991, sec. Editorial.

[461]Robert Perske, *Unequal Justice* (Nashville, TN: Abingdon Press, 1991), 85.

462Margaret N. O'Shea and John Allard, "Justices Overturn Verdict, Retarded Inmate Granted New Trial by High Court," *Columbia State*, 21 June 1990, sec. Metro/Region.

463Ibid.

464"IQs and Execution," *Columbia State*, 15 April 1991, sec. Editorial.

465Ibid.

466The synopses for Senate Bills 241 and 435 as introduced on January 8 and 9, 1991, respectively, state that each bill "provides that a person who is convicted of or pleads guilty to murder and is found to be mentally retarded must be sentenced to life imprisonment; defines mentally retarded; provides a procedure to determine mental retardation; relates to the punishment for murder; prohibits the execution of a person found to be mentally retarded." Similarly, the original synopsis for HB 3095 states that the bill "amends current code to provide that a person who is convicted of or pleads guilty to murder and is found to be mentally retarded must be sentenced to life imprisonment, defines mentally retarded, and provides a procedure to determine mental retardation." South Carolina Bill Tracking, Statenet, Information for Public Affairs, Inc., 1992, Statewide Session.

467R 610, H 3095, An Act to Amend Section 16-3-20, as Amended, Code of Laws of South Carolina, 1976, Relating to the Punishment for Murder, so as to Provide for Mental Retardation as a Mitigating Circumstance, sec. 1 (1992).

468Bill History of H*3095, General Bill by P.B. Harris, M.P. Carnell, J.L. Harris, J.G. Mattos, A Bill to amend Section 16-3-20, as amended, Code of Laws of South Carolina, 1976, relating to the punishment for murder, so as to provide for mental retardation as a mitigating circumstance. - amended title, 1 July 1992.

469Sally Reynolds, Director, Legislative Reference Library, The State of Texas, "Letter to Author," 2 April 1991.

470House Bill No. 55, "An Act Relating to the Exclusion of Mentally Retarded Defendants from the Application of the Death Penalty," Legislative Information System 71(R), 1 April 1991.

471Tex. Rev. Civ. Stat. Ann., Article 5547-300 (Vernon), The Mentally Retarded Persons Act of 1977, was repealed in 1991. The definition of a "person with mental retardation" became a part of Tex. Health & Safety Code Ann. sec. 531.002 (Vernon 1992).

472House Bill No. 89, "An Act Relating to the Consideration of Mitigating Circumstances, Including the Mental Retardation of the Defendant, in the Assessment of the Death Penalty, Legislative Information System 71(1), 1 April 1991.

473Ibid., sec. 1, Article 37.071(b)(4).

474Ibid., sec. 1, Article 37.071(f).

475Legislative General Counsel, H.B. No. 112, Prohibition of Death Penalty for Persons Having Mental Retardation, 1990, General Session.

476Utah Code Ann., sec. 76-3-206 1953, as last amended by Chapter 84, Laws of Utah 1977.

477Utah Code Ann., sec. 76-3-207 1953, as last amended by Chapter 19, Laws of Utah 1982.

478H.B. No. 112, sec. 76-3-206(2)(a).

479Ibid., sec. 76-3-206(2)(b).

480Ibid.
481Ibid., sec. 76-3-206(2)(c).
482Ibid.
483Ibid., sec. 76-3-207.
484Ibid., sec. 76-3-207(1)(a).
485House Bill 112, Utah Bill Tracking, Statenet, Information for Public Affairs, Inc., 1991.
486Michael Hardy, "Linking Death Penalty to IQ Draws Fire in Senate Panel," *Richmond News Leader*, 2 February 1989, sec. Area/State.
487Ibid.
488"In Richmond - No Death Penalty Exemption," *The Washington Post*, 3 February 1989, sec. Metro.
489Hardy, sec. Area/State.
490Sandra Evans, John F. Harris, John W. Anderson and Donald P. Baker, "In Richmond - House Approves Stricter Crime Bills," *The Washington Post*, 8 February 1989, sec. Metro; Tim Cox, "House Panel Refuses to Exempt Retarded from Capital Punishment," United Press International, Dateline: Richmond, VA, 10 February 1990.
491Senate Bill No. 210, "A Bill to Amend the Code of Virginia by Adding a Section Numbered 19.2-264.3, Relating to Sentencing in capital Murder Cases; Mental Retardation," 1990 Session, Offered 22 January 1990. *See also* VA. CODE ANN. sec. 19.2-264.4(vi) (1990).
492Ibid.
493Ibid., sec. 1, 19.2-264.3:29(A).
494"In Richmond - No Death Penalty," sec. Metro.
495House Bill 458, "An Act to Amend and Reenact sec. 19.2-264.4 of the Code of Virginia, Relating to Sentencing Proceedings; Capital Cases," Virginia Acts of Assembly, Chapter 754, 1990 Session, Approved 9 April 1990.
496Senate Bill 5940, Washington Bill Tracking, Statenet, Information for Public Affairs, Inc., 1989.
497Senate Bill 6489, Washington Bill Tracking, Statenet, Information for Public Affairs, Inc., 1990.
498House Bill 1234, *Legislative Digest and History of Bills*, State of Washington, 1992, 118.
499Ibid.
500Senate Bill 5940, Washington Bill Tracking, Statenet, Information for Public Affairs, Inc., 1989.
501Senate Bill 6489, Washington Bill Tracking, Statenet, Information for Public Affairs, Inc., 1990.
502Ibid.
503John White, "Bill Would Aid Insurance Coverage in Terror Cases," *Seattle Times*, 24 January 1991, sec. Northwest.
504H.B. 1234, *Legislative Digest*, 118.
505House Bill Report, H.B. 1234, as Reported by House Committee on Judiciary, 2.
506Ibid.
507WASH. REV. CODE, sec. 10.95.050, as stated in Substitute House Bill 1234, An Act Relating to Imposing the Death Penalty Upon the Mentally Retarded; and Amending RCW 10.95.030, 10.95.070, 10.95.130, and

10.95.140, State of Washington, 52nd Legislature, 1991 Regular Session, sec. 1(2).

[508]Ibid.

[509]S.H.B. 1234, sec. 2(6).

[510]WASH. REV. CODE, sec. 10.95.070, as stated in ibid.

[511]S.H.B. 1234, sec. 1(2).

[512]Ibid.

[513]Ibid., sec. 1(2)(a).

[514]Ibid., sec. 1(2)(b)(c)(d)(e).

[515]Ibid., sec. 3(2)(d).

[516]Ibid., sec. 3(2)(a)(b)(c).

[517]H.B. 1234, *Legislative Digest*, 118.

[518]Roger Nyhus, "Panel Alters Death-Penalty Revision Bid," *Oregonian*, 3 April 1991, sec. North Zoner Washington Coast Zone.

[519]WASH. REV. CODE, 10.95.040 as amended by S.H.B. 1234, Senate Committee Amendment, by Committee on Law & Justice, S-4222.1 (1992), sec. 1(1).

[520]S.H.B. 1234, Senate Committee Amendment, sec. 1(1).

[521]Ibid. *Emphasis added.*

[522]Ibid.

[523]H.B. 1234, *Legislative Digest*, 118.

[524]Ibid.

Index

common law, 48, 49, 80, 91, 116, 127, 131,
170; and lunatics or idiots, 5; and
societal consensus, 5
Common Law, Principle of, 168
communicative skills, 15
Community Legal Aid Society's
Disabilities Law Program,
Delaware, 222
community, 33, 38, 44, 69, 93; corrections,
33; criminal justice, 18; legal, 7, 8
compassion, 7, 155
competent, competency, 18, 37, 49, 50, 79,
85, 120
components, culpability, 20; decision, 180,
181
comprehension, 7, 18, 20, 28, 31, 33, 47, 51,
58, 63, 90, 152
concept(s), 3, 51, 65; legal, 6 of basic facts,
15; of culpability, 20; of
diminished capacity, 16; of mental
age, 14, 47; of proportionality, 6,
22; of retribution.
concern, crucial, 7
conclusion(s), 23, 27, 30, 35, 37, 39, 51, 52,
93, 165, 173, 180; Court's in Penry
case, 6; on legislative initiatives,
249
condition(s), 37, 44, 45, 49, 53, 63, 64;
handicapping, 33, 34; mental, 91,
95, 161; permanent, 17; third, 3;
statutory, 3
conform conduct to requirements of law,
20
Congress, 36, 51, 187, 195, 207, 209
Connecticut, 188, 189, 220
consensus, 33, 34, 35; and common law, 5;
national, 5, 29, 30, 36, 52; political,
29, 61; public, 30; societal, 5, 6, 29,
30, 32, 34, 3 5, 37, 52, 57, 61
consequences, 20, 26, 39, 46, 56, 58, 60, 65,
93, 156; and causation, 18; of
actions, 15, 18, 25
consternation, national 8
Constitution, U.S., 1, 18, 21, 22, 58, 204;
Georgia, 204, 205
context, of national consternation, 8
control, 92, 136; impulse 3, 14, 16, 20, 21,
26, 98, 60, 160
conviction(s), 43, 81, 84, 86, 87, 88, 92, 93,
98, 99, 111, 112, 115, 116, 118, 121,

123, 124, 125, 126, 128, 132, 148,
156; of civilization, 6
convicts, 38; execution of mentally
retarded, 4, 6
countries, Latin American, 6; which have
banned capital punishment, 6
course of action, appropriate, 18
Court of Appeals, District of Columbia,
49; Maryland, 213; Oregon, 240
court's methodology, critique of, 29
court(s), 3, 15, 17, 22, 28, 29, 33, 34, 35, 38,
40, 42, 48, 49, 50, 53, 61, 62, 77, 78,
82, 83, 88, 89, 91, 92, 95, 96, 100,
111, 115, 116, 117, 119, 120, 121,
122, 124, 125, 128, 134, 148, 149,
158, 160, 192, 195, 196, 197, 198,
202, 203, 204, 205, 208, 209, 211,
213, 214, 215, 216, 217, 221, 222,
223, 225, 226, 227, 230, 231, 232,
235, 236, 237, 238, 240, 242;
procedure(s), 231; proceeding(s),
146, 152, 155, 242, 244, 245, 250;
process(es), 77, 120
Court, Circuit, Eleventh. See Eleventh
Circuit Court of Appeals.
court, Georgia district, 17
Crank, John, 24
Crawford, Representative William of
Indianapolis, 229
crazy, 17
Crime Control Act of 1990, 35, 36, 48, 51,
53, 63, 188
crime(s), 2, 15, 17, 18, 20, 21, 22, 23, 24, 25,
28, 31, 36, 39, 40, 42, 43, 44, 45, 46,
47, 49, 50, 51, 60, 62, 63, 77, 78, 79,
80, 81, 82, 83, 84, 85, 86, 87, 88, 89,
90, 91, 92, 93, 94, 95, 96, 98, 99,
100, 112, 113, 115, 116, 119, 120,
121, 122, 123, 124, 125, 126, 127,
128, 129, 130, 131, 134, 135, 136,
147, 148, 149, 152, 153, 154, 155,
156, 158, 159, 161, 165, 166, 167,
168, 169, 170, 171, 174, 175, 177,
178, 179, 180, 182, 192, 193, 196,
197, 201, 202, 203, 204, 208, 219,
226, 227, 233, 247, 248;
circumstances, 149, 161;
legislation, 188; let punishment fit.
18; locus of, 149; relationship to
culpability and punishment, 18,

About The Author

Emily Fabrycki Reed was born in South Bend, Indiana, and lived there throughout most of her childhood. She studied Philosophy and Political Science at Marquette University, Milwaukee, Wisconsin and received her Bachelor of Arts degree *cum laude* from Marquette. She earned her Masters of Public Administration Degree from the University of Hartford, West Hartford, Connecticut, and her Ph.D. in Political Science from the University of Massachusetts, Amherst.

Since 1985, Dr. Reed has been employed as a management analyst by the Delaware Criminal Justice Council, the State's criminal justice planning and grants management agency. Her work there led to her interest in how persons with mental retardation interrelate with the criminal justice system.

Most of the time, Dr. Reed resides in Wilmington, Delaware with her husband of thirty years, Thomas J. Reed, Associate Dean of the Widener University Law School. When she can, she spends time at her *pieds à-terre* in Dewey Beach, Delaware, where the view of the ocean is magnificent and inspirational. Much of this book was written there and at other beaches along the Atlantic coast.